Newborn Socialist Things

NEWBORN SOCIALIST THINGS

Materiality in Maoist China

Laurence Coderre

Duke University Press
Durham and London
2021

© 2021 Laurence Coderre
All rights reserved

Text designed by Omega Clay
Cover designed by Aimee C. Harrison
Typeset in Huronia and Franklin Gothic by Westchester Publishing Services

Library of Congress Cataloging-in-Publication Data
Names: Coderre, Laurence, [date] author.
Title: Newborn socialist things : materiality in Maoist China / Laurence Coderre.
Description: Durham : Duke University Press, 2021. | Includes bibliographical references and index.
Identifiers: LCCN 2020046224 (print)
LCCN 2020046225 (ebook)
ISBN 9781478013396 (hardcover)
ISBN 9781478014300 (paperback)
ISBN 9781478021612 (ebook)
Subjects: LCSH: Socialism—China—History—20th century. | Mass media—Political aspects—China. | Mass media and culture—China. | China—History—Cultural Revolution, 1966–1976. | China—History—1976–2002.
Classification: LCC DS778.7.C63 2021 (print) | LCC DS778.7 (ebook) | DDC 951.05/6—dc23
LC record available at https://lccn.loc.gov/2020046224
LC ebook record available at https://lccn.loc.gov/2020046225

Cover art: xu zhen® 徐震®, *Things I See Every Morning When I Wake Up and Think of Every Night Before I Sleep*, 2009. Several replicas of Middle East antiques, security steel wire mesh, 213 by 213 by 213 centimeters. Courtesy James Cohan, New York.

For my parents

CONTENTS

- ix   Acknowledgments
- 1   **Introduction**
- 27   Chapter 1 **The Sonic Imaginary**
- 54   Chapter 2 **Selling Revolution**
- 82   Chapter 3 **Productivist Display**
- 112   Chapter 4 **Illuminating the Commodity Fetish**
- 139   Chapter 5 **Remediating the Hero**
- 170   Chapter 6 **The Model in the Mirror**
- 190   **Coda**
- 197   Notes
- 221   Bibliography
- 241   Index

ACKNOWLEDGMENTS

As I write this on the thirty-first anniversary of the Tian'anmen Square Massacre, the United States of America is rife with civil unrest in the face of George Floyd's murder, Donald Trump's fascist flirtations, and the ravages of COVID-19. Another Black man killed at the hands—knee—of police; another peaceful protest forcibly disbanded; another thousand lives blithely sacrificed for the economy. New York, the city I call home, likes to think of itself as the center of the universe—well, it is at the national forefront here. One cannot hear George Floyd's pleas to breathe without recalling those of Eric Garner. The NYPD, the country's largest police force, continues to deploy aggressive tactics against protesters, engaging in militarized overpolicing on a grand scale night after night. Meanwhile, just under one in five hundred New York City–area residents have died of the novel coronavirus to date—disproportionately high numbers of people of color among them. New York University, the institution I call home, finds itself in the middle of all this, rocked by public health and economic uncertainty, much like the rest of higher education. The siren call of disaster capitalism beckons. We do not know what the fall semester will look like—on any level.

This book is the culmination of eight years of work, undertaken with the help and support of countless friends and colleagues. It has loomed so large in my mind for so long, but now, in this moment, it feels small, almost trivial. I try to take solace in the fact that at its essence this book is about a utopian project, a utopian project then called *socialism*. I think it is fair to say that that project failed to achieve its own stated goals and ambitions in the Chinese Cultural Revolution (1966–76). For most, this period offers yet another violent, cautionary tale of revolution run amok. But I confess, I take strange comfort in the impulse to imagine otherwise to which it speaks. This is the very propensity we must draw hope from now in our dystopian present. We must do better than this.

Newborn Socialist Things was first conceived with the help of Andrew F. Jones, Sophie Volpp, and Jocelyne Guilbault. I could not have asked for a better trio of mentors—I continue to work and live by their example, even as I have flown the Berkeley nest. The foundational research for this project was facilitated by the UC Berkeley Center for Chinese Studies, the Social Science Research Council, and the Fulbright-Hays program. I also received support from the American Council of Learned Societies and the UC Berkeley Doreen B. Townsend Center for the Humanities at the initial drafting stage. I would additionally like to acknowledge the generosity of the UC Berkeley Department of East Asian Languages and Cultures.

Crafting a book is an arduous and sometimes painful process of seemingly endless reconceptualization, revision, and expansion. I am grateful to have had the time and space to think, write, and travel afforded me by a Postdoctoral Fellowship in the Study of China from the Lieberthal-Rogel Center for Chinese Studies at the University of Michigan. My time in Ann Arbor was incredibly fruitful. Indeed, to the extent that I have been able to go to press relatively quickly, I credit my postdoctoral experience at Michigan. My thanks to Erin L. Brightwell, Yasmin Cho, Madhumita Lahiri, Sonya Ozbey, Glenn D. Tiffert, and Emily Wilcox, among many others, for making that experience at once joyful and productive. S. E. Kile, my spiritual twin in so many ways, remains indispensable. I would surely have lost my way by now without our essential "writing group" meetings.

I continue to be humbled by the support of my NYU colleagues, both inside and outside my home department of East Asian Studies, who, with humor and perspective, have helped me navigate the choppy waters of an incipient academic career. A particular shout-out goes to Eliot Borenstein, Lily Chumley, Faye Ginsburg, Monica Kim, Yoon Jeong Oh, Moss Roberts, Jini Kim Watson, Hentyle Yapp, Xudong Zhang, and Angela Zito on this score. Todd Foley has been an incomparable partner in crime. Rebecca E. Karl and Bruce Grant have been uncommonly generous with their time, volunteering hard-won advice on many occasions. Both provided detailed feedback on an early manuscript draft as part of a workshop facilitated by a First Book Colloquium Grant from the NYU Office of the Dean for Humanities. Tina Mai Chen and Paola Iovene also offered invaluable feedback as part of this event, flying all the way to New York to do so. (Melissa Lefkowitz took excellent notes.) The final publication of *Newborn Socialist Things* was made possible by a Book Subvention Grant from the NYU Center for the Humanities.

My sincere thanks to the staff of the following libraries and archives: Sichuan University, Wuhan University, the Jingdezhen Ceramic Institute, the National Library of China, the Shanghai Library, the Shanghai Municipal Archives, the Universities Service Centre at the Chinese University of Hong Kong, the Hoover Institution, Harvard University, UC Berkeley (especially Jianye He, Deborah Rudolph, and Susan Xue), the University of Michigan (especially Liangyu Fu), Columbia University (especially Chengzhi Wang), and NYU (especially April Hathcock and Beth Katzoff). I owe a particular debt to Mira Golubeva and Jiaqi Wang for scanning and acquiring materials on my behalf in Moscow and Beijing, respectively. Caitlin MacKenzie Mannion and Qinghua Xu of NYU Shanghai were instrumental in obtaining publishable images in the midst of the global pandemic.

Over the years I have been privileged to present my work at numerous conferences and events, from Hong Kong to London, Denmark to Denver. The Weatherhead East Asian Institute at Columbia University has been the site of more than its fair share of these. My thanks to Eugenia Lean and Ying Qian, among other faculty, as well as Gavin Healey, Yanjie Huang, and Ben Kindler for welcoming me into their community. In 2018 and 2019 I participated in a series of tremendously productive conferences organized by Jennifer Altehenger and Denise Y. Ho on the material culture of the Mao era. The conversations at these events have been invaluable. A very contentious one, with Karl Gerth, continues to provoke and, at times, enrage—good-naturedly, of course. I regret that Karl's most recent book did not come out until after *Newborn Socialist Things* was essentially finalized. I look forward to engaging with and critiquing his argument in the future.

Other important interlocutors since I first conceived this project include: Robert Ashmore, Jonathan Bach, Patricia Berger, Marjorie Burge, Corey Byrnes, Chris Chang, Paul Clark, Alexander C. Cook, Jacob Eyferth, Matthew Fraleigh, Maggie Greene, Katie Grube, Margaret Hillenbrand, Christine I. Ho, Isabel Huacuja Alonso, Erin Huang, Wan-Chun Huang, Dorothy Ko, Fabio Lanza, Haiyan Lee, Andrew Leung, Angelina Lucento, Jie Li, Song Li, Xiao Liu, Jason McGrath, Jeffrey Moser, Michael Nylan, Katherine O'Brien O'Keefe, Laikwan Pang, Meredith Schweig, Evelyn Shih, Marc Steinberg, Andreas Steen, Jonathan Sterne, David Der-wei Wang, Kathryn VanArendonk, Paula Varsano, and Judith Zeitlin. I am deeply indebted to them all.

Finally, to my parents: I am so lucky to have you in my corner. You have moved mountains to make this possible for me. This book is for you.

Introduction

In the fall of 1974, Shanghai People's Press released *Storm at the Counter* (*Guitai fengbo*), a remarkable collection of new short stories.¹ Attributed to the Shanghai Number 1 Department Store composition group (Shanghaishi di yi baihuo shangdian chuangzuozu), the collection comprises fictionalized accounts of retailers' experiences working in the People's Republic of China's (PRC's) oldest state-owned department store.² Taken as a whole, the volume reads like an implicit rejoinder to the notion that commerce and those who engage in it are ideologically suspect. The stories have something to prove—See! Retailers can be revolutionary too! On the one hand, this claim to revolutionary status is put forth on the basis of ongoing class struggle: Making revolution means discovering the malign influence behind an engaged couple's shopping spree, unmasking the black market profiteering ring at work in an old lady's purchases, and unraveling a renegade clerk's plot to steal from the store. With a pitched battle against capitalist restoration raging on both sides of the shop counter, retail workers present themselves as the tip of the proletarian spear to be applauded and encouraged. On the other hand, in addition to fending off class enemies, the Shanghai Number 1 retail force also attempts to distinguish itself in these stories through its dedication to diligently serving its worker-peasant-soldier (*gong nong bing*) clientele.

To this end, consider the practices described in "Pairing Socks" ("Pei wazi"), a story entirely devoted to one of the store's recent service initiatives.³ A student worker in the sock department, Xiao Fang, arrives at his new post just as an initiative is getting off the ground. In response to a suggestion from "the masses," the sock department now does more than sell pairs of socks; it also sells singles. Should a customer have only one sock—perhaps the other has been lost or is too worn to be darned—the customer can drop off the solitary good sock at the store. Store staff will then take it upon themselves to match said used sock with a new one, forming a now wearable pair at half the price.[4] It is a tremendously labor-intensive process, Xiao Fang soon learns. Master Bu, who seems to be something of a sock whisperer, makes clear that matches must be made in terms of color, yes, but also thread count and thickness, length of cuff, pattern, and general size. Should the store's own sock inventory not yield a match, one must be pursued elsewhere, either in other stores or in factory remnants. Xiao Fang and Master Bu, for example, visit a local sock factory in search of a pattern no longer carried by Shanghai Number 1. Tellingly, they are warmly received at the factory as fellow proletarian workers.

The ardent spirit of service encapsulated in this story is closely tied to a much-touted contemporaneous expansion of the store's purview, which included not only selling goods but repairing, replacing, renting, and recycling them as well.[5] By 1975, store cadres publicly claimed to offer more than 180 such services, ranging from advice on removing stains to collecting spent toothpaste tubes.[6] In each case, the retailers were said to put the masses' convenience (*fangbian qunzhong*) ahead of the profit motive, thereby further distinguishing themselves from capitalist purveyors. In the mid-1970s, this, alongside the omnipotence of the centralized plan, is what supposedly defined China's commercial sector as socialist. All these demonstrable "advancements" were consequently promoted as "newborn socialist things" (*shehuizhuyi xinsheng shiwu*).

Although it is now colloquially used in the more general sense of an emerging phenomenon, as a technical term, expounded by party theorist Sun Dingguo (1910–64) in 1959, "newborn thing" was not to be deployed in reference to a passing fad. Newborn things, by definition, were necessarily much more consequential than that. Specifically, they had to pass four tests: They had to struggle against "old things" (*jiu shiwu*); forge their own path; be in accordance with developmental principles; and have a long, bright future. Only then could something earn (*yingde*) the right to be called a newborn thing.[7] At once emblems of their own time and heralds of the future, newborn things were therefore understood—especially in the wake of Mao Zedong's (1893–1976) 1957 disquisition "On the Correct Handling of Contradictions among the People"—as a key engine of history's forward progress. Newborn things' struggle with old things was particularly crucial to the creation of a developmental dialectic whereby the struggle itself would help pave the way for ever newer—and therefore ever more advanced—newborn things.[8] Indeed, this evolutionary process was ultimately rooted in a notion of planned obsolescence. Newborn feudalist things inevitably became old things under capitalism; newborn capitalist things became the object of socialist struggle; and one day, with the arrival of the communist Promised Land, even newborn socialist things would become dangerously outdated.

Of course, at the time of Sun's canonical essay and at least until Mao's death in 1976, the future was not meant to look like what we see in China today, a condition sometimes deemed to be postsocialist. Postsocialism, loosely defined as an economic and cultural shift away from the direct control of a Leninist party-state to the purportedly autonomous workings of global capitalist markets, could never constitute historical advancement.[9] A perversion of the developmental assumptions of the revolution, a resurgence of capitalism could be seen only in revisionist terms as a kind of backward historical motion. Anything associated with such retrogradation was, necessarily, an old thing. Indeed, the identification and destruction of old things of this type—especially when they pretended to be newly emergent—became one of the major focal points of the Cultural Revolution (1966–76). Newborn things pointed the way forward such that the only possible progressive post- to socialism was communism.[10]

We arguably still see traces of this attitude in the PRC's official pursuit of "socialism with Chinese characteristics" (*Zhongguo tese shehuizhuyi*). Although contemporary Chinese socialism is increasingly seen as a misnomer—the party's vain attempt to maintain ideological appearances despite, for all intents and purposes, having given up the dream of a communist future—here, the claim to socialism remains significant in and of itself. It speaks to a fraught relationship with the Maoist past, its unfulfilled promises, and its ongoing legacy in a way that the arguably more accurate economic descriptor "capitalism with Chinese characteristics" does not. What happens, to that end, if we begin to take seriously the purported capaciousness of a Chinese socialism that, as an experience and an idea, successfully encompasses the apogee of Maoist fervor, the Cultural Revolution, and the increasingly extreme marketization of the early twenty-first century? How, for example, might that change the way we think of contemporary China's service sector and its relationship to Shanghai Number 1 Department Store's newborn socialist things of yesteryear? What would it mean, moreover, to truly think of that relationship as a dialectic?

It may be argued that such an expansive understanding of Chinese socialism effectively stretches the notion beyond its breaking point, that in order for it to be applicable to such radically different historical circumstances as the Cultural Revolution and the current cultural moment, it must also apply to everything and therefore mean nothing. Perhaps. But even if only as a short-lived thought experiment, I believe this approach, especially vis-à-vis what initially appear to be the trappings of the Chinese turn *away* from the

Mao period, can nonetheless prove productive in recapturing the richness and contradictions that have always already been part of the Chinese socialist condition. Chinese socialism has always been something of a moving target.

This study essentially constitutes a wager—of considerable time and energy both on my part and the reader's—that the movement of that target is worth mapping, particularly during the period just prior to the onset of market reforms in the late 1970s and 1980s: the Cultural Revolution. In the pages that follow, then, I pursue a line of inquiry suggested by the concept of the newborn socialist thing itself, its expansiveness and heterogeneity, its ambiguous relationship to the material world, and its anticipated usurpation of historically dominant forms of interaction, like the commodity. More precisely, my focus is the media environment of the Cultural Revolution and the ways in which its constituent elements engaged with contemporaneous discourses of materiality and material culture.

A Brief History of the Newborn Thing

The fight against the old has become a critical component of the popular imagination of the Cultural Revolution, especially abroad. The campaign to "smash the Four Olds" (*po sijiu*), at the high tide of Red Guard activity (1966–68), has proved remarkably compelling for such imaginings and is consistently blamed for the widespread destruction of Chinese cultural heritage perpetrated during this period—cultural heritage that must now be recovered or reinvented in various ways. Most notable for my purposes here is the fact that this loss is typically represented in material terms. Consider the iconic photograph of burning Buddhist relics or depictions of the literal smashing of objects in posters promoting the campaign (see figure I.1). This despite the fact that the Four Olds were, at least explicitly, very little concerned with material particularities. Lest we forget, each of the Four Olds— old customs (*fengsu*), old culture (*wenhua*), old habits (*xiguan*), and old ideas (*sixiang*)—seems much more preoccupied with behavior than concrete objects in isolation. Indeed, it is easy to see why, when each "old" is so abstract and difficult to disentangle from the other three, they were typically referred to as a group. In the aggregate, the Four Olds became all-encompassing, an umbrella term on a par with the equally expansive "old things," itself a rhetorical holdover from the late 1950s. I would suggest, in fact, that we consider the two terms as part of the same larger, tempestuous history of negotiating the past that has always been at the heart of socialist construction as a political project. For although the notion of the Four Olds may have been short-lived, the Four Olds themselves, like the "old things" targeted before and after

Figure I.1 "SHATTER THE OLD WORLD, BUILD A NEW WORLD," poster (unsigned), circa 1967, 37 by 26 centimeters. International Institute of Social History / Stefan R. Landsberger Collection, chineseposters.net.

them, were pitted against a class of forward-looking "newborn things" in very much the same way.

This should alert us to the fact that, in a sense, both old and newborn things were, as a rule, remarkably un-thing-like. More precisely, we might say that they tested, stretched, and exceeded the bounds of materiality. They are perhaps best thought of as constellations—of objects and bodies brought into relation with each other, of institutions produced by and through those objects and bodies, and of the social formations they helped to construct. In other words, instead of distinguishing an object from its production, usage, and discursive apparatus, an old or newborn thing brought all these together into a single conceptual entity, comprising both human and nonhuman actors. Defining the boundaries of a particular thing therefore becomes a matter of scale—of how many connections one wishes to trace.[11] A salesclerk pairing socks or a peasant driving a tractor could be thought of as a newborn thing in this sense, but so could collectivization writ large. By the same token, the smashing of the Four Olds, as abstract as those Four Olds may initially seem, in practice could be equated with the smashing of physical objects, the dismantling of institutions, and the reconfiguring of social relations. In theory, at least, the capaciousness of the old or newborn thing—now so much more than a mere object—unified all these facets under one conceptual roof. Thus, in his famous "On the Correct Handling of Contradictions among the People," mentioned above, Mao could refer to the agricultural collective as a newborn thing, and two years later, Sun Dingguo could likewise tout the recently formed people's communes as the most glorious of newborn things to date.[12]

When progressive constellations emerged in the old society they were promptly quashed, a consequence of the natural threat they posed to the status quo. Under socialism, by contrast, newborn things were now to be nurtured in order that they might take root and grow. Moreover, they had to be defended from the many class enemies who would see them crushed underfoot. Fully articulated during the years of the Great Leap Forward (1958–60)—and further buoyed by the unbridled optimism of the time—properly carrying out one's responsibilities toward newborn socialist things became one of a good communist's chief concerns. In some ways it was a remarkably easy job since, at the end of the day, newborn things were, by definition, guaranteed to prevail over the old things of the pre-revolutionary era. The Sun Dingguo essay to which I have been referring, for example, is tellingly titled "Newborn Things Are Invincible" ("Xinsheng shiwu shi bu ke zhansheng de"). Even so, overconfidence and complacency would not do either. For all his bombastic assurances of victory, then, Sun also has to strike a more cautionary note: Although the new would necessarily win out over the old in the long run, vigilance still needed to be maintained on a day-to-day basis.¹³ There was no room for historical fatalism.

This tricky two-step remained a staple of discourse pertaining to newborn things when it returned to prominence in the Cultural Revolution. After the official close of the Great Leap Forward in 1960, as President Liu Shaoqi's (1898–1969) more centrist policies gained a better foothold, the praise of emerging newborn things decreased substantially, only to make a comeback in 1966. Red Guard publications like *Red Guard Report* (*Hongweibing bao*), emanating from Beijing, regularly couched their implied readers' activities—particularly when it came to the formation of new groups and troupes—in terms of support (*zhichi*) for newborn things and opposition to the Four Olds and old things.¹⁴ The official press also increasingly began using this terminology to refer to "advancements" in many areas, including progress in the arts. It was not until the 1970s, however, that official invocations of newborn things—more often than not now appearing with the modifier *socialist*—grew exponentially. This was especially true of the period between the onset of the Criticize Lin, Criticize Confucius campaign (Pi Lin pi Kong) in 1973 and the arrest of the Gang of Four—Jiang Qing (1914–91), Zhang Chunqiao (1917–2005), Yao Wenyuan (1931–2005), and Wang Hongwen (1935–92)—in 1976, during which time the most radical elements in the party were trying to retain or regain power. Their chief concern in these years was to promote what had taken place during their often-meteoric rise in the late 1960s, before the Ninth Party Congress in 1969 and the "end" then declared to the Cultural Revolution. Thus, in March 1975, *People's Daily* (*Renmin ribao*) published an article calling on its readers to continue building on recent achievements for the good of the dictatorship of the proletariat.

> The process of social development is precisely the process by which newborn things progressively vanquish old things. Our socialist revolution and the victories of our established enterprises are precisely the result of newborn socialist things vanquishing rotten capitalist things. Bourgeois right can only be restricted under the dictatorship of the proletariat. Only in doing so during the lengthy process of socialist revolution can we gradually narrow the three great distinctions [between town and country, industry and agriculture, and mental and physical labor], reduce class difference, and incrementally create the material and spiritual conditions whereby these distinctions can be eliminated completely. Since the dawn of the Cultural Revolution, newborn socialist things have sprung forth in large numbers: cadres, workers, soldiers, peasants, students, and merchants taking the May 7 road [this refers to Mao's "May 7 Directive" of 1966]; educated youth going up to the mountains and down to the countryside; collectivized

healthcare and barefoot doctors; workers, peasants, and soldiers participating in theory groups; and so on. These newborn things represent the inevitable course of historical development and are of deep significance for narrowing the three great distinctions and restricting bourgeois right. Our great leader Chairman Mao has always emphasized the importance of newborn socialist things. He has afforded them high praise and given them warm support. Every party member, cadre, and poor or lower-middle peasant must diligently study Chairman Mao's directives and promote the advancement of newborn things.[15]

By the mid-1970s, ironically enough, supporting the newborn things that pointed the way forward to communism looked very much like backtracking to an earlier state of affairs—the implication being that China had been led astray by revisionists (yet again) in the intervening years. It was therefore time to go back to the future—as it were—with, as always, the newness of the newborn things the measure of progress.

One of the most intriguing formations with which the newborn things of the Cultural Revolution were to coexist and do battle was the commodity (*shangpin*)—or, more precisely, the commodity form—as described in the opening chapter of Karl Marx's *Capital*. According to a 1974 dictionary of political economic terms, a commodity is something consumed by someone other than its producer and acquired through exchange. That exchange is made possible by the commodity form's dual nature, which brings together use value and exchange value, as a function of labor power measured in labor time. "Thus, as Marx emphasized, a commodity is not a thing, but a kind of social relation amongst people hidden underneath the exterior appearance of a thing [*wu de waihu*]."[16] It is a familiar definition that nonetheless tells us little about the appropriate role—or lack thereof—of the commodity under (Chinese) socialism. Indeed, while the eventual withering away of the commodity would coincide, according to Karl Marx and Friedrich Engels's pronouncements, with the arrival of communism, a number of key questions about what should happen in the interim were left maddeningly open by canonical communist theoreticians.[17] There were many gaps to fill in the study and practice of political economy, including the reinvention and demystification of holdovers from the ancien régime, most notably, the commodity and its close cousin, money. These tasks were undertaken in the PRC in the name of a transitional period that brought together temporarily necessary vestiges of the past with the inchoate developments of the future. It was the combination of these things that helped define socialism as a liminal age, where the trick was learning to distinguish what was retrograde (in order to keep it in check) from what was progressive (in order to encourage its growth).[18]

Indeed, I would suggest it is no accident that the briefest of histories of the newborn socialist thing outlined above in many ways mirrors the Chinese Communist Party's (CCP) contentious history of negotiation with the (socialist) commodity. The two stories are rhetorically and conceptually linked. During the Cultural Revolution, if not before, socialist commodities and newborn socialist things often formed a developmental dialectic in precisely these terms. Consider Mao's assertion, made only a month before the article quoted above, that the socialist economy was "a commodity system."[19] Or consider the fact that, whereas socialist retailing and its innovations—for example, pairing customers' used socks—may have been hailed as newborn things, the (socialist) commodity form per se, as opposed to its exchange and circulation, was seen as a danger to socialism even as it helped to build it.[20] The commodity under socialism was a critical advance, to be sure, but it was still not quite new enough. Socialist commodities bespoke the limits of remaking the past—that is, they testified to the need for continuously birthing newness. Thus the need to support ever newer and more up-to-date things.

The connection between the commodity form and newborn socialist things also extends well beyond this dialectic, however. At base, each constitutes an arguably failed attempt to grapple with the same problem: How does one bridge the gap between material specificity and social relations without subsuming one into the other? As I argue in this book, in the early 1970s the threat posed to socialism by the commodity form—that is, its latent potential to pull history backward—was rooted in a suspicion that its defining capitalist relations of production could not be wholly overcome. This was true even in a PRC in which such social relations had been dramatically altered by revolution and were constantly demystified by the popularization of Marxist political economic theory. Still, the latter project remained an important way to manage the destabilizing danger of the commodity, and it is particularly key here because, as a coping mechanism, it relied on discourse and abstraction, leaving material specificity by the wayside. As for the newborn socialist thing, it could counter the dangerous relationality of the commodity dialectically with its own appropriately future-oriented relationality, but doing so discursively seems to have come at a tremendous cost to it as well, namely, at the cost of its materiality. For although newborn socialist things were theoretically conceived as comprising constellations of objects, people, and practices—of merging the material and the social—the objects within those constellations were also consistently overlooked. One notes, for example, that the newborn things enumerated in the aforementioned *People's Daily* article show little to no concern for the objects these newborn things purportedly encompass. Materiality is conveniently jettisoned, thereby effectively reproducing the very problem it was meant to solve. In this sense, the newborn socialist thing, meant to form a developmental dialectic with the commodity form, could not break free of its mold; it could not seem to square the material specificity–social relations circle in a fundamentally different way. As a result, it became difficult to imagine concrete new social relations in anything other than the commodity form—despite that having been the goal.

Given all this—given what would appear to be a crucial flaw in the historical deployment of the newborn socialist thing as a concept—it may seem a rather odd source of inspiration for a book such as this. But in truth, it is not the actual usage of the term in the Cultural Revolution that primarily interests me. Rather, I am more interested in the potential it holds as a way of thinking about interactions among people and things. What would it mean, in fact, to extend the newborn thing's relationality from the social to incorporate the material, as I believe it was originally intended to do and, on rare occasions, succeeded in doing? What new affinities could we see? And how would that change our understanding of Chinese socialism? This study attempts to answer these questions by examining Cultural Revolution media systems, their constituent elements and forms, because when we think about media relationally—especially when we do so in terms of equivalence and exchange—we begin to see deep connections with the commodity, connections that have hitherto gone unnoticed.

The Political Economy of Mediation

In *The Chinese Cultural Revolution*, film historian Paul Clark traces the complex lineages of the period's key performances and cinematic works, illustrating at length just how far from a cultural wasteland the decade actually was. In fact, the richness and sheer pervasiveness of the period's cultural production prompts the following observation: "The commercial commodification of culture that has characterized Chinese artistic life in the last quarter-century was made possible by the ideological commodification of culture in the Cultural Revolution."[21] The implications of this statement are not fully explored in Clark's work, nor for that matter is the notion of the "ideological commodification of culture" wholly unpacked. But what makes this claim so potent is not some new, implied typology of commodification so much as the recognition on which the claim is predicated, namely, that there is a formal similarity between the radically intermedial proliferation and endless repetition of what might loosely be called "official cultural production"—rhetoric, sound, images, objects, and performances directly produced or tacitly endorsed by the CCP cultural and propaganda apparatus—during the Cultural Revolution and the ways in which commodities circulate and multiply.

The expansive notion of the newborn socialist thing—as a habit of mind and critical lens—is helpful here insofar as it allows us to investigate this fundamental insight, precisely by conceptually bringing together that which is typically kept separate, when acknowledged at all: official Cultural Revolution–era cultural production and the workings of the (socialist) commodity. The justification for the conventional separation of these two spheres is, more often than not, quite simply provided by the fact that economic considerations, like production costs or potential returns on investment, were seldom, if ever, meant to enter into the equation when making socialist culture. Why, then, worry about such things now? The implication is that doing so would in some sense be missing the point. The areas of overlap, influence, and collision of the official cultural realm and the commodity explored in this book, however, are not as straightforward as all that. I do not wish to venture into discussions of the *economics of culture*, for lack of a better term, or otherwise restrict myself to adjudicating the commodity status of any particular cultural work. The promise of the newborn socialist thing lies elsewhere—specifically, it allows us to identify and articulate a cluster of formal, relational affinities and logics operative in both the cultural and the economic domains.

The sprawling scope of this goal accounts for my emphasis on the commodity form and its permutations in the Cultural Revolution rather than on tracing the production, circulation, and consumption of particular commodities. As a function of this, I am less interested in actual, historical economic activity than in the formation of an avowedly socialist field of political economy, its theories, contradictions, and material manifestations. To that end, it bears repeating here that the making of socialist culture and the making of socialist political economy were very much contemporaneous projects. One might even go so far as to say that they were two sides of the same coin, that coin being the forging and negotiation of new social relations across the board. The language of political economy was particularly crucial insofar as it provided explanations and alibis for an array of phenomena that, though proudly labeled as socialist, looked suspiciously capitalist, the continued reliance on commodities chief among them. In other words, political economic justifications were a very effective way of giving apparently old things a new lease on life. Taking these justifications seriously, then, means forcing ourselves to consider the relationship between culture and political economy differently and, notably, more expansively than has hitherto been done with regard to the Cultural Revolution.

I have found inspiration for this endeavor in a number of unexpected places, including in studies of English and American literature by Walter Benn Michaels, Lynn Festa, and Jonathan Lamb.[22] I say "unexpected" simply because of the manifest historical and cultural distance between these scholars' immediate subject matter and mine. Putting this issue to the side for the moment, each of these literary critics has succeeded in doing what I aim to do here: They have sussed out the political economic in the cultural and vice versa, isolating common problematics of identity, personhood, and ownership, among others. I will touch on some of these areas myself, particularly as they concern bodies and subjectivities (chapters 5 and 6), but my primary focus remains the question of relationality itself. More specifically, my focus lies on the prescriptive form of relationality constitutive of both the commodity form and the material construction of Chinese socialist culture.

I approach this particular form of relationality in terms of *mediation*, a notion I invoke with a view to the word's multiple associations in common parlance. First, *mediation* is often used in reference to media—to that which media *do* in a performative sense—and to the extent that Clark's original observation pertains to the proliferation, circulation, and repetition of mass media objects, including films and recorded sound (chapter 1), this implicit connection is crucial. Indeed, one of the things that sets the Cultural Revolution apart from the Mao era is the increased number of people (especially those in or of the cities) for whom the mass media were an integral part of daily life. That said, I approach media and the cultural work of mediation in purposefully broad material terms, terms so broad, in fact, that mediation must really be understood as a situationally derived function of materiality as such. This sense of context-driven functionality is grounded in the second notion of mediation as processes of in-between-ness, in other words, as that which makes particular relations not only *possible* in the abstract but *operative* in a given situation. And here it is worth noting that these relations need not necessarily be friendly, nor indeed need the processes by which relations are enacted be smooth. When one mediates a conflict, for example, one tries to bridge a gap between two or more parties; the bigger the gap, the more work is required to overcome it. Mediation, in this sense, while dialogic by definition, can also be dialectical insofar as it is processual and, at least potentially, the stuff of opposition and contradiction.

This understanding of mediation clearly applies to monetized systems of commodity exchange, which are grounded in a process that renders one thing equal to another in terms of something else. This situation is crystalized in the commodity form, which, as Marx taught us, is, at its core, relational: The commodity form implies and engenders social relations between individuals as well as material relations between things.[23] That the former is regularly effaced by the latter is, famously, Marx's explanation for commodity fetishism (the focus of chapters 3 and 4). What is of interest to me here, however, is the way in which the relational nature of the commodity form makes it particularly promiscuous. The kind of mediation it emblematizes and facilitates is difficult to limit to the realm of actual exchange or to quantify with the standard tools of economics as an empirical discipline. Mediation crosses boundaries by virtue of its very structure; in order to get the full measure of the commodity form—whether capitalist or socialist—we must do so as well.

If this discussion of mediation and the commodity form smacks of ahistorical or universalist abstraction, allow me to clarify at the outset that my goal in this study is to explore the *material—and therefore culturally and historically specific—articulations* of this type of relationality in the Cultural Revolution. Remarking on the promiscuity of the commodity form is a condition of possibility for this investigation, not its end point. The implications of doing so, however, are intentionally wide-ranging, for the historiographic stakes of fully grappling with the socialist commodity, let alone mediation in the context of the newborn socialist thing, are unquestionably high. Despite popular conceptions of the Cultural Revolution as both a cultural and a commodity desert, there is little doubt that the political economic order of the day—even for the most radical faction of the CCP during the Cultural Revolution, the Gang of Four, and their followers—was not the elimination of commodities, but rather, monitoring their appropriate function. In short, the dangers posed by commodities, including commodity fetishism and revisionism, needed to be properly managed, that is to say, with an eye to the communist future.

This compromise should sound familiar; determining the appropriate role of the commodity under Chinese (post)socialism continues to be a difficult task for the CCP. And yet, the ongoing nature of this struggle is regularly ignored in favor of a historiographic narrative positing the commodity's sudden emergence in the era of reforms. In his treatment of the "Mao craze" (*Mao re*) of the early 1990s—a fad that saw a resurgence in the popularity of all things Mao—for example, Michael Dutton speaks of an emerging Mao industry. Despite the use of iconography from the Cultural Revolution, however, Dutton argues that there is no political power to be found in these recycled images, that they present no imminent danger to the party Mao had once nearly destroyed from within. Rendered as commodified kitsch, the objects of the Mao craze have supposedly been politically neutered. "The commodity form seduces rather than challenges. One can challenge a claim to truth, but how does one challenge a theme park?"[24] For Dutton, the commodified Mao can neither challenge nor be challenged, to the detriment of all. This understanding is predicated on the notion that the commodification of Mao is a wholly new phenomenon, but what if it weren't? What if we approached the proliferation and circulation of Mao's likeness during the Cultural Revolution through the lens of mediation à la commodity form? What if the millions of Mao badges produced in the late 1960s, for instance, were understood as more than a cult of personality run amok? What if they spoke to the fact that Mao has been commodity-like, if not precisely a commodity per se, all along?

These questions are intended to be provocative, and, I confess, I am likely giving Dutton short shrift here, stretching his argument beyond its intended scope. My point in doing so, however, is this: (Socialist) commodities were seductive and insidious long before Deng Xiaoping's (1904–97) market reforms. Indeed, they were recognized and criticized as such, even as they remained integral to the socialist enterprise and the logic of the commodity continued to suffuse everyday life in the Cultural Revolution. Although the material conditions of daily existence have undoubtedly changed dramatically for many Chinese in recent decades, that underlying logic persists to this day. What this ultimately means, then, is that we need to reevaluate what we think we know about Chinese socialism, commodities, and the way they continue to inform and resonate through the interactions of media, people, and things. At a time when commodities were regarded with suspicion as threats to the socialist enterprise, how and to what extent did the workings of the highly saturated, Cultural Revolution media environment nonetheless activate and engage the unsettling potential of the commodity form? How did the constituent parts of this increasingly omnipresent media environment—LPs, radio broadcasts, films, lantern slides, newspapers, magazines, comic books, posters, paper cuts, porcelain figurines, wallets, product packaging, ornamented mirrors, household appliances, and human bodies, to name just a few—themselves participate in that process? To what extent do they bear the imprint of that participation? And how might that impact the way we understand these media objects and their role in the construction of Chinese socialism then and now?

A Material (Re)turn

These motivating questions—and my attempts to respond to them in the coming pages—enact a material (re)turn of sorts—back to the specific media and particular objects of a historical and cultural moment. I find the notion of the newborn socialist thing helpful, as I suggest above, insofar as it has the potential to effect just such a (re)turn in combination with an emphasis on mediation—on material, social, and political economic relationality—and/as historical development. Basic as it may seem, the (re)introduction of material concerns constitutes a much-needed departure from the heretofore dominant approach to Cultural Revolution culture. Consider, for example, the existing scholarship on one of the mainstays of the media of this period, the so-called *yangbanxi*. A notoriously tricky term to translate, the word was coined in 1966 to refer to a group of five Beijing operas, two ballets, and one symphonic work intended to be the vanguard of the performing arts revolution.[25] More precisely, as *yangban* (models)—a term first used in the context of agricultural fields during the Great Leap Forward—these pieces were endorsed as exemplars of what the socialist arts could be. Yangbanxi therefore initially denoted a status—in contradistinction to *shiyanxi* (experimental performances)—more than a repertoire, though it has since acquired the latter connotation.[26] Each work was meticulously crafted and relentlessly revised, often over a period of many years, under the auspices of Jiang Qing, Mao's third wife and a former Shanghai actress. By 1976, a total of eighteen works had earned the "model" designation, with the original eight yangbanxi, in particular, holding an unparalleled position of prominence within the official cultural sphere.

In keeping with their cultural importance, the yangbanxi have been the subject of considerable scholarship over the past few decades, most of it written in Chinese by PRC researchers.[27] Much less has been written in English, no doubt due to the (until recently) prevailing sentiment that, as propaganda, the model works could be of little value to literary and film scholars.[28] Despite its Cold War inflections, this stance is understandable insofar as the approach typically deployed in the analysis of these works has, more often than not, heavily relied on symbolic readings. Explicitly designed in adherence to a totalizing system of signification—the yangbanxi were models precisely because their every aspect was ideologically and semiotically overdetermined—attempts to decode the yangbanxi in semiotic terms tend (unwittingly?) to reproduce official CCP interpretations. In other words, these works were meant to be read in a manner very much in keeping with the majority of contemporary scholarship, and as a result, it should not surprise us to discover that such scholarship tends to emphasize the univocality and self-evident simplicity of the yangbanxi. The model works are merely operating the way they were meant to operate, yielding a very particular reading as a product of a particular hermeneutic approach. In humanistic disciplines that valorize and thrive on polysemy and ambiguity, like literary and film studies, the yangbanxi have therefore often seemed too readily interpretable, too manifestly easy to understand, to be worthy of our attention.

Rather than casting aside these works—and the realm of official cultural production to which they belong—what is required is a new approach that does not jibe quite so neatly with the Cultural Revolution's prescriptive modes of reading. In a sense, we need to learn to willfully mis-read and misinterpret in a way that is nonetheless culturally and historically informed. Enter the newborn socialist thing. More specifically, my gambit in this book is that a renewed attention to the material specificity of official cultural products, broadly construed, and to the work of mediation in which they are engaged affords us just such a possibility, and it does so, ultimately, with great implications for our understanding of Chinese socialism past and present.

Again, the yangbanxi are a case in point, for their reach extended well beyond the professional performing arts of stage and screen. As part of the popularization campaign, begun in 1970, that resulted in the films extant today, yangbanxi-related paraphernalia was produced spanning every conceivable media form, including those discussed in the pages that follow: recorded sound (chapter 1), porcelain statuettes (chapter 3), amateur performance (chapter 5), and mirrors (chapter 6). Little of the interest the yangbanxi have garnered thus far has sought to address either the proliferation of yangbanxi ancillaries or the material environment in which yangbanxi were shown or performed.[29] Rather, as I have suggested above, the yangbanxi have generally been treated semiotically as texts to be read, with little regard for the materiality of any given text, which, through the act of interpretation, is rendered into a series of apparently dematerialized signs. In point of fact, however, we know that the model works and their related objects took on particular media forms and were experienced (and interacted with each other) in terms of the specific properties and possibilities attending those media forms. To read the film version of *The Red Lantern* (*Hong deng ji*) or a plate emblazoned with its protagonist, Li Yuhe, as simply a string of signs or a sign in itself in this way is to lose sight of the film as film, the plate as plate, and their fundamental material incommensurability.

As Bjørnar Olsen notes, this is a danger present in all purely semiotic approaches to things, but it is especially problematic in the context of the Cultural Revolution, where the reduction of material things to abstract signs threatens to forsake the experiential in the name of highly crafted official discourse.[30] By overlooking the level at which a thing was interacted with, that is, the thing as thing, one is left precisely with the system of signification CCP propagandists, for lack of a better term, were so at pains to construct. One is left, in other words, with the intended message as opposed to the thing as it was experienced; the plate with Li Yuhe's image becomes a symbol of CCP power and thereby ceases, in a sense, to also be something on which one might eat. In this particular case, then, a de facto blindness to things does more than restrict our hermeneutic horizons: It also serves to reinforce a notion of propaganda as a fundamentally top-down instrument of ideological indoctrination, strangely divorced from the material conditions of its own existence.

By contrast, *Newborn Socialist Things* seeks to turn this notion on its head. Examining cultural products as materially specific components of the Cultural Revolution media environment—that is, maintaining their "robust materiality" as a source of meaning, as Krisztina Fehérváry puts it[31]—forces us to ask a fundamentally different type of question: What did yangbanxi ancillaries mean, but also, *how* did they mean it? What did they do, and *how* did they do it? How did different media interact with one another, and what kind of subjectivities did these interactions make possible? Note that these are not precisely questions of audience reception, a topic that presents significant methodological challenges at the best of times. Trying to get a handle on the reception of official cultural works in the Cultural Revolution is a veritable methodological minefield.[32] Instead, what I carry out in this book remains a hermeneutic enterprise at heart, and in that sense it, too, is invested in semiotics. My reliance on *mediation* as a notion as opposed to, say, an economy of signification, however, is intended to foreground the materiality of the sign, not to efface it. This study is thus every bit an interpretative project but one in which I nonetheless approach media and discursive objects as materially specific, interactive, and productive.

That being said, I remain mindful of two particularly insidious pitfalls. First, there is the issue of whose materiality is at stake: whose vocabulary—whose ontological and epistemological frameworks—can we call on as we seek to engage the material specificity of this historical moment? On the one hand, we must be careful not to simply reproduce—much as I have just accused other approaches of doing—socialist discourses about things and, by extension, about the circulation and consumption of state-socialist goods. While the goal may be to engage socialist material culture in a manner informed by its own assumptions, priorities, and contradictions, it is still imperative "to dislodge the actual experience of state-socialist material culture from its more admirable ideological claims—whether genuine or convenient."[33] With this in mind, Fehérváry, for one, makes very pointed, often anachronistic use of such terms as "branding" and "commodities" in her work on the material culture of socialist Hungary, a move that is in keeping with much of the scholarship on socialist consumer culture in Eastern Europe and the former Soviet Union.[34] This is perhaps in part because these discussions often address, in one way or another, the reemergence of socialist-era goods, styles, and designs within the context of postsocialist/postcommunist nostalgia or, in (East) Germany, *Ostalgie*.[35] The use of such terminology also serves as a corrective of sorts in the face of a prevalent view, heavily influenced by János Kornai's assessment of communist political economy as fundamentally structured by shortage and scarcity,[36] "in which the absence of a 'capitalist' economy somehow implie[s] the absence of consumer culture—with its accompanying panoply of dreams and frustrations, forms of sociality, and social distinctions."[37] Within this context, the use of such terms as *consumer culture*, *brand*, and *commodity* is purposefully ahistorical in the name of scholarly intervention, but we must be cognizant that this tactic has its own risks, namely, of merely replacing one theoretical apparatus, equally unconcerned with the historical thingness of things, with another.

I attempt to negotiate this dilemma in a manner suggested by the newborn thing itself, that is, by juxtaposing objects with contemporary discourses of materiality (and political economy) in order to consider them in relation to each other. I therefore deploy the notion of the commodity, for example, in a manner and with an aim very different from Fehérváry. My goal here is to examine and recuperate the term as it was used during the Cultural Revolution rather than as a destabilizing and decentering mechanism. In other words, my interest in the commodity form is deeply historical. When I speak of the *socialist commodity* in the coming pages, I am referring to the concept as it emerged and evolved within Chinese socialist discourses of political economy and material culture. In this sense, it is meant as a culturally and historically specific indigenous term, the clarification and understanding of which—through the examination of particular objects—are principle motivations for this investigation. That Marx's theory of the commodity figures prominently in this book should not be surprising, then, for it is precisely this theory that informed the materials under examination, and its shortcomings were no less frustrating in the Cultural Revolution than they are to us today—which is exactly the point.

The second major pitfall threatening this study and its incipient material (re)turn is all the more serious for being more fundamental than the first. Regardless of the discourse I ultimately deploy, the underlying tendency of language to usurp the place of things remains.[38] I am, after all, engaged in a linguistic act; I am writing—have written—a book, one comprising material elements, true, but mostly one comprising words. Much as I may peg my scholarly project in contradistinction to those exclusively reliant on symbolic texts, then, at the end of the day I must own that I am as hamstrung by the semiotic structure of language as anyone. And though I seek to use the notion of the newborn socialist thing in a way that fulfills its potential to think the material with the social, I must also own that the historical failure to consistently do so offers little hope for prolonged success. In Elaine Freedgood's words, "We cannot outsmart our own forms; indeed, we can scarcely read them."[39] It may well be that the best we can collectively hope for is to disturb, however fleetingly, not just the totalizing claims of a particular discourse but of discourse tout court. This, then, is my goal here—undertaken with a little help from my material friends.[40]

Harnessing the Fugitive

Faced with a similar linguistic predicament in her study of things in the mid-Victorian novel, Freedgood proposes an albeit temporary recourse to metonymy in an attempt to stave off the substitutive logic of metaphor. That is, she is principally interested not in what a thing stands for or represents—mahogany furniture as merely an avatar of Jane Eyre's newly acquired wealth, for example—but, rather, in the constellation of relations in which a given thing, literally rendered, participates (as part of a larger whole). To read a realist novel metonymically is, for Freedgood, a way out and beyond, a way to unsettle and complicate: "Metaphor defines and stabilizes; metonymy keeps on going, in any and all directions. It threatens: to disrupt categories, to open up too many possibilities, to expose things hidden."[41] As a methodology, metonymy involves chasing fugitive connections and going down rabbit holes. This is precisely what makes metonymy so potently unruly and the reason why, ultimately, we must rely on metaphor to rein it in, to foreclose its seemingly endless array of options.[42] As scholars, we prioritize some texts and case studies above others; in order to communicate an idea with relative clarity, we use conventionally circumscribed language—in this case, printed and bound between the two covers of this book—to build a directional argument with a beginning, a middle, and an end. Metonymy may well offer a reprieve from these strictures—of language, of thought, of representation—but it cannot last. In the end, metaphor will always win the day.

Freedgood's metonymic reading has much in common with the methodological inspiration I am drawing from the newborn socialist thing and its seemingly limitless capacity for relational expansion. The newborn socialist thing is also unruly, testing the bounds of conceptual and material cohesion, and it, too, must ultimately be brought to heel in the name of linguistic and argumentational conventions. This inescapability notwithstanding, my hope is that the purposeful combination of tracing fugitive connections and the substitutive imperative of language, deployed in methodological tandem, can itself be a productive tack. I would like to suggest that our recourse to metaphor, inevitable as it may be, need not necessarily be understood as metonymy's failure in Freedgood's sense. Indeed, my emphasis on mediation very much depends on our ability to read both metaphorically *and* metonymically, to pay attention to relations of exchange and equivalence as well as the material incommensurabilities on which such relations rely. On the one hand, the following chapters engage—through the crucial notions of the newborn socialist thing and mediation—not with a group of literary texts but with a historical and cultural period: the Chinese Cultural Revolution. Whereas Freedgood concerns herself with textual interpretation through a process of literalizing, and then fanning out from, the material objects referenced within a novel's pages, I am interested in what the material components of a media environment can tell us, through what amounts to a similarly rhizomatic approach, about a historical moment. On the other hand, insofar as this study is interested in how that media environment was structured and how it shared a formal affinity with commodity exchange and the commodity form, substitutional logic is more than inevitable; it is also invaluable. I could not approach Chinese (post)socialism—past and present—as a developmental dialectic of old and newborn things without it.

Having said that, the inclusion of the fugitive in my methodology in this way has had two important consequences for the structure of this study, both of which should be mentioned here. First, there is the question of periodization. Throughout *Newborn Socialist Things*, I refer to the Cultural Revolution as the decade spanning May 1966, when the movement was officially endorsed by the politburo, to the arrest of the Gang of Four in October 1976. This is in keeping with the periodization endorsed by the CCP in its 1981 verdict on party history, but it is not without its drawbacks.[43] On the one hand, the Cultural Revolution was officially brought to an end at the Ninth Party Congress in 1969, and indeed, the 1970s did not witness anywhere near the level of open chaos and destruction that characterized the ascent of Red Guard factionalism in 1967. Moreover, many sectors of the economy, including the publishing and film industries, resumed operation in the early 1970s after being shut down in the late 1960s, meaning that the media environment of the former varied quite significantly from the latter. The ten-year periodization therefore elides differences that a narrower designation—from 1966 to 1969—would serve to highlight. On the other hand, there is an argument to be made that the Cultural Revolution never really existed as a discrete historical formation, even in the late 1960s. What we conventionally call the Cultural Revolution merely corresponds to a handful of disparate political campaigns—in a very long series of such campaigns—targeting cultural reform. I have decided to deploy the 1981 designation largely because it is still dominant in the PRC (and abroad) today, but I remain very cognizant of its constructed, if not wholly arbitrary, nature as a heuristic. In fact, my approach here consistently draws attention to the porousness of temporal boundaries even as I invoke them rhetorically. I spend much of my time tracing connections back in time, before the beginning of the Cultural Revolution proper, such as I have defined it. This is by design.

Second, given the newborn thing's penchant for the contingent, the media and exempla I examine in the following six chapters may at times seem strange or unmotivated. They require a plethora of interpretive tools, usually deemed the purview of disparate disciplines. But insofar as this variety nonetheless manages to produce a compelling account of a historical moment and its relationship with the China of today, this, too, is by design. To be sure, my choice of materials is not entirely haphazard; I have selected examples that are central to and emblematic of the workings of the media environment and commodity economy of the Cultural Revolution. Even so, this seems as good a place as any to own the role of serendipity in determining the final shape of this project. To the extent that the crux of my methodology—as inspired by the newborn thing—is thinking *with* or *through* things rather than speaking straightforwardly on their behalf, then the apparently contingent structure of this book is very much as it should be. *Newborn Socialist Things* does not claim to be exhaustive. Instead, it focuses on objects and texts that have spoken to me such that I have felt compelled to engage them—to work with and through them—here.

The Road Ahead

The six chapters that follow are loosely grouped into sets of two, each exploring forms of mediation related to conceptual tensions at the heart of the Cultural Revolution as a period and the newborn socialist thing as a critical lens. Although the chapters also resonate with one another beyond these pairings, my hope is that these groupings help create a more navigable structure for the reader. Taken together, chapters 1 and 2 focus on issues of modernization and developmental progress as measured through access to media technologies and consumer commodities, respectively. In the first instance, demands for newness mapped quite easily onto socialism. The second instance proved much more difficult to negotiate. Chapters 3 and 4 then examine this negotiation with an eye to the relationship between ideological discourse and materiality. What makes a socialist thing socialist? What makes it a thing? I address these questions from the vantage points of productivist commodity display and political economic texts meant to counteract commodity fetishism. Finally, chapters 5 and 6 take us from things to bodies and back again. What happens to subjectivities when bodies become implicated in vast systems of (re)mediation? Within this general framework, allow me to briefly sketch out each of the chapters.

Chapter 1 examines the central role of recorded sound—a crucial component of the Cultural Revolution media environment—in the CCP's efforts to build and consolidate the PRC as a modern socialist nation. Specifically, I focus on the dominant sound technologies of the loudspeaker and the record player and the ways in which these technologies worked to produce the nation as a sonic space of mass publicity and socialist modernity. This sonic topography suggests a desire to sonically territorialize the nation and purportedly civilize the minority peoples of the frontier. It is precisely at the figurative and literal margins of the socialist enterprise—in representational spaces of developmental backwardness—that we see the extent to which the modern national subject was still imagined as a consumer of both media and socialist commodities.

I build on this argument in chapter 2 with an analysis of the paradoxical figure of the socialist retailer, for whom making revolution meant selling commodities in the name of the Communist Party. The socialist department store was as much a site of class struggle as it was a place of consumption in the Cultural Revolution; indeed, these were often described as the same thing. As media and commodity consumption on the frontier became a paradigmatic mark of the modern socialist nation, the traveling broadcaster and the traveling salesperson—who brought the store counter to the people—were called on to enact, occupy, and patrol the same marginal, so-called underdeveloped spaces. In fact, the latter figure was so vital to the construction of a socialist modernity in the mid-1970s that the mobile retailer became the focus of many cultural products, including the nationally promoted northern *pingju* opera *Xiangyang Store* (*Xiangyang shangdian*). The role of the idealized salesperson as depicted in these works is critical to the function of the retail system as a whole. The vast array of customer service she provides is meant to mediate a fundamental contradiction of socialist economics: On the one hand, she casts consumer desire as not only politically acceptable but also emancipatory; while, on the other hand, she educates the masses (her prospective customers) about the dangers of frivolity, overindulgence, and the beguiling nature of commodities.

In chapter 3, I discuss the politics of productivist commodity display. Demonstrations of consumer plenty, as found in shopwindows, were meant to glorify production rather than fetishize consumption, but this was much easier said than done. Department stores, for one, inherited the architectural legacy of republican shopping, and the commodity on display remained exceedingly valuable as a representational form, quite apart from issues of a given commodity's actual use value. Moreover, the legibility of certain kinds of labor as production was not itself a given. I turn to the making of decorative porcelain in Jingdezhen, China's porcelain capital, to examine the tensions between different regimes of value as they played out in the organization of labor and the realm of sculptural aesthetics. Despite porcelain's historically elitist associations and the figurine's ties to petit bourgeois interiors, porcelain statuettes representing revolutionary heroes were churned out in Jingdezhen throughout the Cultural Revolution. A rewriting of porcelain-making historiography, the creation of massive new factories, and the construction of porcelain producers as members of the proletariat helped rehabilitate porcelain as a politically acceptable medium in the Mao period. At the same time, this process also worked to make production visible in ways that purportedly usurped the position previously held by consumption and consumer desire.

Chapter 4 follows this up by examining a number of pedagogical texts and efforts to popularize political economy as part of a massive production of discourse intended to unmask the inner workings of the commodity form and thereby diffuse its latent, counterrevolutionary potential as it was understood in the Cultural Revolution. The idea was to try to counteract the dangers of commodity fetishism through the spread of political economic knowledge. In practice, however, rather than focus on use value, for example, as we might expect, this discourse itself fetishized the commodity as an abstraction, doing little to grapple with the materiality of social relations as was purportedly its aim. Jing Chi's 1975 *A Commodity's Tale* (*Shangpin zishu*) is a case in point. A Marxist history narrated in the first person by a commodity, the text is cast as the inside scoop on how commodities work and, therefore, as the ultimate weapon against their thrall. But in reality, *A Commodity's Tale* does little to imagine an alternative relationship between people and material things. After all, the narrator is less a specific material commodity than an abstracted dematerialized commodity form.

In chapter 5, I move to the world of amateur performance, which I approach as a crucial part of the Cultural Revolution media environment. Seen from this angle, the bodies of amateur actors become a medium much like vinyl or porcelain. The key to this reframing is a notion of performance as a technology of transformation, which acts on the plastic bodies and, ideally, the subjectivities of the masses to produce a nation of revolutionary heroes in the model of the porcelain figurines discussed in chapter 3. Playing a character in a yangbanxi, for example, thereby becomes a way to actually produce that character in real life, much as the kiln effects the transmutation of clay and glaze into porcelain. Anxiety remains, however, over the possibility that this process might fail, allowing the would-be saboteur—the class enemy hidden in plain sight—an opening to undermine the revolution. The transformation sought through performance is predicated on the complete correspondence of appearance and essence, but what if the faith placed in that correspondence is exploited by the counterrevolutionary? In fact, the constant vigilance required to prevent such sabotage paradoxically guarantees that the transformation will never occur to specifications. In other words, a Cultural Revolution *hermeneutics of suspicion* necessarily begets this technology's failure.

Chapter 6 draws this study to a close with an examination of Cultural Revolution tabletop and wall-hanging mirrors in an effort to grapple with this central question: To what extent does the amateur performer's participation in networks of Cultural Revolution mediation, as described in the previous chapter, implicate that performer in and expose her to the vicissitudes of the commodity economy? Mirrors, ornamented with images of socialist models and produced for the home in massive numbers, operated very much with the same goals and logic as performance during this period, and they therefore allow us to think through the mechanisms and consequences of media proliferation. Not unlike the amateur performer, as the gazer interacts with the mirror, her body is rendered as alienable and exchangeable as a commodity.

The Stakes

Taken together, these six chapters are intended to map key aspects of the Cultural Revolution media environment, to analyze its underlying problematics, and to articulate the ways in which these problematics hark back to, and engage with, the commodity form. As a group, they also attest to the fine line between restricting the scope of commodity production under the dictatorship of the proletariat and the proliferation of commodities in the name of teleological progress or modernization, not to mention the difficulty of policing that line since the beginning of the Chinese socialist enterprise. The political and economic predicament with which the CCP has so obviously struggled in its market dealings since the 1980s is by no means new. What may well be new, however, is that, the market having long since usurped the plan, the purported uniqueness of contemporary China's socialism/capitalism—its defining Chinese characteristics—now more often than not amounts to an alibi for the unexpected persistence of the CCP in the era of the market.[44] Daniel Vukovich has even suggested that the widely held belief that the People's Republic of China will inevitably become the same as "us," that is, the (Anglo-American) West, constitutes a prevailing form of Orientalism in the twenty-first century.[45] To the extent that this is the case, the Communist Party is cast as developmentally out of step with the Chinese market and the sole obstacle to the fulfillment of the PRC's liberal destiny. When, to paraphrase Yiching Wu, "actually existing" socialism is understood as a mere "detour in the long history of capitalism," an aberration to be overcome in this way, questions concerning the CCP's continuing hold on power and legitimacy present themselves as something of a puzzle: Having outlived the Leninist party-states of Eastern Europe and the Soviet Union, the continued survival of the CCP—well in excess of its life expectancy, if the basic assumption of economic liberalization and global precedent are to be believed—cries out for explanation.[46]

One such explanation contends that commodity consumption, particularly since Deng Xiaoping's Southern Tour (*nan xun*) in 1992, has acted as a social palliative. Consumption is said to have filled the ideological void left in the wake of Mao's death while also having the benefit of "[keeping] the population satisfied when the previous certainties collapsed in the reform period. Communism and class struggle, the foundations of political understanding in the People's Republic since 1949, may have been left behind, but the rewards they had always promised were to be found in the present rather than postponed to some never arriving future."[47] This argument has been all the more persuasive for jibing neatly with a widely held explanation for the collapse of the USSR and the communist regimes of Eastern Europe. In her influential *What Was Socialism, and What Comes Next?*, for example, Katherine Verdery argues that the failure of socialism was rooted in the mismanagement of consumption and consumer desire, mismanagement that fostered much more than mere shortage. It produced an abiding tension: "Even as the regimes prevented people from consuming by not making goods available, they insisted that under socialism, the standard of living would constantly improve. This stimulated consumer appetites, perhaps with an eye to fostering increased effort and tying people into the system. Moreover, socialist ideology presented consumption as a 'right.' The system's organization exacerbated consumer desire further by frustrating it and thereby making it the focus of effort, resistance, and discontent."[48] Discontent led to collapse. Insofar as that discontent can be quelled through economic growth, commodity consumption becomes a social palliative, a means to maintain the CCP's hold on power.

There is something decidedly self-defeating in this line of reasoning, however. On the one hand, the purportedly free exchange of commodities is saddled with the responsibility of political liberalization, whereas, on the other hand, by dissipating the political potential of frustrated desire, the consumption of those same commodities is blamed for the persistence of an illiberal regime.[49] In other words, the revolution must be marketized—even if to its own inevitable detriment. And *revolution* is precisely the term, for if Maoist socialism has become capitalism with Chinese characteristics, the process by which this has taken place is often described as a sudden, irrevocable change very much on the order of 1949.[50] Such "rhetorics of transition," predicated on a notion of market development, may well, as Kevin Latham suggests, "enable the Party to defer utopia, or the new range of utopias, into the future once again," thereby maintaining its legitimacy.[51] But in reality, these rhetorics depend on a denial of contemporary China's indebtedness to the Mao era as much as they do on a vision of tomorrow as a consumerist paradise.

The failure to acknowledge and investigate the precise ways in which Chinese socialism has become what it is (and is not) today has been described as "a [deep] critical lacuna," namely, "the absence of a historically grounded understanding of the vicissitudes of Chinese socialism, with all its complexities and contradictions."⁵² Given the political expectations and burdens so often placed on marketization and consumption in characterizations of contemporary China, few vicissitudes of Chinese socialism could be more worthy of our attention—or have been so consistently misunderstood—than its fraught relationship with the commodity form in the Cultural Revolution. The future utopia currently espoused by the CCP may well be littered with commodities, but we have yet to fully come to grips with the extent to which the socialist imaginary of the Mao period—constructed in large part by and through processes of mediation—was bound up with them and their underlying logic as well. *Newborn Socialist Things* seeks to remedy that situation.

1 The Sonic Imaginary

> The utopian potential of the acoustic lies in its intensified mimicry of the process of exchange itself, now the mark not of seriality and the subordination of commodities to the single abstract equivalence of the money-form, but the anticipation in the interior and exterior reorganization of the senses of a more polymorphous transformation of value.
> —Steven Connor, "The Modern Auditory I"

Sound. Not the most obvious place to start this historical foray. I could have easily begun with something much more tangible—the porcelain statuettes discussed in chapter 3, for example, have the pleasing solidity of a cornerstone about them. To contemporary eyes, they are immediately engaging, cutesy, kitsch—a great writing hook if there ever was one. And yet, I begin with sound, sound that so often strikes us as ephemeral in the extreme, its materiality almost incidental. Almost. I begin with sound because it is much more than simply one among many components of the media environment of the late Mao period. As Steven Connor notes, the acoustic is defined by relationality, the very relationality that I argue is constitutive of newborn socialist things.[1] Sound is the realm of vibration, transmission, and sympathetic resonance; it necessarily brings entities into relation with one another, forcing us to rethink the thingness of things. Even the "modern auditory I," the self conceptualized in relation to sound instead of vision, cannot escape its implications: It teeters on the edge of disintegration, "imaged not as a point, but as a membrane" subject to—and participating in—the tuning of the world.[2] This reorientation of the self is, for Connor, the source of "the utopian potential of the acoustic" insofar as it enacts a form of relationality and anticipates an understanding of value distinct from those attending commodity exchange. I begin with sound, then, both because it speaks to the essence of mediation itself and because, to the extent that Connor is correct about the ways in which sound and a commodity-free utopian imaginary might be intertwined, we would expect the acoustic to figure prominently in constructions of Chinese socialism and dreams of the communist future. And so it does, as we shall see. In this sense, the task of this chapter is to probe the sonic imaginary of the Cultural Revolution, its imbrication with multiple media, and its role in the broader pursuit of developmental/historical progress—that is, of ever-newer newborn socialist things.

I use the term *sonic imaginary* advisedly, here, in order to go beyond the question of what the Cultural Revolution sounded like in some quantitative sense. Since listening cultures change over time, attempts to reconstruct historically accurate soundscapes by relying solely on recordings or audiometer readings strike me as beside the point.[3] Much more intriguing and productive are questions of how sound is conceptualized, what power and importance it is afforded, and the cultural valences it accrues at any given moment. In other words, I am interested in how and to what end sound is imagined and understood, and I therefore rely on a very different kind of archive.

Consider by way of example Ma Dayou's contribution to the 1959 volume *Scientists Discuss the Twenty-First Century* (*Kexuejia tan 21 shiji*), in which he complains that modernity is too noisy. For all the wonders of mechanization and industrial production facilitated by socialist advancement, the din of heavy equipment and transport vehicles leaves much to be desired. Development, in other words, comes at the cost of what we might today call noise pollution. But whereas the emergence of such a concept in North America and Western Europe in the early twentieth century was met with new legal and societal apparatuses of noise abatement,[4] Ma Dayou imagines a future in which the offensive sounds of modernity become something else entirely: "In the twenty-first century, not only will our factories have been transformed into 'concert halls' [*yinyueting*], but forms of transportation, including trains, buses, ships, and airplanes, will no longer emit monotonous, ear-piercing roars [*housheng*]. They will each be able to perform their own marvelous music [*yuequ*]. They will make people feel carefree and happy and raise work spirits a hundred-fold."[5] The drawing accompanying Ma Dayou's essay (see figure 1.1) suggests that the machines of the future would produce recognizable music much as they would produce objects on the assembly line. It is not listening that evolves here but, rather, the quality of sound itself, rendered intelligible and, therefore, by implication, pleasing. The definition of music, as opposed to noise, and the desirability of the former over the

Figure 1.1 Music-making machine of the future. In *Kexuejia tan 21 shiji* (*Scientists Discuss the Twenty-First Century*), 27. Courtesy of the Shanghai Library.

latter are taken very much for granted, and tellingly, silence, or the absence of sound, is not perceived as a viable option.[6]

Ma Dayou's fantasy is just that, of course—a fantasy—born of the Great Leap Forward. As such, Ma's flight of fancy speaks, more than anything, to the conceptual possibilities of that particular moment as well as its attendant cultural assumptions and associations. These include a fundamental link between mechanization and progress.[7] Technological innovations, emblematized in never-before-seen or -heard machines, lent themselves well to claims of advancement, separate and apart from alleged political distinctions between socialism and capitalism. There was little sense that technology per se might be anything other than a developmental boon, much as music is here assumed to be an improvement over noise and (implicitly) silence. Mechanized production processes are in this sense assumed to be inherently better than manual ones, and the (re)production of intelligible sound is deemed superior to an indecipherable racket. The factory–cum–concert hall is necessarily an improvement over the factory as it currently stands.

The machines of Ma's dreams may not have come to pass, but they did have something of a real-world corollary: the loudspeaker. Recorded sound technologies—chief among them the wired loudspeaker network—were used in the furtherance of a project very much in keeping with Ma Dayou's. The continued expansion of the network in the 1960s and beyond, sounding centralized radio, music records, and local broadcasts, was tied to a developmentalist discourse, much as "radiofication" (*radiofikatsiya*) had been a "keyword of socialist modernity" in the Soviet Union of the 1920s and 1930s.[8] In other words, in the terms of this book, the network and its related institutions, forms, audiences, and, yes sounds can be considered a newborn (because technologically novel) socialist thing. The particular aspect of this formulation I want to pursue in this chapter, however, concerns not only the issue of technological modernity but also its role in contesting, defining, and ultimately producing different kinds of space. Ma Dayou's fantasy is spatialized; the space of the factory is remade through sound into something new. I take this as a reminder that the sonic imaginary of Chinese socialism was bound up with a quest for modernity to be sure, but it was also very much enacted in and through space. And not all spaces were deemed developmentally or discursively equal. What follows is essentially my attempt to map the complexities of this acoustic topography in the Cultural Revolution so as to better understand both the mechanics of socialist sounding as well as its resonating spatialities.

Total Ambitions

As the repertoire of model performances—of revolutionary Beijing operas, ballets, and symphonic works—most closely associated with the Cultural Revolution, the yangbanxi initially belonged to the world of the stage and the live concert. But most people did not have the opportunity to attend full, professional yangbanxi stagings. Instead, they went to amateur performances of yangbanxi excerpts, performed selected arias themselves, or, beginning in the early 1970s, attended local screenings of the film versions.[9] The cinema, brought to the countryside by the efforts of mobile film units, proved crucial to the popularization and standardization of the yangbanxi and Cultural Revolution culture more broadly, but throughout that process going to a screening remained an event. Seeing a yangbanxi film—even if for the umpteenth time—meant taking a break from the monotony of one's job, endless political meetings, and the mass mobilization campaign du jour. It is difficult to argue that the ballet film *The Red Detachment of Women* (*Hongse niangzi jun*) was still fresh in 1974, but as millions of teenage boys, mesmerized by the ballerinas' short shorts, could attest, both it and film as a technology managed to retain some of their escapist charm. Yangbanxi audio recordings, by contrast, were played so often and sounded in so many quotidian spaces as early as 1967 that they became truly enmeshed with the everyday. It is in the context of such aural repetition that the yangbanxi, along with other revolutionary works, were most often consumed.

Nicole Huang understands this form of aural saturation as foundational to the "total soundscape of Mao's China." Huang adds the modifier *total* to Emily Thompson's reworking of the term *soundscape* in order to highlight the extent to which "every corner of social life was thoroughly saturated with centrally ordained and politically charged sound bytes [sic]. Sounds stemmed from the Centre and radiated to all corners of the society, including those where light failed to penetrate."[10] The implication is that mechanically (re)produced sound operated as a powerful complement to better-known mechanisms of work unit, village, or neighborhood visual surveillance. This supplementary role is not uncommonly attributed to sound. In his "acoustemology" of a Scottish hospital, for example, Tom Rice theorizes an aural equivalent to—and crucial inversion of—the Panopticon to capture this point. A "Panaudicon," Rice argues, is "an acoustics of power which, unlike the Orwellian notion of the 'never-sleeping ear,' is not manifested in the possibility of being heard by a listening presence, but in hearing an authoritarian presence. The Panaudicon operates actively through the subtle infiltration of sound into the patient's awareness."[11] This is a way of performing centralized power and enacting perpetual control not through the threat of overhearing—of unexpected sonic capture—but of audible omnipresence. Technologically speaking, it is the purview of amplification rather than that of clandestine recording or "bugging."[12]

While I share Huang's desire to emphasize the ubiquity and pervasiveness of centralized sound bites during this period, her invocation of the "total" gives me pause. For one thing, the "total" lends itself all too easily to an unproductive discussion of totalitarian cultural production and an excavation of totalitarian realism in sound, much as Igor Golomstock has attempted in his study of Nazi, Stalinist, Italian Fascist, and Maoist art.[13] In other words, it may be tempting to approach the "total soundscape" as a product of a particular sonic—and especially musical—aesthetic. We could posit, in short, not only a Cultural Revolution soundscape but also a particular Cultural Revolution sound, thereby assuming the existence of sound or music as a discrete, analyzable, aesthetic object in the process. Although this has not been Huang's own tack, it is not unfamiliar to scholars of music from this era.[14] My concern is that efforts to determine the musical characteristics of a repertoire in this way already presuppose the existence of a coherent aesthetic formulation or project with set ideological associations.[15]

As Brian Currid convincingly argues with regard to the German National Socialist case, this manner of assumption is troublesome, for if a "Nazi sound" can be said to have existed at all, it was made, not given. It was produced over time. The politics of fascism alone did not preordain a particular musical aesthetic, nor can they alone account for the aesthetic tendencies that eventually came about under the Nazi regime. The key for Currid is not only to "concentrate on questions of *what* was listened to; equally important to our analysis of musical mass culture is the study of *how* listening took place."[16] How music was consumed and the terms under which that consumption was imagined and represented are critical to understanding both the cultural work (popular) music has done and continues to do and the meanings sound and music acquire as they circulate. Currid's own particular interest is in historicizing the production of Nazi-era "unisonality," which he approaches as a historically specific mediated form of what he calls the "acoustics of publicity."[17] He is interested, in essence, in sound and its involvement in the production of—specifically national—publics and their attendant qualities, that is, publicity.

There is ample reason to be wary of relying on scholarship pertaining to Nazi Germany in discussions of New China, despite some similarities in the apparent aesthetic traits favored by the regimes.[18] Often lumped together under the nebulous banner of "totalitarianism," as indicated above, Hitler's Germany and Mao's China differed widely in terms of the availability of radio and other home devices, not to mention differences in expectations as to standards of living and the consumption of (luxury) consumer commodities.[19] These dissimilarities notwithstanding, Currid's provocative methodological intervention remains instructive for those of us interested in the popular culture of the Chinese socialist period. It is incumbent on us not to approach works of cultural production and media systems as static but, rather, as part and parcel of dynamic social processes. More specifically, we must attend to a given medium's "forms of address and... structures of publicity," which are socially constructed and change over time.[20] Better, then, to speak of sounding the Cultural Revolution rather than of an a priori Cultural Revolution sound—a process of making and imagining rather than a ready-made entity.

My second concern with the invocation of the "total" in regard to Cultural Revolution sounding is its tendency to collapse the necessary conceptual gap between the aspiration to centralized sonic totality that we see and hear in the period in myriad ways and the inevitable historical failure to fulfill that aspiration. Ironically, an increased attention to the particular technologies of sonic (re)production used at the time, and their attendant forms of address, can be misleading here, if such attention comes at the expense of a concept of listener agency, for there is little doubt that the dominant technology in the PRC soundscape up to and beyond 1976 was the (mostly wired) loudspeaker system. Even after the transistorization of radios in the 1960s, private radio usage "lagged behind loudspeakers as a form of mass communication."[21]

This was partly the result of pricing, as household loudspeakers remained cheaper than even transistor radios. It was also partly due to the continued suspicion of individualized listening and the flexibility radios afforded in receiving shortwave foreign or "enemy" broadcasts.[22] This was in fact one of the main reasons initially given for developing a wired—as opposed to wireless—system on a national scale in 1955.[23] It was not until the 1970s that private radio ownership was encouraged by officials, and by that point, the wired loudspeaker network was already ubiquitous.[24] Although official statistics cannot be taken at face value, estimates concerning the number of loudspeakers in the network remain instructive in terms of the scale and pervasiveness of the system. Andrew James Nathan reports, "By 1974 there were 141 million speakers in use, widely available in cities and reaching into 90 percent of the production brigades and teams and 65 percent of rural households."[25] That amounts to roughly one loudspeaker for every six people.[26] Even if we assume that these numbers are inflated, they speak to the centrality of loudspeakers within the CCP's larger project of integrating revolutionary China through sound.[27]

The underlying logic of the loudspeaker itself bespeaks a compulsory egalitarianism that also seems to further these "total/totalitarian" goals. Those within range of the loudspeaker are all subject to the same aural stimuli, regardless of individual choice or social hierarchy, to say nothing of the fact that listeners are unable to affect or modify the sound to which they are exposed. The CCP's use of the loudspeaker emphasized precisely those aspects of the technology that most restricted listener agency. Loudspeakers were most typically fixed to immovable architectural elements, like electrical posts or buildings, high above listeners' heads. The volume could not be adjusted, nor could the loudspeakers be turned off. Finally, it goes without saying that while some of the content played on the loudspeaker network may have been up to the discretion of local work units and brigades, it was most assuredly not up to individual listeners. To the extent that we might think of the music and sound emanating from officially sanctioned loudspeakers as a means of ideological interpolation, the way in which the technology operated—its technologically mediated modes of address—(re)produced and (re)enforced fundamental communist claims about equality, collectivity, and the integrity of the proletarian masses as a cohesive entity.

It is precisely because of this logic that the loudspeaker has often stood as a perfect aural metonym for totalitarianism: It makes listeners of us all, regardless of our individual wishes. As the sound studies commonplace puts it, though we can close our eyes, we cannot close our ears, and it is precisely the difficulty of keeping sound at bay that the loudspeaker exploits. Moreover, this aspect of the loudspeaker is all the more evident in the wake of new devices—from the Sony Walkman to the Apple iPod—that afford listeners the opportunity to consume their own music regardless of where they happen to be or whom they happen to be with, that is, devices that allow for what Rey Chow has called "miniaturized listening."[28] By virtue of its portability and headphones, the Walkman—Chow's paradigmatic technology of this new way to listen—offered perhaps the first of many technological approximations of a would-be "deaf[ness] to the loudspeakers of history": the production of one's own sound world as a tactical counter to a "hailing" that cannot otherwise be denied.[29]

The problems with this formulation are themselves twofold. On the one hand, it gives the loudspeaker far too much credit; we must allow for the possibility, if not the inevitability, of failure. Although there were no Walkmans during the Mao era—Sony first released the Walkman in 1979—the Mao-period soundscape could nonetheless be navigated and negotiated in important ways, ways that must not be overlooked. On the other hand, considerations of sonic contestation must not be reduced to a facile dichotomy whereby relatively cheap transistor radios, for example, allowing clandestine access to foreign stations, are pegged as resistive and take the place of Chow's Walkmans, fighting the good fight against the sonic totalitarianism made possible by the loudspeaker. The lines between hegemony and counterhegemony and between politics and pleasure are not so easily drawn, especially in discussions of soundscapes, which are porous and permeable by definition. Positing and seeking out an opposition between what Chow calls the "gigantic history of the public" and "miniaturized music" limits the terms of their possible interplay from the outset.[30] Moreover, we risk lapsing into a technologically determinist argument in which the specifications of the loudspeaker necessarily act on passive listeners unprotected by headphones or earbuds. The question of mass publicity, from this perspective, would simply be reduced to the logic of the loudspeaker, outlined above, a logic understood to be inescapable and independent of listener agency and social interaction.

Making Space

I would like to suggest something different: The CCP's investment in and reliance on the loudspeaker network for the dissemination of official discourse, both musical and linguistic, may have been undertaken in the pursuit of forming what Carolyn Birdsall, building on Benedict Anderson, has called an "imagined listening community."[31] However, the notion that the party could unilaterally impose the terms and character of this imagined community, of this particular form of mass publicity, was more fantasy than reality—more goal than fait accompli, more sonic imaginary than historical soundscape.

This is not to say that the logic and technical constraints of the loudspeaker can be overlooked; they were crucial to the ways in which revolution and counterrevolution were sounded and sonically conceptualized, both in terms of the development and shape of the broadcasting network and in terms of the aesthetics favored in official sounding. As Andrew F. Jones has argued in relation to quotation songs—a popular form in the first few years of the Cultural Revolution in which Mao's quotations were set to music—recording practices appear to have taken the specifications of the wired loudspeaker network into account.

> The production is perfectly suited to unison singing, melding choral voices and orchestral accompaniment together into a monophonic wall of sound, one pitched high enough and with enough amplitude to penetrate the public spaces in which these songs were usually broadcast on monaural in-line loudspeaker systems. The shrillness of the music, with its tendency to emphasize the frequencies well above the midrange, almost certainly reflects the inability of compact loudspeakers and megaphones to reproduce low-frequency band with any degree of fidelity. The lack of stereo separation and internal space between the instruments or individual voices is also an artifact of this technology.[32]

In this way, record production took the sonic limitations of the loudspeaker, the record's primary mode of intended dissemination, into account from the very beginning, such that the loudspeaker network could be put to the most effective use. Insofar as the sonic qualities of quotation songs, despite being a relatively short-lived phenomenon, are indicative of a more generalizable Cultural Revolution proclivity, the technical specifications of loudspeakers go hand in hand with ideological justifications for a "monophonic wall of sound." The emphasis on homophonic choral settings of important political texts, for example, is often understood as evoking the unity of the masses exacted by the CCP. In drawing our attention to the technology by which this music was sounded, Jones complicates such (largely semiotic) interpretations of an a priori Cultural Revolution sound, much as Currid urges us to do.

Beyond this, however, I want to emphasize Jones's observation concerning the spatialized aspect of this music and its dissemination as particularly crucial. Both Jones and Huang speak of Cultural Revolution sound "penetrating" (already existing) space(s)—and with good reason. The fantasy of uncontested, centralized sonic dominion and aural saturation depends on the twin notions that space exists, out there, irrespective of its resonant actualization, and that walls of sound can trump walls of brick and mortar. Like the Panaudicon, sound in this formulation permeates and infiltrates. It does not produce space; it fills it, just as a liquid takes the shape of its container.

We see these assumptions at work in the general statistical record of the era itself. What percentage of brigades have loudspeakers? What is the ratio of households to loudspeakers in the countryside? The goal implicit in these statistical enquiries is always completeness, 100 percent, 1:1. On occasion, this predilection for the complete is baldly spelled out, as in a draft 1965 report by the Shanghai People's Radio (Shanghai renmin guangbo diantai) on the state of the PRC's broadcast and listening network. The document lays out a fifteen-year plan for the expansion of the national broadcast system: By 1980, the average rural ratio of households to loudspeakers, for example, was to be brought down from 18.4:1 to 1.5:1, with 63 percent of the countryside populace having access to broadcasts in their own homes.[33] (If Nathan's calculations are correct, these "penetration" rates were achieved by 1974, six years ahead of schedule.[34]) And that was just the beginning. The quality of the loudspeakers would improve, requiring less power and operating with ever greater fidelity. These new specifications would allow the network to piggyback on already existing and newly built infrastructure systems, including railway, telephone, and electric lines. Meanwhile, a renewed push toward sonic omnipresence in the cities would focus on increasing the number of street-side loudspeakers and amplifying broadcasts on public transportation.[35] Each of these initiatives speaks to an apparent need to sonically fill every nook and cranny of a preexisting, fixed topography.

And yet, despite the evident historical investment in this understanding of the relationship between sound and space, we need not follow suit. Indeed, I would suggest a much more phenomenologically informed approach whereby sound does not penetrate as much as it constitutes, organizes, and defines space(s). In this way, the CCP push toward aural saturation might be understood not (only) as an exercise in centralized power but rather as a mechanism that helped conceptualize and produce the nation as an acoustic space. The question for us then becomes one of balance: How do we reconcile these two apparently disparate—even conflicting—conceptions of sound and space, one historically informed, the other a product of a more contemporary phenomenological approach?

My reliance on the notion of a historically and culturally specific *sonic imaginary* is partly in response to this question. It would behoove us at this juncture, however, to draw an additional distinction between the concepts of *space* and *territory*. More specifically, drawing on the insights of Gilles Deleuze and Félix Guattari, I want to suggest that while sound, by virtue of its resonant properties, is forever spatial and spatializing, it need not necessarily be a territorializing force.[36] Territories require organization, borders, and power differentials; they are the stuff of complex, multifaceted, and multimodal architectonics. Consider the role of Muzak as an architectural component of the Mall of America or the amplification of the *azan* (Islamic call to prayer) as a means to reorganize urban geographies in Singapore, Pakistan, and Nigeria.[37] These constitute efforts to instrumentalize sound's ability to produce space in the name of much larger conceptual entities and projects (consumerism, religion, etc.). It is not enough, therefore, to recast sound as a productive spatial force during the Cultural Revolution; it was also quite consciously deployed as a tool through which the ongoing processes of national territorialization could be supplemented. In other words, despite its essentially phenomenological nature, the production of the Chinese nation as an acoustic space did not come about spontaneously. An idea of national territory preceded it, like a blueprint or architectural plan. It is precisely this understanding, taken to be a preexisting actual space—rather than its conceptual precursor—on which the notion of aural saturation is predicated. The goal of such saturation is to ultimately render an acoustically produced territory *coextensive* with cartographical norms, resulting in a process not unlike the elementary school assignments of my youth in which I was asked to color in maps of the world. We should know better than to believe that cartography simply and objectively reflects an ontologically independent geography; maps make geography in the name of facile reflection. So, too, in the Cultural Revolution was acoustic space actively produced in the name of penetrating every inch of an assumed national territory.

Sounding the Nation

The ties between broadcast sound technologies—notably, radio—and the arduous process of nation building are well known, especially as they pertain to the formation of explicitly national "mass publics" and "imagined listening communities."[38] Studies of state broadcasting organs, of both liberal democratic and authoritarian regimes, lend themselves uncommonly well to the examination of these ties, since, in these cases, the media apparatus is manifestly part of the national bureaucracy. Still, I want to argue that, even in the instance of centralized broadcasting, the impact of recorded sound and its dissemination on nation building ultimately has less to do with state organization and integration than it does with the fostering of imagined communities in national terms. The imprimatur of the central government is not nearly as crucial here as the ability of sound to facilitate the production of homogeneous empty time, its corollary understanding of simultaneity, and a belief that the listening public, though scattered and unseen, has something essential in common. These abilities, which Benedict Anderson so famously attributed to modern newspapers, novels, and, more generally, print capitalism, have unquestionably been exploited by official broadcasters far and wide, but such organs are not alone in this.³⁹ This clarification is important, for it requires us to focus on sounding and listening in active and productive terms as part of the underlying justification for the national PRC broadcasting bureaucracy in the first instance, as opposed to its mere by-product.

Consider, in this vein, the proliferation of loudspeakers during the Cultural Revolution as both instruments of compulsory egalitarianism and a unitary sense of time. Listeners were made simultaneous, as well as equal, actors, a fact exploited by the organization of the system as a whole. Each wired loudspeaker was linked to a local broadcast station, which received wireless signals from Central People's Radio (Zhongyang renmin guangbo diantai) in Beijing in addition to signals from the provincial capital. These local broadcast stations were typically located in the county seat or, in some cases, in individual factories and production brigades, disseminating one of Central Radio's three feeds through the locality's wired system. Central Radio I and II offered the most extensive daily programing schedules, each coming on the air in the early morning hours (4:00 a.m. and 5:00 a.m., respectively) with a choral rendition of "The East Is Red" and a preview of the day's upcoming broadcasts. News and cultural programming—presented under the catchall term *geming wenyi* (revolutionary literature and art)—filled the bulk of Central Radio I's and II's air time, broken up at various points throughout the day with more specialized programming, including morning calisthenics, children's shows, and broadcasts intended for the military, among other targeted demographics.⁴⁰ This system was undoubtedly meant to promote the centralization and standardization of ideological content, but its greatest impact on everyday life likely had little to do with the dissemination of authorized sound bites per se. Rather, the daily repetition of the Central Radio schedule, sounded across the broad expanse of the PRC, ultimately (re)structured time itself, much as early BBC radio (and then television) have been credited with doing in the United Kingdom.⁴¹ More precisely, it reorganized local temporalities according to an explicitly national rubric. Not for nothing does Guo Qingsheng credit radio with popularizing "Beijing time" outside military circles in the early months of the PRC. Broadcasters were charged with keeping time for their publics; when they switched over to the new standard, they helped produce the very nation in whose name that new standard was enacted.⁴² The repetitive and predictable parceling of airtime, characteristic of the schedule as a form, is an extension of this same logic over the course of the day.

If there is something of a chicken-and-egg quality to all of this, it is perhaps rooted in the paradox of the nation itself. On the one hand, we speak of the birth of a nation and nation building while, on the other hand, nationhood is also rooted in a notion of the eternal. The PRC, as a nation, therefore both does and does not have a beginning. Given our focus here, it should come as no surprise that the construction of this nonbeginning beginning is inextricably tied to sound and, more specifically, to Central Radio. Consider the very moment of the PRC's conjuring: Mao's declaration, made atop the rostrum of the Gate of Heavenly Peace on October 1, 1949, that the People's Republic of China was established. The statement itself is a perfect example of J. L. Austin's "performative utterance" whereby the enunciation of the words accomplishes the fact; in a very real sense, Mao's words called the PRC into being. They did so, crucially, not because of their semantic meaning, but because of the "felicitous" circumstances under which they were uttered.[43] As the microphones surrounding Mao in figure 1.2 suggest, these circumstances involved a form of sonic reproduction and mediation. Indeed, it is no accident that this bit of word magic—this mediated summoning—should make up the first Central Radio broadcast, the (re)production of which, as sound, helped constitute the nation acoustically. Lest we think this sonic process a minor side note, we should remember that the precise formulation of Mao's declaration has not survived in the Chinese popular imagination. That is to say, Mao has consistently been misheard by history, a claim that "the Chinese people [had] stood up" erroneously placed in the chairman's mouth.[44] Truth be told, it is difficult to begrudge the then inchoate national public its collective aural hallucination: Mao's Hunanese accent was so strong, and Mandarin was spoken by so few, that the semantic meaning of his statement was (relatively) rarely understood. In other words, perhaps this defining moment is better characterized not as word magic, but as sound magic. It is the sounding and resounding of the utterance *as a performative act* that ultimately matters more than the precise lexical composition of the utterance itself.

The importance of mediated sounding, as opposed to linguistic communication, at this crucial and explicit instance of national formation has a number of consequences for the way we might approach the sonic imaginary of the Cultural Revolution. Most importantly—and fortuitously, given the current restrictions of the archive—it once again draws our attention to the means through which sound was produced and the underlying conceptualization of that process rather than the aesthetic particularities of any given broadcast.[45] It also requires us to shift our focus from listeners to broadcasters, to the interaction between human actors and technologies, like the loudspeaker and the flexi disc, in the production of sound as well as its consumption. From the perspective of the party-state, there is a sense in which that initial conjuring of the PRC in 1949 must be perpetually reenacted, such that the nation can be sonically reforged. Every radio broadcast, every centrally ordained sound bite blared through the wired loudspeaker system is a performative invocation and remaking of the nation, as an epistemic and lived category, as well as

Figure 1.2 Mao Zedong proclaims the founding of the People's Republic of China atop the Gate of Heavenly Peace in Beijing, October 1, 1949. His words were broadcast on Central Radio. AP photo.

a performance of centralized CCP power. With stakes such as these, it should not be surprising, then, that the fantasy of sonic saturation became so enticing or, for that matter, that access to the instruments of (national) sounding became such contested terrain.

At the heart of that terrain lies the local broadcast station. In the case of Central Radio programs geared toward a national audience, as in the schedule outlined above, local stations essentially functioned as mere relay posts, extending the wireless network, emanating primarily from Beijing, outward throughout the countryside via wired technology. It was also the case, however, that local broadcast stations could, to a certain extent, control local content. In some situations, this might mean broadcasting in local topolect, thereby overcoming language barriers commonly faced in rural areas where Mandarin remained unfamiliar, if not incomprehensible, to peasants.[46] In other cases, it permitted the communication of information pertaining to local news and events as well as the broadcasting of live performances by local propaganda troupes. Areas still relatively far removed from the closest location broadcasting over the wired system also sometimes complemented this sonic network with stand-alone broadcast stations in order to provide more localized information and programming.

The control of both types of broadcast station became very contentious in the factional Red Guard violence of 1967–68, with different groups, each claiming to defend Mao, fighting over the means of sonic information dissemination.[47] After this phase of the Cultural Revolution had passed and order was—albeit tenuously—restored, broadcast stations retained their status as key loci of struggle in the discourse of continuous revolution, if not in its reality. In Wang Cuilan's short story "Red Broadcast Station" ("Hongse guangbozhan"), for example, the Criticize Lin Biao, Criticize Confucius campaign translates into a battle over local broadcasting between a twelve-year-old and a former landlord. Inspired by the sound of Beijing and the attacks on the traitor Lin Biao (1907–71), the intrepid Tiezhu (literally, "iron pillar") dreams of joining a local voice to that of the faraway capital. Between 1966 and 1969, everyone in Tiezhu's northeastern hamlet installed a loudspeaker in their homes, but they had no broadcast station of their own with which to address local issues. Tiezhu and his friends set out to remedy this situation and establish a small outpost at the foot of the Great Wall from which amplified sound can reach every household. Tiezhu's father, the requisite revolutionary adult of the piece, solemnly warns his son at the outset not to "belittle this broadcast station! Your broadcast station is a dissemination point [xuanchuanzhan] for Chairman Mao's revolutionary line. You must earn the praise of all poor and lower-middle peasants and the fear of every class enemy."[48] Tiezhu predictably succeeds in doing just that. He so rattles and angers the evil Zhou Guangfa by involving the latter's granddaughter in the revolutionary enterprise that Zhou is forced to show his true colors. He resorts to sabotage and loosens a stone on the mountain path to the station in an effort to do Tiezhu bodily harm. It doesn't work; Tiezhu is too vigilant to be taken in by such tricks. Instead, he manages to turn the tables on Zhou Guangfa, fooling him into admitting his crimes and getting him arrested.

As we see in this short story, the expansion of local broadcast stations, both as part of the wired loudspeaker system and in addition to it, as in the case of Tiezhu, was promoted not just as a way to extend the reach of Central Radio and increase centralization—though that was undoubtedly a prime motivating factor. It was also seen as a way to encourage and carry out class struggle at the local level. That is, it was a tool with which to continuously remake the revolutionary masses and, therefore, the nation as an imagined community free of class enemies.

Focusing on the production of sound rather than its consumption, however, we might also understand the local broadcast station and broadcaster as the architect of the nation as an acoustic space in addition to a listening collective. Tiezhu's importance would therefore reside in his desire to performatively expand the nation's sonic (re)production on its territorial margins, that is, to supplement the spaces engendered by the sound of Beijing. Technologically speaking, this role could be achieved with only a microphone. An additional amplifier or loudspeaker would be necessary when operating outside the wired system, but these were relatively inexpensive and easy to obtain. The poorest rural communes and communities could make do with this to broadcast news and political reports, as Tiezhu does in his village. But we know that many slightly richer localities equipped their stations with "elaborated banks of receivers, recorders, microphones, and amplifiers."[49] After 1968, these rural broadcast stations were often run by urban youth with an interest in radio and audio technology sent down to the villages (*xia xiang*).[50] These broadcast stations also typically boasted record players and collections of politically acceptable records fit to be played for the public in an official capacity. As with most commodities, work units in both urban and rural areas remained the major purchasers of record players and records throughout the Cultural Revolution. It is in this context, fueled by the desire to produce, expand, and saturate national territory, that the crank-operated turntable and the flexi disc emerged in the late 1960s as key recorded sound technologies.

Records and Record Players

This phenomenon is borne out in the few published photographs of record players in the late Mao period. A remarkable example is found in a 1974 collection of photographs of youngsters sent to the northeast (see figure 1.3). Two teenage girls are shown sitting under a tree on the edge of an agricultural field—laboring peasants are just barely visible in the background. The young women are hard at work too. They are surrounded by audio equipment: a microphone, a record player, stacks of records, a loudspeaker hidden among the leaves. The girl in the foreground is in the midst of reading a report, while the other looks on with a smile, ready to change records when her

Figure 1.3 Broadcasters in the field. From Jiefangjun Heilongjiang shengchan jianshe budui zhengzhi bu, *Zhishi qingnian zai Beidahuang* (*Sent-Down Youth in the Northeast*), 51. Courtesy of the Shanghai Library.

comrade is finished. They are broadcasters in the mold of little Tiezhu. Here, at the end of the world, they are beyond the reach of the wired loudspeaker network and the electric grid, but they must nonetheless find a way to sound the nation. Luckily for them, the great migration of sent-down youth to the countryside coincided with a renewed interest in the manually powered record player and the invention of a new, more durable type of record, one eminently better suited to the rugged outdoors.

Production of any kind of record in the PRC during the Cultural Revolution was the sole purview of the China Record Group (Zhongguo changpian she), better known since 1985 as the China Record Corporation (Zhongguo changpian zong gongsi). China Records traces its roots back to the Great China Record Factory (Da zhonghua changpian chang) of republican Shanghai. With initial financing from Japanese businessmen—a detail conveniently left out of official China Records histories—obtained by none other than Sun Yat-sen (1866–1925), the proverbial father of the republic, the Great China Record Factory was one of the few relatively successful domestic and explicitly nationalist attempts to compete with transnationals like Pathé-EMI.[51] After Shanghai was taken over by the Communists in May 1949, Great China was placed under the control of the new municipal government and quickly released seven records of revolutionary songs for radio stations to play on air.[52] The Great China Record Factory was then initially rechristened the People's Record Factory (Renmin changpian chang) and put under the direction of the Central Broadcasting Administration (Zhongyang guangbo shiye ju). After a series of short-lived mergers and record labels in the early 1950s, all PRC record production was consolidated under the People's Records facility, now the China Record Factory (Zhongguo changpian chang), and the China Records (Zhongguo changpian) label in 1955. The overarching China Record Group was officially founded in 1958, taking Shanghai as its headquarters and establishing subsidiaries in Beijing, Chengdu, and later Guangzhou. The group brought together every step of the record-making process under one organization, which, as of 1963 and the establishment of the China Record Distribution Company (Zhongguo changpian faxing gongsi), included getting the finished product into the hands of (in-country) broadcasters and consumers.[53] The China Record Group also incorporated record player and needle production and released a line of electric record players, mainly for use in broadcast stations. Beginning in 1964, the most popular of these was the Zhonghua 206, a four-speed (16, 33⅓, 45, and 78 rpm) record player produced in the Shanghai factory until 1987.

Prior to the emergence of the Zhonghua 206, the Shanghai factory had been closely associated with two manually powered turntable units: the Zhonghua 102 and the Zhonghua 103. According to research conducted by the China General Goods Company (Zhongguo baihuo gongsi), these were in fact the only hand-operated record players domestically produced in 1963 and 1964.[54] This was partly because of new restrictions placed on the use of necessary raw materials, but it was also a reflection of the fact that, by this point, the Shanghai factory's sixty-thousand-unit annual production rate was well in excess of demand. Those in charge of commodity acquisitions in state department stores chalked this situation up to a number of factors, including reductions in individual purchasing power and limitations on discretionary spending at the work-unit level. But the underlying cause of the manually powered record player's demise was ultimately pegged on the increased electrification of the countryside—why get a manual model when a more advanced electric model becomes an option?[55] Whereas the early 1960s were characterized by a marked tendency toward the development of electric record players, however, beginning in the late 1960s, hand-cranked record players returned to prominence.

This apparent comeback had everything to do with shifts in the radio industry. The Beijing Radio Factory (Beijing wuxiandian chang), for example, had achieved great success in the late 1950s with its line of Peony (Mudan) luxury brand radios.[56] In 1959, it began offering a new combination model: The Peony 1201 added a four-speed record player with a diamond-tip needle to its Peony radio base and frame. It was a console-style unit and was endorsed by the likes of then president Liu Shaoqi. In 1961, the Beijing Radio Factory took the concept to the next level by adding an audio recorder and a television. Transistorization then changed the game completely, and in the mid-1960s the bulk of the industry shifted from making large, console models to small, portable devices. But how does one combine a transistor radio with a record player and maintain flexibility of operation outside the home or broadcast station? Reenter the hand-crank, once pooh-poohed in favor of electricity. Thus, in 1968, the Beijing Radio Factory began producing the East Is Red (Dongfang hong) 101: a two-speed (33⅓ and 78 rpm), hand-crank-operated record player with built-in battery-powered transistor radio and amplifier, perfect for the most intrepid broadcaster or rusticated music lover.[57] (See figure 1.4.) Other record player manufacturers began offering similar devices as well. A national industry forecast for 1970 made by the military suggests that these new combination models quickly overtook electric record player production: Whereas thirty thousand electric units were on the production docket, 132,750 multiuse devices (*duoyongji*) were slated for 1970. These numbers indicate a tremendous change in the industry's priorities.[58]

Just as these new combination units became available in the late 1960s, China Records began producing a new kind of record: the flexi disc. As the name suggests, a flexi disc is a flexible record usually made from thin, malleable sheets of polyvinyl chloride (PVC) plastic. Eva-Tone Inc., based in Clearwater, Florida, and its licensees (Lyntone in the UK) began producing the first commercially available flexi discs—the format was trademarked Soundsheets—in 1962. China Records first successfully produced its own 33⅓ rpm

Figure 1.4 The East Is Red 101 record player, circa 1970. Weltmuseum Wien.

seven-inch flexi disc—*bomo changpian* in Chinese—in 1966 and achieved full-scale production in 1968. The records came in red, blue, and green, could hold about six minutes of music, speech, or other sound per side, and were practically indestructible. The sound quality may well have been horrible— yet another indication that the act of sounding was just as important, if not more so, than the particularities of what was being sounded—but the new format was much more affordable than the typical ten-inch micro-groove LP. Flexi discs quickly became the dominant format in the PRC, with a full and varied—at least by Cultural Revolution standards—catalog. Returning our attention to the young broadcasters in figure 1.3, we might note the appearance of yangbanxi heroes on the record sleeve in the lower left of the photograph. This is precisely the sleeve used for yangbanxi flexi discs.[59] The girls have taken to the fields, and thanks to the flexi disc, they have no need to worry about the stacks of music they have brought with them. Like the return of the hand-crank, the flexi disc facilitates a conceptualization of the farthest reaches of the PRC as an acoustic space. This is the record player territorializing the national frontier.

Given China Records's relationship with the central broadcasting apparatus, it is perhaps no surprise that the company's primary target audience was the broadcasting network itself. Record players in individual homes were a rarity throughout the Mao period. Like most luxury leisure items, they were in short supply, and their cost, when available at all, put them well out of reach of the average urban worker, to say nothing of the average peasant.

Beginning in the mid-1950s, the China General Goods Company categorized record players, along with products as varied as waxed paper, harmonicas, ping-pong balls, typewriters, and sewing machines, as *fenpei shangpin* or distributed commodities—commodities that were in limited supply and therefore needed to be controlled.[60] As time went on, a number of (increasingly, electric) record player models went on the market, including those put out by China Records, but they nonetheless retained their status as high-end, elusive consumer goods. Indeed, in 1967, electric record players were among a number of luxury commodities (including typewriters, furniture, bicycles, loudspeakers, amplifiers, and watches) made off-limits for both work units and individuals without the expressed permission of the local revolutionary committee or its military equivalent.[61]

By contrast, the hand-crank-operated record player, newly reemerged in the late 1960s, seems to have served something of a different discursive function. It became primarily associated with itinerant broadcasters and others seeking to supplement and expand the performative sounding of the national wired loudspeaker network and the nation as an acoustic space; that is, it became tied to the project of frontier territorialization. In this sense, images of record players out in the countryside are reminiscent of the discourse surrounding mobile film projection teams and, to a certain extent, touring propaganda and opera troupes. In the case of traveling projection units, which first emerged in the early 1950s, the medium of film and collective viewing practices sought to forge new national subjects while producing and organizing national space.[62] The peregrinations of the mobile and mobilized record player appear to have served much the same purpose. Despite the similarities in the ways in which the mobility of film projectors and record players were harnessed by the CCP, however, it is nonetheless important to bear in mind that the two technologies had very different cultural associations, to say nothing of their distinct forms of address. Film viewing was always something of an event outside the (urban) home—thus the importance of the cinema as a quintessentially modern, public space and, conversely, the very different appeal of television—whereas sonic broadcasting, in the words of Kate Lacey, could be "woven into the warp and weft of everyday life."[63] More to the point, film as a medium did not readily lend itself to fantasies of saturation and penetration in the way that recorded sound did; film projection teams were not in the business of achieving perpetual omnipresence. Broadcast teams, on the other hand, implicitly were. The depiction of record players *en plein air* and in the far reaches of a preconceived national territory attest to this aspect of the Cultural Revolution's sonic imaginary all while establishing the record player's new domain on the margins.

Sonic Oases

This is not to say that sonic totality was achieved, of course—quite the opposite. As the concerted emphasis on the territorializing capabilities of performative national sounding, somewhat counterintuitively, suggests, alternative sonic modes and soundings—and therefore alternative spaces and spatialities—continued to vex fantasies of total saturation, even as the number of loudspeakers and broadcasters grew ever larger. Indeed, one might even suggest that the more invested in omnipresence the centralized sonic regime became, the more it was guaranteed to fail. In late 1968, for example, a great wave of urban youth began to descend on the countryside—from the borderlands of Inner Mongolia to the tropical island of Hainan to the frigid expanses of Manchuria—that is, to the margins of national (acoustic) space. Many brought with them an interest in technology, music, literature, and the performing arts; some could boast skills and training in these areas; and a precious few carried radios, record players, records, and books with them on their journey out of the cities. These materials ran the gamut from official cultural products to hand-copied, restricted novels. In some cases, distance from the cities resulted in the relaxation of restrictions on cultural consumption, allowing the very same population of youngsters who were called on to broadcast the sound of the center ever louder and ever farther to also create an increasing number of rather subversive, impromptu *shalong* (salons). There were fewer eyes to surveil and fewer ears to overhear, which made tuning in to enemy radio stations emanating from Hong Kong or listening to a recording of Debussy's "Clair de Lune" far less dangerous in the countryside than in densely populated areas. There was, in this regard, much more room to maneuver on the frontier.

Such salon gatherings also took place in urban environments, albeit at greater risk to the participants. Indeed, they feature prominently in the poet Bei Dao's (1949–) recollections of records, despite the fact that he also worked as a broadcaster at the East Is Red Oil Refinery on the outskirts of Beijing in the early 1970s.[64] His three favorite records? Strauss's "The Blue Danube," Tchaikovsky's "Capriccio Italien," and Paganini's Violin Concerto No. 4 in D minor. The fact that these are all Western classical music records should remind us that listening to records privately was, more often than not, part of an elite cultural practice, both in the sense that the materials required were luxury items and that listeners often had designs on a certain musical erudition. If one was lucky enough to own or have access to a record player for personal use, chances are one was not listening to the yangbanxi or anything else that might be broadcast over the loudspeaker network. In this might be found a form of distinction. But what interests me most here is the way in which this kind of clandestine sounding produced spaces that constituted themselves in contradistinction to those of official mass publicity.

> We closed the heavy curtains, filled our wine glasses, lit our cigarettes, and let the music shatter the night around us, taking us far away. Because we'd listened to it so many times, the needle first had to cross a scratchy expanse before reaching the glorious work. A short pause. Kang Cheng gestured to emphasize his words as he started to explain the second section [of the Tchaikovsky]: "At the crack of dawn, a small band of travelers crosses the ruins of ancient Rome.…" It was late. The music was finished, but nobody left. We slept, strewn about left and right, the needle slipping at the end of the record with a *zila zila*.[65]

The closed curtains and the record player combine to produce a space beyond the purview of the official cultural apparatus—a sonic haven of decadent leisure and individual choice. This is a fantasy of the record as "desert island."[66] It is also a fantasy of "record listening" as "contribut[ion] to a hermetic world walled by favorite recorded sounds."[67]

In truth, of course, any such approximated hermeticism is and was necessarily imperfect. The boundaries of these precarious worlds remained porous, the space created short-lived—even more so in the cities than in the countryside. The means of their (re)production—that is, records—were always subject to seizure by the authorities. Bei Dao, for example, was relieved of his Tchaikovsky after an official search. Where and when this space was engendered it took on the fleeting, oppositional character of Hakim Bey's "Temporary Autonomous Zones" or TAZs, which exist "not only beyond Control but also beyond definition, beyond gazing and naming as acts of enslaving, beyond the understanding of the State, beyond the State's ability to see."[68] But a TAZ can operate in this "beyond" only for so long: It "is like an uprising which does not engage directly with the State, a guerilla operation which liberates an area (of land, of time, of imagination) and then dissolves itself to re-form elsewhere/elsewhen, *before* the State can crush it."[69] The alternative bubble must sporadically shift and reconstitute, lest it be summarily popped once and for all.

In a sense, the hermeticism is imperfect here, too, in that Bei Dao listens in the presence of others. Strictly speaking, this is not one of Evan Eisenberg's "ceremonies of a solitary."[70] A group of listeners are constituted as such through sound. More to the point, however, this particular group of listeners is also implicated in a larger imagined listening community, extending far beyond the confines of a single, dark room—an imagined listening community that, to use William Howland Kenney's evocative phrase, listens "alone together" as more than, or other than, national subjects.[71] To the extent that this scene invokes the fantasy of the desert island, that island is part of a vast archipelago, a network of TAZs forged in unsolicited sounding at the apparent expense of the explicitly *national* territorialization project.

The New Frontier

Despite what seems to be the inevitable failure of the total sonic territorialization of the PRC—and the persistent (re)constitution of TAZs, especially on the geographical frontier—the officially endorsed project continued throughout the Cultural Revolution. The production of national territory as (ideally) a saturated acoustic space was wedded not only to the nation but also to the notion that the recorded sound technologies required for this process were *quintessentially modern technologies*. In other words, the territory produced through the (re)sounding of official broadcasts and records was meant to be that of a *modern socialist* nation, specifically; just any old kind of territorialized nation would not do. While I have been arguing that the performative act of sounding was at least as important as the specific musical and semantic content of what was sounded, this content undoubtedly aspired to a certain ideological consistency. It prescribed, or was interpreted as prescribing, a particular understanding of the nation it acoustically engendered. The reliance on the modern media qua *modern* media supplemented this prescribed view. Singing "The East Is Red" in a field is not, in this sense, quite the same thing as broadcasting a record of the very same anthem in that very same field. Moreover, the difference between the two is not reducible to volume or standardization per se. Rather, it is a function of the more fundamental idea that increased volume and standardization are both helpful to the national territorialization project *and* testaments to technological—and therefore historical—progress.

It should come as little surprise, therefore, that loudspeakers, record players, and mobile broadcast outfits were—in addition to their actual sounding—often representationally deployed as emblems of national development. Again, the technological display seen in figure 1.3 is a prime example. These technologies were depicted on the frontier precisely because they were at their most performatively powerful when they sonically produced territory that had not been there before, that is, when they added to the territorialized expanse of the PRC rather than simply maintaining it. The frontier, after all, is constituted by the notion that territory ends, that it has an edge. Acoustic saturation demands omnipresence both at the center and the margins, but the romance of the latter lies in its expansionist potential: The sonic edge can and must be pushed back; it must be coextensive with the cartographic border.[72] The desire to expand by filling in the map, by territorializing the nation in accordance with a preconceived conceptual geography, in turn goes hand in hand with a sense of ideological superiority and historical inevitability that we might think of as the manifest destiny of modern (because mechanical) sound.

I invoke the notion of manifest destiny here with considerable wariness, but I do so precisely because of its damning (neo-)colonial/imperialist connotations. Sonic saturation during the late Mao period acquired many similar associations, now wedded to an avowedly socialist modernity rather than to capitalism, Christianity, and whiteness.[73] The central discursive place afforded the (sonic) frontier is a testament to this, as is a related issue: the characterization of ethnic others as primitives in desperate need of modernization. If the acoustic frontier evoked a sense of spatial expansion in the name of the modern socialist nation, nominally internal ethnic minorities constituted both real bodies and representational terrain on which developmental progress could be simultaneously enacted. Recorded sound technologies were key to the latter process as well as to the former.

Images of people gathered around listening devices were not hard to come by in the Cultural Revolution or the Mao period more broadly. Photographs of families sitting around radios and loudspeakers, for example, are quite commonly found on the pages of such publications as *China Pictorial* (*Renmin huabao*) and *Nationality Pictorial* (*Minzu huabao*).[74] Among other things, these official organs sought to promote the PRC as a modern, multiethnic country to both an international and domestic readership. At the same time, proof that socialism had brought modernity to China's most backward places (the border regions) and people (minorities) powerfully testified to the CCP's power and beneficence. These twin missions necessitated the regular depiction of minorities—always dressed in traditional garb rather than Mao suits or army uniforms—engaging in ideologically and developmentally advanced behaviors. Listening to or broadcasting the politically correct, technologically (re)produced sound of the center seems to have qualified. Photographs of the sort seen in figure 1.5 proclaim the participation of recorded sound technologies in the creation of what Ralph Litzinger has called the "developmental double bind" of minority groups in the PRC.[75] These groups "experience a contradiction between modernization goals and the expectation that they maintain traditional identities as a basis for incorporation into the Chinese nation."[76] The result is a profusion of always ongoing "civilizing processes," in Sara Friedman's words. The juxtaposition of the device as an avatar of modernity and the by definition as-yet-uncivilized minority broadcaster or listener whose status as such is sartorially marked perfectly encapsulates this. Such images primitivize non-Han groups while confirming the superiority of the implicitly Han revolutionary enterprise.[77] What better way

Figure 1.5 Monpa broadcast studio (Tibet). From *Nationality Pictorial*, no. 9 (1975): 8. Photo by Liu Qian'gang.

to model socialist modernity—for the Han viewer and the world at large—than by promoting it as a civilizing process marshaled by the party?

The use of recorded technologies in this way—or, more precisely, the strategic instrumentalization of their modern cultural connotations—was by no means a CCP innovation, of course. As Michael Taussig makes clear in *Mimesis and Alterity*, all around the world "colonial photography" and "colonial phonography" thrived on making purported distinctions between the civilized and the savage both visible and audible. "Primitives" astonished by "frontier rituals of technological supremacy" were standard colonial fare.[78] To the extent that the Western fascination with credulous colonial others in the phonographic age Taussig describes is a redirection of sound magic in the name of power, the same might be said of the CCP's penchant for photographs depicting minorities with record players and loudspeakers in the late 1960s and 1970s. It had not been that long, after all, since Han Chinese had found themselves on the wrong end of the phonograph horn. Shanghai had been the semicolonial frontier for transnational record conglomerates in the early twentieth century.[79] Now—via the China Records monopoly—it was at the heart of a modern, socialist sounding carried out on a new set of frontiers. In this reversal of fortunes, we find something of a repetition with a telling difference: The developmental tropes required of the revolutionary project are not exactly of a piece with those Taussig examines in that the socialist primitive is not quite as awed by technology as colonialism once required. Rather than testify to the magic of technology per se, the socialist primitive figures a process of *demystification*, a recent—because still behind the times—awakening and, therefore, the righteousness of revolution.

This chapter has attempted to capture the sonic imaginary of the Cultural Revolution, particularly in relation to the problematics of space, national territory, and modernization with which it is intimately linked. That this imaginary should be so reliant on media(ting) technologies should come as no surprise, given my focus on the relationality of newborn things in this book, but it is especially in regard to the question of (national) development and the frontier—both territorially and ethnically conceived—that we are reminded that socialist progress pursued through an increased engagement with media technologies is predicated on availability and access. It is worth noting, therefore, that this coincided not only with increased access to cinema and recorded sound but also to such public services as healthcare and education. It also, fundamentally, meant access to certain material objects. It is with this in mind that I would draw our attention to another kind of access, used as evidence of socialist advancement by the CCP: consumer commodities, the dissemination of which is the subject of the next chapter.

2   Selling Revolution

In 1974, China Records released M-1022, a collection of songs on ten-inch vinyl exported as *Where the Motherland Needs Us Most, There Is Our Home*. The original Chinese title, *Geming qingnian zhi zai sifang*, has a slightly different connotation, literally translating to something like "the intent of the revolutionary youth is all around." Neither title, however, gets at the record's unifying theme and purpose: the glorification of the staunch revolutionary young person engaged in the unglamorous tasks of the everyday. To this end, the album features songs in praise of an unlikely pantheon of heroes, including youth team members, rusticated youth, tractor drivers, truck drivers, teachers, newspaper delivery boys, and kitchen workers. These figures are lauded precisely because they display unflagging revolutionary fervor in jobs commonly thought to lack revolutionary romanticism and urgency. The daily grind of socialist construction, often confronted on the frontier, does not dampen these individuals' spirits; they methodically and tirelessly forge ahead, armed only with their righteous conviction. In other words, they are heroes of a remarkably tame and mundane sort.

One might well see in this record, therefore, a turn toward the banality of revolution or, more to the point, a renewed acknowledgment of a banal undercurrent central to revolution's very success. Not so long ago that undercurrent had been deemed tainted by revisionism. At the dawn of the Cultural Revolution in 1966, the operating thesis was that the CCP had grown bloated, bureaucratic, and, above all, content. It had lost its way precisely because it had begun acting as if the revolution were over, as if the engine of history were happily idling in place. Some individuals bore more blame than others in this turn of events, of course—counterrevolutionaries were said to have actively and intentionally aided this process along. But in the end, the solution to the overarching problem demanded more than a straightforward purge of political/class enemies. It demanded continuous revolution, chaos, and upheaval; the entire ossified bureaucracy—including and perhaps especially the party bureaucracy—needed to be destroyed, the headquarters bombarded (*pao da silingbu*), in Mao's famous phrase. There was, in this sense, nothing banal about the Cultural Revolution's raison d'être and still less about its methods. Not only did every aspect of the heretofore mundane suddenly take on an out-sized political importance—what class crime might you have unknowingly and unthinkingly committed in the course of daily life?—but a whole new generation of young people, who had missed out on the romance and glory of the founding struggle of the PRC, was called to extraordinary action in order to ensure the country's survival. The Red Guards criticized, ransacked, and assaulted; they went on pilgrimages and quests and reenacted historic victories; they breathed rarified ideological, political, and aesthetic air.

China Records M-1022 speaks to the ensuing aftermath of that initial Cultural Revolution cataclysm. Complacency in the face of banality—dare I say boredom?—is still the enemy, but the appropriate recourse has changed. If the period from 1966 to 1968 was driven by a need to upend and eradicate that which had become uncomfortably mundane, that is, the quotidian status quo, the period that followed did not share such spectacular ambitions. The early to mid-1970s were much more politically and aesthetically invested in a newly established order than they were in chaos. (Ironically, they had that in common with the so-called seventeen years, 1949–66.) Even nominally mass movements like the Criticize Lin Biao, Criticize Confucius campaign of 1973–74 were clearly pushed and organized from the top in a way that the Red Guards had not been.[1] This new order of things was just as susceptible to the dangers of eroding revolutionary ardor as the old one had been, however. Short of overturning the newly emerging status quo through romantic and glorious means, the approach to the problem embodied in this long-playing record involves recasting that status quo as itself inherently romantic and glorious.[2] Want to be a revolutionary hero? No need to engage in disruptive and destructive behavior. Be the very best truck driver you can be and help the continuous revolution advance that way.

Some of M-1022's stable of extraordinarily ordinary revolutionary figures are familiar enough. Tractor drivers—especially female tractor drivers—were prominent in the cultural production of the pre–Cultural Revolution period, for example.[3] That the tractor drivers on the album are lauded alongside retail salespeople, on the other hand, may come as something of a shock to the twenty-first-century listener. In fact, two of the record's twelve songs are dedicated to retailers, a move wholly in keeping with other cultural products of the time. With an indomitable spirit reminiscent of the US postal worker, the idealized PRC salesperson brings people what they need no matter the meteorological or topographical obstacle. As the female chorus of "Going up the mountain, a basket on my back" ("Shenbei beiluo shangshan lai") jauntily proclaims, "I don't fear the rainstorm, I don't fear the hot sun, my feet tread the winding road, my breast as wide as the sea. I am a people's retailer, over the mountain and across the range I go, a red heart for the people, Chairman Mao's teachings etched in my heart."[4] Socialist trade was desirable and commendable—somewhat ambivalently so given the waste and exploitation associated with capitalist trade in communist ideology but desirable and commendable nonetheless—when undertaken "for the people." Retail services directed at the most materially and developmentally needy among "the people"—those tucked away "over the mountain and across the range," for instance—were especially meritorious. Under such circumstances, even selling the most basic sundries, from condiments to enamel basins, could be worthy of song.

As we saw in chapter 1 in the context of sounding the PRC as a modern socialist nation, geographical and ideological backwardness was often attributed to those populating the frontier or to minority groups, and indeed, in this sense, we should think of broadcasters and salespeople as fellow travelers, crisscrossing the same developmentalist terrain. To wit, when one peruses *China Pictorial* and *Nationality Pictorial* issues from the 1970s, one notes a recurring motif: The very same "exotic" peoples shown huddled around radios and loudspeakers are also regularly photographed while shopping. They consistently find themselves awash in commodities (see figure 2.1). If, as Ann Anagnost has suggested, the "civilizing processes" directed at minorities in the post-Mao period include the modeling of prescriptive modes of consumption, of the "correct" ways in which commodities should be consumed, such official, Cultural Revolution–era images suggest that shopping was understood and promoted as a "civilizing process" before the transition to a more market-driven economy as well.[5] One might even go so far as to argue that the modern, national, socialist subjects envisioned in these photographs are fundamentally consumers—of media, of newfangled technologies, of commodities—much like their capitalist cousins.

This is not to say that such tantalizing and persistent similarities were always openly acknowledged, of course; on the contrary, what similarities and continuities with capitalism and the old society did exist were typically very carefully and quietly managed while the apparent differences were touted as evidence of hard-won progress. The initial, chaotic period of the Cultural Revolution was in large part an exception to this rule, as we shall see, as Red Guards spied capitalism at work where it had gamely been ignored up through

Figure 2.1 Shopping in Inner Mongolia. From *Nationality Pictorial*, no. 3 (1966): 26. Photo by Cui Yaoxian.

the early 1960s. Despite attempts to banish the unnerving capitalist tendencies of socialist trade, however, a significant tension remained between the pull of modernity and prosperity—measured in consumer goods—and the dictates of socialist ideology and thriftiness. This is precisely the domain of the newborn socialist thing, forged by the often-contradictory imperatives of technological/industrial development, the pursuit of a communist utopia, and the material interactions of bodies and the objects in their midst. All of these played out front and center in the official retail sector, with sales personnel tasked to implement a self-styled socialist approach and continuously reassert the PRC's anticapitalist nature on behalf of the party, even as they labored in the famously bourgeois arena of domestic commerce. As I argue in this chapter, the figure of the retail salesperson became a discursive linchpin within a system attempting to repackage consumption into a benign—that is, neither revisionist nor counterrevolutionary—component of Chinese socialism.

Domestic Commerce 101

As is the case throughout this book, most of my attention in this chapter is focused on discursive constructs and dominant modes of representation pertaining to material and consumer culture as opposed to making a systemic determination or argument about how things "really" worked on the ground. But whereas we might draw a distinction between the two as objects of study in theory—not only with regard to the Cultural Revolution and the PRC but also in general—they are not so easily disentangled in practice. The ways in which officially sanctioned cultural products characterized socialist commerce to the populace necessarily helped produce the experiential reality of both consumers and retailers, on the one hand, while the depictions of interactions between salesclerk and customer—as well as between person and thing—were themselves to some extent constrained by what was actually happening, on the other.[6] I think it important, therefore, despite my typical emphasis on prescriptive ideals and their material manifestations, to begin this discussion with a brief sketch of the official PRC commercial apparatus during the late 1960s and 1970s. It will be brief in part because it is extremely difficult to capture the totality of the relevant state bureaucracy. Writing about Chinese industrial society in 1969 (itself an exceedingly complicated topic), Barry Richman found the retail sector such an uncommon challenge to analyze that he prefaced his discussion of it with this disclaimer: "I must admit that even after interviewing several Chinese commercial and retail executives I am still quite hazy about the general organization of this sector. This is the chief reason why I have not even attempted to draw organization charts for this sector."[7] There will be no streamlined organization charts from me either.[8] Even so, it is possible to reconstruct a rough schema, "close enough that only someone concerned with minutiae need fear for his sanity."[9]

The system itself, to say nothing of the policy it enacted, is something of a moving target. Over the course of the Mao period, commerce-related ministries and bureaus merged, split, and reorganized constantly, but it is precisely the complexity, heterogeneity, and unexpected dynamism of the system that I wish to emphasize here.[10] This was partially a function of overlapping jurisdictional entities, the most important of which, during the Mao period as a whole, was arguably the Ministry of Commerce (Shangye bu), operating under the direction of the State Council (Guo wu yuan).[11] In addition to overseeing national economic planning and the service sector (which included hair salons, restaurants, hotels, etc.), the Ministry of Commerce was responsible for an ever-evolving number of corporations, each one dedicated to a particular type or family of good. One corporation controlled textiles, for example, while another dealt exclusively with liquor and tobacco. The corporation with the vastest portfolio in terms of the variety of its offerings was the China General Goods Company, which, beginning in 1950, mostly traded in items for daily use and catered to the PRC's network of department stores.[12] Each corporation oversaw the procurement of its respective class of goods from industrial or agricultural production units, transportation, storage, and final distribution to retail outlets. The actual wholesaling and retailing facilities, however, were under separate administering units, also under the Ministry of Commerce. This bureau-corporation structure was also reproduced at both the provincial and municipal levels, with each level subject to both the layers of bureaucracy above it and more local institutions, including municipal and district governments or, when such structures were dismantled in the Cultural Revolution, revolutionary committees (*ge wei hui*). Under the umbrella of the relatively straightforward central commercial apparatus, then, was a complex and uneven system comprising large numbers of reduplicative administrative units, each with competing interests. On the ground, this meant that any individual store was subject to layers upon layers of municipal, provincial, and national bureaucracy, impacting everything from the pricing of its goods to its workers' salaries. Moreover, jurisdictions changed over time, and locally managed goods could be dealt with very differently from place to place, making it exceedingly difficult to generalize about prices and rations, among other things, on a national scale.[13]

All of this is to say that although it would be accurate to claim that state-owned (or co-owned) and -operated—in addition to cooperative—entities developed a virtual monopoly of the domestic trade sector *in aggregate*, no single organization dominated the official commercial landscape.[14] To wit, "domestic trade [was] substantially more decentralized down to the municipal and district levels in China than [was] the case in the Soviet Union."[15] We are not talking about a great bureaucratic monolith, here; this was a patchwork. And lest we imagine that this heterogeneity was experienced only behind the scenes—in procurement and wholesaling activities, perhaps—we find a similar mishmash of official retail outlets serving individual consumers. In the countryside, the most important venue from which peasants purchased consumer goods produced by state-owned enterprises was the local supply and marketing cooperative (*gong xiao she* or *hezuo she*), which at various times was directly linked to commune governance.[16] Communes and, during periods of economic relaxation, individual peasants also sold their agricultural output and handicrafts back to the state through these same cooperatives. Some urban areas had similar cooperatives as well, but state-owned stores as well as joint public-private retailers were much more common in the cities. Such stores varied widely with regard to size, amenities, and specialty—or lack thereof. A quick perusal of *Trade Work* (*Shangye gongzuo*), a biweekly journal published by the Ministry of Commerce in 1964 and 1965, indicates an astounding amount of diversity on this score, from brand new megastores to recently socialized family businesses with centuries-long histories.[17] Generally speaking, in addition to revamped family shops, so-called *menshibu* supplied goods, at times via direct links to factories, in specific domains (cloth shoes, hats, lightbulbs, etc.) while *baihuo shangdian*, or department stores, provided a range of basic sundries as well as certain luxury items. To these shopping options one must also add licensed peddlers (*shangfan*)—not to be confused with unlicensed black-market traders—who were permitted to sell their wares door-to-door and at occasional markets and festivals. So reminiscent of past retail practices, such peddlers often took the brunt of ideological attacks on the commercial system writ large, but they continued to be an important conduit for the distribution of goods. Finally, we must also add that some portions of the system were exclusively dedicated to particular segments of the populace. Those in the upper echelons of the party as well as individuals in positions deemed to be of particular national importance—scientists and athletes, for example—had access to special supplies (*texu gongying* or simply *tegong*), a privilege that persists to this day.[18] The military oversaw (and continues to oversee) products for its personnel while foreign visitors were directed to shop at so-called friendship stores (*youyi shangdian*), where they were encouraged to pay in hard currency.[19]

This turn to restricted outlets brings us to one of the Mao period's most important methods for controlling the flow of goods, namely, rationing. Despite the variety of establishments and people involved in the retail sector, overall, given the size of the country's population, China's official distribution channels were extremely limited, and with so many competing bureaucratic interests in the mix, what channels there were often were clogged with red tape. Economic planning emphasized heavy industry and agriculture over the production of consumer goods (essentially, the Soviet model), resulting in widespread shortages of the most desirable items. At the same time, because of the general lack of feedback to production units about the strength or weakness of consumer demand—information implicit in fluctuating prices within a market system—inventories of undesirable items could pile up, taking up warehouse space and creating massive gluts at the expense of ongoing procurement work.[20] None of these issues is particular to the PRC; we see them crop up throughout the socialist world. Indeed, one could argue that such problems stem from the fundamental epistemological impossibility of planning an economy.[21] It bears remembering, however, that the prerevolutionary wartime economy was also racked with shortages as well as skyrocketing prices for staples, including grain.[22] That is to say, the PRC inherited a number of supply deficiencies, which were then arguably compounded by its own Soviet-inspired policies.

In the face of these ongoing shortages, whatever their origin, and the price pressure exerted by excess demand for a whole variety of products, the CCP relied on a system of ration coupons (*piao*) and certificates (*zheng*). To this end, goods were divided into three categories. Category I goods—grain, cooking oil, and cotton cloth—were subject to planned purchase and planned supply (*tong gou tong xiao*) and therefore centrally controlled and centrally rationed under the direction of the Ministry of Food and the Ministry of Commerce. Nationwide grain rationing was first mandated in 1955.[23] It continued in some areas of the country until 1993.[24] Edible oils were rationed as of November 1953, while formal cotton cloth rationing began as early as 1954.[25] Category II comprised goods whose distribution was also subject to quotas but whose rationing, when needed, was controlled locally, whereas category III products could be traded freely, albeit at set prices.[26] Goods were regularly moved from category III to category II in economically difficult times and in the opposite direction in times of strong economic growth. By all accounts, the Cultural Revolution was characterized by widespread rationing, but given the decentralized treatment of category II goods, which included such basic necessities as pork, for example, individuals in different parts of the country naturally had divergent retailing experiences, not to mention varying amounts of purchasing power.[27] This is to say nothing of the fact that the vast majority of ration coupons and certificates were only valid for a limited amount of time within a limited geographical area, according to one's work-unit or commune registration. Functionally, this helped keep many displaced urbanites in the countryside in the 1970s, when they would otherwise have preferred to return to the cities. Without the proper urban registration, they would not have received ration coupons valid for use in their home-city districts. Expiration dates also made it difficult to hoard coupons or save them for future use, since they needed to be redeemed within a rather short time frame.[28]

In addition to the limitations placed on when and where ration coupons and certificates could be used, it is also critically important to note that these purchasing tools were valid only when used in conjunction with money, that is, *renminbi*.[29] Ration coupons were not in and of themselves currency; rather, they worked alongside currency to further restrict access to goods. To that end, rations were issued in denominations relating to purchasable quantities (for foodstuffs, typically in units of weight, such as *jin* and *liang*) as opposed to a fixed monetary value (see figure 2.2). It has become something of a truism that during the Cultural Revolution all the money in the world was useless without a ration coupon, but we should not lose sight of the fact that the reverse was also a no-go. A coupon without money—and urban wages were indeed paid in renminbi, not in coupons or in kind—was equally useless in the state retail sector. What a coupon actually provided was not a guaranteed amount of a certain good, but permission to purchase *up to* a given amount at an artificially reduced price. The difference is subtle but crucial. It means that

Figure 2.2 Provincial-level grain ration coupons, Guangdong: (*above*) 5 jin, 1968; (*below*) 30 jin, 1969. Weltmuseum Wien.

domestic trade remained thoroughly monetized even when rationing was widespread. There is a compelling argument to be made that the system as a whole was designed in order to downplay this continued monetization and that barter and gift giving were central to the PRC economy as a whole.[30] My point, however, obtains: money remained key to the official retail experience.

Not only did this continued reliance on money help fuel a suspicion that socialist commerce was politically problematic, that it had inherited the exploitative character of capitalist trade, but it also indexed, in the most mundane way, the commodity status of traded goods. According to the Stalinist position adopted by the PRC in the mid-1950s, the commodity (*shangpin*), as defined by Marx in *Capital*, remained dominant under socialism because, among other things, the collectivized peasantry would not accept any other form of economic relation with state-owned enterprises. In this sense, the commodity was critical to the socialist economy as a whole, but it needed to be reinvented, demystified, and managed in the appropriately "socialist" way.[31] I will leave the extensive theoretical and discursive gymnastics required by such processes to future chapters. Suffice it to point out for now that, elaborate political-economic arguments of radical difference aside, the mechanics of buying and selling goods with money enacted commodity relations in a very familiar, tactile manner. This familiarity proved troublesome. As long as filthy lucre was in circulation, it was feared, the profit motive could continue to exert an *eminently quantifiable*, corrupting influence on those who engaged in exchange even when they purportedly did so in the name of the party and the people.

New China, New Commerce

Just being around retail shops—especially if those shops were selling high-end goods and luxuries—could spell ideological trouble. Consider the campaign to Learn from the Good Eighth Company of Nanjing Road (Xiang Nanjing lu shang hao ba lian xuexi), which came to a head in 1963–64, and "in its ideological agenda, rhetoric, and organizational structure... helped to set the stage" for the Cultural Revolution.[32] The Eighth Company had participated in the liberation of Shanghai in May 1949, and though it had not actually been stationed on Nanjing Road at that time, in the reimagining of the 1960s campaign the company found itself on the frontline of the battle against bourgeois decadence. The soldiers' post in this formulation, Nanjing Road, had long been known as the great shopping street of republican Shanghai's International Settlement and thus as a powerful emblem of Chinese colonial modernity and its constitutive consumer culture.[33] During the interwar period, Nanjing Road boasted, among other attractions, the great multistory homes of Shanghai's "big four" department stores: Sincere (Xianshi) (established 1917), Wing On (established 1918), Sun Sun (established 1926), and Sun Company (established 1936).[34] The department store, an invention of late nineteenth-century industrialized France and the United States, was more than a retailing novelty; it comprised not only the spectacle of consumerism but also the myriad inducements of the self-consciously modern.[35] The Nanjing Road department stores had much to offer by way of amusement: "with escalators leading to variegated merchandise on different floors, together with dance halls and rooftop bars, coffeehouses, restaurants, hotels, and playgrounds for diverse entertainments, these edifices of commerce combined the functions of consumerism and recreation."[36] Indeed, the department stores were directly tied to veritable amusement parks and amusement park publications.[37] In the 1964 feature film *Sentinels under the Neon Lights* (*Nihongdeng xia de shaobing*), directed by Wang Ping, Good Eighth Company soldiers are tempted by glitz and glam at every turn. In fact, some of them temporarily succumb to all the moral corruption the city has to offer, including the corruption wrought by an overabundance of pretty things on display. That these peasant-soldiers eventually find their way back to moral rectitude is to be expected, given the circumstances of the film's production. Even so, the men's momentary lapse is important insofar as it sets us all on notice, as viewers and (potential) consumers, that we too might be corrupted by the retail world of modern delights. The film as a whole also clearly puts forward the notion that the everyday is a battlefield, a battlefield very much on the order of the Korean front, to which the Good Eighth Company is dispatched after its time in Shanghai. The Nanjing Road of the 1960s and 1970s may have been remade for the Chinese masses, but the underlying threat faced by the men of the Good Eighth Company persisted.[38]

If simply being in proximity to commercial spectacle could itself be morally and ideologically risky, the prospect of actually working in this economic sector, which entailed basking in bourgeois temptation at length, was all the more daunting. In addition to having to stave off the siren call of money and luxury commodities, the socialist retailer would need to grapple with an unwieldy bureaucracy as well as a particularly volatile policy landscape and the enduring stigma of the profession.[39] As evidenced by the Good Eighth Company of Nanjing Road, vigilance over and in this environment was key, especially when dealing with a class enemy as famous for its reliance on material incentives (*wuzhi ciji*) as the bourgeoisie. To make matters worse, the bourgeois saboteurs were said to thrive on the very sense of complacency and contentment afforded by displays of abundance. Consider Mao's warning, originally made on the eve of Shanghai's liberation in May 1949 and recirculated in the 1960s as part of the Little Red Book (*hong bao shu*).

> With victory, certain moods may grow within the Party—arrogance, the airs of a self-styled hero, inertia and unwillingness to make progress, love of pleasure and distaste for continued hard living. With victory, the people will be grateful to us and the bourgeoisie will come forward to flatter us. It has been proved that the enemy cannot conquer us by force of arms. However, the flattery of the bourgeoisie may conquer the weak-willed in our ranks. There may be Communists, who were not conquered by enemies with guns and were worthy of the name of heroes for standing up to these enemies, but cannot withstand sugar-coated bullets; they will be defeated by sugar-coated bullets. We must guard against such a situation.[40]

Woe betide the "weak-willed" person surrounded by "sugar-coated bullets" of the kind shelved on the shop floor. Such an employee would be turned—in spite of herself, perhaps—against the people she was meant to serve, lapsing into the famously exploitative retail practices of the old society: speculating on basic necessities, price-gouging, badgering customers, knowingly selling faulty wares, and so on. Consider, too, that retail employees, with their money and their abaci, hardly cut the figure of the physically laboring proletarian worker the party was said to represent.

Given these circumstances it is no great wonder that the PRC retail sector came in for added political scrutiny when class struggle was particularly high on the CCP agenda.[41] The sector could not be done away with completely, however. Commerce as a whole could be—and was—modified and controlled by a massive, complex bureaucratic structure, but the fundamental need to distribute goods to individual consumers—even if some of those goods might have deleterious ideological and political effects—persisted. This was the fundamental problem posed by consumption in the socialist world writ large: "It was both needed, given the pursuit of a communist utopia, and endlessly problematic."[42] In fact, access to and acquisition of consumer goods continued to function as a benchmark of historical progress in the PRC, even as the mechanisms that facilitated development in this area raised significant questions about the overarching socialist project. This tension was putatively resolved by subsuming the former into the latter, that is, by configuring the definition of revolutionary work to include trade.

An oft-repeated quotation from Chairman Mao speaks to this endeavor as well. In a speech given to the Second National Congress in 1934, Mao made clear the importance of addressing the material concerns of the masses to the revolutionary enterprise and the war effort against the Guomindang.

> If we only mobilize the people to carry on the war and do nothing else, can we succeed in defeating the enemy? Of course not. If we want to win, we must do a great deal more. We must lead the peasants' struggle for land and distribute the land to them, heighten their labor enthusiasm and increase agricultural production, safeguard the interests of the workers, establish cooperatives, develop trade with outside areas, and solve the problems facing the masses—food, shelter and clothing, fuel, rice, cooking oil and salt, sickness and hygiene, and marriage. In short, all the practical problems in the masses' everyday life should claim our attention. If we attend to these problems, solve them and satisfy the needs of the masses, we shall really become organizers of the well-being of the masses, and they will truly rally around us and give us their warm support.[43]

That remedying the practical material problems of the masses, including access to basic foodstuffs at affordable prices, should become part of the CCP's organizational purview was not a foregone conclusion in 1934, but Mao's statement casts the CCP as would-be "organizers of the well-being of the masses" in such a way that the distribution of goods becomes crucial to the broader war effort and the pursuit of its attendant ideological goals.[44]

This implicit framing of domestic commerce—more specifically, retail—as integral to the revolution was a source of empowerment and political cover for those involved in the commercial sector after 1949, who could rely on this statement as evidence of the fact that they were doing the people's business. In 1960, for example, the central party organ *Red Flag* (*Hongqi*) published an essay by then First Party Secretary of Chongqing Ren Baige extolling the value of commerce as important, explicitly *revolutionary* economic work, precisely by referencing Mao's 1934 pronouncement.[45] The effort to tie retailing to the CCP's broader mission, to cloak domestic trade in the discourse of political—and therefore historical—advancement, also effectively placed salespeople and cashiers in the de facto position of representing the party to the populace on a daily basis, whether or not they actually were party members. As a result, commercial workers were under tremendous pressure to treat shoppers with all due proletarian respect, if not outright deference. This was made all the more important by the fact that consumers had to rely on salespeople in order to inspect and ultimately purchase store merchandise at counters (*guitai*). Mao-period retail outlets overwhelmingly eschewed self-service, flying in the face of a global trend away from salesclerk-reliant practices that coincided with the rise of the (US) supermarket format.[46] The continued emphasis on counter service guaranteed that prospective consumers' relationship with store merchandise was mediated by sales personnel. The frequency with which shop-floor personnel were instructed, through targeted publications like *Trade Work*, to improve relations with their customers suggests that this pressure was of limited use. Even so, given the inclusion of everyday economic concerns within the revolutionary sphere, customer service as well as the state of store infrastructure (refrigeration, ventilation, cleanliness, etc.) and the quantity and quality of available goods became inextricably linked with the party in such a way that the consumer experience elicited great official attention.[47]

All of this put retailers in a very precarious position: On one hand, they were encouraged to do their work—to sell goods, thereby facilitating consumption—while, on the other hand, that work was considered perilously close to bourgeois in both character and aim. It became extremely important for the party as well as tradespeople, therefore, to try to draw a clear line between capitalist retail and consumption and socialist retail and consumption, especially when they often seemed to be rather the same thing. A 1970 *People's Daily* editorial, for example, makes the case for the radical difference of "new-style trade" (*xin xing shangye*) as follows: "Socialist trade is in the service of proletarian politics; it is not purely buying and selling [*zuo maimai*]. Socialist tradespeople are the revolutionary warriors [*geming zhanshi*] of the proletariat. They are not capitalist business people [*maimai ren*]."[48] Whereas capitalist-style commerce chased profits and thus catered to those with money to spend, socialist trade was ostensibly geared toward strengthening the worker-peasant alliance (*gong nong lianmeng*). "Socialist trade is the bridge [*qiaoliang*] connecting industry and agriculture, production and consumption."[49] This bridge was meant to be definitively slanted in favor of producers, its overall purpose to "develop the economy and safeguard supplies [*baozhang gong gei*]," as the slogan went. In a strange reversal, the selling of commodities was said to be more closely associated with production than consumption, the former, of course, being much more consonant with PRC ideology.[50]

In addition to this large-scale reinvention of the commercial sector, circulating discourse concerning retail heavily relied on some tried and true techniques. "Recalling bitterness" (*yi ku si tian*) accounts from shopworkers were helpful in that they narrativized difference as progress in personal and emotional terms, typically for an audience of fellow retail professionals. There were stories of abuse from bosses and customers, of horrible work conditions, and of being forced to cheat people out of their money.[51] These things were then said to have been stamped out under the new order, replaced by fair labor practices and responsible interactions with customers. In addition, such tales of past pain were coupled with the elevation of models, worthy of emulation. As was typical of this ubiquitous tactic, models were promoted at both the level of the unit—in this case, the store—and the individual. Outlets such as Changchun's Number 2 Department Store (Changchun di er baihuo shangdian) and Beijing's Tianqiao General Goods Emporium (Tianqiao baihuo shichang) were extolled in the press in the late 1950s and early 1960s for their efficiency in serving the masses, while salespeople like Zhang Binggui (1918–87), who worked the confections counter in Beijing's Wangfujing Department Store (Wangfujing baihuo shangdian), and Yang Jinyu (1943–), a textile and cosmetics retail worker in Xi'an, were praised for going the extra mile for their customers.[52] Bizarrely, one of the key figures retail workers were instructed to learn from on the eve of the Cultural Revolution was the Chinese athlete Xu Yinsheng (1938–), whose advice on how to play ping pong, endorsed by *People's Daily*, was apparently deemed eminently translatable into the language of commerce in 1965.[53]

The tension between promoting modernity through the distribution of consumer goods and promoting ideologically correct behavior, including acts of economic solidarity among the peasantry and the proletariat, persisted, in the commercial sector, throughout the Mao period and beyond. In some cases, the models meant to mitigate this tension had very long discursive lives. The aforementioned Zhang Binggui, for example, and his "blazing" (*yi tuan huo*) spirit continue to be a model of good customer service to this day. Although he emerged as an exemplary figure in the 1960s, Zhang published an essay in *Red Flag* much later in 1977.[54] His subsequent book on the art of counter service was released in 1983.[55] Scores of biographies have been issued since, including one published as recently as 2016.[56] This is to say nothing of the memorial hall housed in his former employer's building or the fact that the Wangfujing Department Store "formally enshrined the 'yi tuan huo' spirit as its supreme principle and guiding force" in 1987.[57] The problem that models like Zhang Binggui were meant to solve—the underlying push and pull of the socialist modern and its contradictory impulses—did not disappear with Mao's death or, for that matter, with the onslaught of economic reforms. More concretely, responsive customer service continued to be emphasized as a marker of (increasingly less emphatically socialist) modern commerce.[58] That Zhang Binggui could be deemed worthy of emulation in times of such divergent economic policies is indicative of important continuities in the retail sector throughout the Mao era and the ensuing decades.

The Cultural Revolution

While the predicament posed by socialist trade for the Chinese Communist regime—and even the tools and rhetoric addressing that predicament—have been rather consistent, the kinds of policies enacted in this area as well as the range of behaviors that qualified as appropriately socialist or destructively capitalist at any given moment were in constant flux. In fact, because commercial activities were so ideologically fraught, they were particularly sensitive to shifts in the political winds.[59] It is in this regard that the Cultural Revolution—and especially the high tide of Red Guard activity in 1966 and 1967—stands out, as the line between revolution and counterrevolution moved sharply to the left. That is to say, activities that had been advocated in the early 1960s in an effort to recover from the Great Leap Forward, for example, were the subject of great, in some cases violent, criticism a few years later, picking up additional steam when their original proponents in the party fell from grace. Thus, when President Liu Shaoqi was attacked in 1967, his economic policies were attacked as well. Two of his major rural economic initiatives, now discredited, were directly tied to the commercial sector: the "three freedoms and one guarantee" (*san zi yi bao*) and the "four freedoms" (*si da ziyou*). The former promoted private land plots (*zi liudi*), free markets (*ziyou shichang*), independent accounting for small enterprises (*zi fu yingkui*), and the use of household output quotas (*ban chan dao hu*). The four freedoms, on the other hand, permitted individuals in the countryside to freely lease land, lend money, hire labor, and engage in trade (*maoyi*). Each of these facets impacted the commercial arena in some way, and each was understood by 1967 as a revisionist attempt to dismantle communes and allow capitalism to reemerge. They were quickly replaced by a renewed emphasis on politics and class struggle, but the retail sector as a whole became that much more ideologically and politically problematic as a result of the designs that so-called capitalist-roaders (*zouzipai*) had purportedly held on this portion of the economy.

Even prior to these tectonic shifts in national economic policy and elite party politics, however, department stores and service providers, including hair salons and photography studios, were early targets of Red Guard ire, featuring prominently in the campaign to smash the Four Olds—old thoughts, old culture, old customs, and old habits—in the late summer and fall of 1966. Many businesses were forced to change their names, for example, because of their residual, feudal implications.[60] Wangfujing Department Store became the Beijing Department Store, a name officially accepted by the municipal government in 1968, two years after Red Guards removed the store's original sign.[61] Likewise the famous Wing On Department Store on Shanghai's Nanjing Road—by that point a joint public-private enterprise—caused consternation because of its name: literally, "everlasting peace" (*yong an*). Peace was no longer something to be pursued in 1966, so Wing On was promptly renamed: First it became the East Is Red Department Store and then, in 1969, the Shanghai Number 10 Department Store.[62] Similar changes were undertaken nationwide; indeed, they were encouraged by the central party apparatus.[63]

This attention to naming and renaming on the part of Red Guards was combined with a push to cease the sale of goods and services they deemed particularly offensive to proletarian sensibilities. Such apparently noxious items included pornographic (*huangse*) books and music, old- and Western-style clothes, and women's jewelry and cosmetics. In this last vein, perfume, lipstick, and face creams were often singled out by Red Guards for explicit criticism as luxury items (*shechipin*) not intended for the broad masses.[64] Central authorities echoed this move as well when they called for an end to domestic sales of high-end cosmetics (*gaoji huazhuangpin*) to the general public (stage and screen actors who relied on makeup for their work were granted an exception).[65] According to one source, ideological objections to items associated with the feudal past (popular religious markers, historical figures, etc.) or (foreign) capitalism led to a 21 percent reduction in the number of items stocked by the newly renamed Beijing Department Store. That is, during the Cultural Revolution, over 6,583 products available to store customers for purchase prior to 1966 disappeared from the shelves.[66] One suspects that similar drops in product variety occurred throughout the PRC. For their part, the service industries were called on to drastically curtail their offerings as well. Hair salons in Shanghai, for example, were instructed by a group of Red

Guards not only to stop providing transgressive hair styles but also to "immediately desist from providing services specifically intended to benefit the bourgeoisie, including manicures, makeovers, and facials."[67] A Beijing Red Guard manifesto likewise called on bathhouses to cease servicing "bourgeois sons of bitches. Don't scrub them down, massage their feet, or pound their backs." Launderers were also told to stop washing the bourgeoisie's dirty "underwear, socks, and hankies."[68]

All of these admonitions, dating to the early period of the Cultural Revolution, speak to a shrinking range of politically acceptable commercial and consumer behaviors, both with regard to particular goods and to particular practices undertaken at the customer's behest. The extent to which problem products and services are overwhelmingly targeted at female consumers is striking. It suggests a particularly acute narrowing of acceptable behaviors for women as well as the effeminization of class enemies and the bourgeoisie more generally. It also reminds us that shopping has long been the domain of women, who, ironically, were often thought to be particularly susceptible to the moral corruption wrought by things and their display. One need only think here of the paradigmatic depiction of the newly invented department store, Émile Zola's *Au bonheur des dames* (*The Ladies' Delight*) (1883), for which the author did extensive research at Paris's Le Bon Marché, to get a sense of the anxiety surrounding the department store as a quintessentially female space,[69] a space of female shoppers and female workers.[70] Lest this all seem rather removed from Mao's China, consider the looming shadow of the republican "modern girl" (*modeng nüzi*), inheritor of the West's late nineteenth-century female-consumer mantle, as both a purchaser (or coveter) of newfangled things and a hallmark of the *advertising* for many of those things.[71] From this perspective, the Red Guards' apparent disdain for relatively recent classes of such female-oriented commodities as cosmetics makes perfect sense. Both they and their would-be consumers were well placed to be emblematic of politically problematic consumption writ large.

While undoubtedly significant, this tightening of acceptable bounds should in no way be misconstrued as an indiscriminate attack on commerce and consumption of all kinds. The trade sector continued to operate as such; store names may well have been forcibly and disruptively changed, but in the vast majority of cases, it seems, those stores also remained open for business. Systemically speaking, the policy advocated by the center in September 1966 was to fully nationalize as many retailers as possible, including heretofore public-private ventures, but those outlets or peddlers (*xiao shang xiao fan*) for whom that was not feasible were permitted to ply their trade under the umbrella of state stores and the supervision of the masses. Such entities and individuals were "useful for the distribution of commodities" and, in general, helped to facilitate "the establishment of a commercial network and commercial outlets that is convenient for the masses."[72] Although the weight of this kind of pronouncement from the State Council was somewhat attenuated during these the most radical years of the Cultural Revolution—Yao Yilin (1917–94) was removed from his post as minister of commerce in January 1967, and the commercial sector operated without anyone in that position until the summer of 1970, when a revolutionary committee led by Fan Ziyu (1914–2002) took the reins—this directive nonetheless speaks to a simple, oft-misunderstood fact: the Cultural Revolution as a movement was not anti-commerce per se.[73] It was, rather, anti-bourgeois and egalitarian in a way that demanded a reorientation and reorganization of existing commercial practices.

At the very top of this radically egalitarian, Red Guard/rebel agenda was anything that smacked of special treatment, including items and services the masses were priced out of—the bourgeois luxuries identified above—and, predictably, the restricted-access, special supply system that catered to VIPs. The latter target had the advantage of bringing the fight against undue privilege directly to the most odious capitalist-roaders in the party. The criticism directed at the so-called Black Number 7 (Hei qi hao) shop—the special supply outlet located on the fourth floor of Beijing's Wangfujing Department Store, exclusively frequented by party leaders—is a case in point. By the spring of 1967, Black Number 7 was being denounced as a secret stronghold of decadence and bourgeois restorationism, supposedly operating under the direction of Liu Shaoqi and Deng Xiaoping.[74] The alleged consumer practices of these leaders, their families, and their acolytes became class crimes in and of themselves as well as evidence of these individuals' fundamental moral bankruptcy. Officials who had promoted particular stores as model retail units in the late 1950s and early 1960s found themselves vulnerable to similar attacks. The ousted mayor of Beijing, Peng Zhen (1902–97), for example, was accused of elevating the Tianqiao Department Store to national prominence in order to amass power, speculate on commodities meant for the masses, and line his own pockets.[75] Liu Shaoqi was denounced for similar malfeasance at the Guangfudao Store in Tianjin.[76] These were extremely incendiary accusations; indeed, few charges were as damning during this period as "profiteering and speculation" (*touji daoba*) at the expense of the people.

Even as these erstwhile models and their patrons were being toppled, however, new models of politically appropriate retail were also put forth. That is, certain kinds of commerce were actively endorsed by the very same forces best known for attacking commercial practices as bourgeois. Thus, in the spring of 1969, a Beijing rebel group could write glowingly about the changes recently implemented at Xidan Department Store in Tongxian. Xidan had by that point apparently been transformed into a veritable "new-style store that served the workers, peasants, and soldiers."[77] Of course, socialist commerce had claimed to be dedicated to the masses and innovative—powered by newborn socialist things—since its very inception. Improved customer service, encompassing delivery to people's homes, for example, had already been emphasized as a hallmark of proletarian retail for years. Service initiatives had long proved a relatively easy way to remake the commercial sector into something developmentally progressive without restructuring the system's fundamental reliance on the exchange of commodities for money. To the extent that the model retail units of the Cultural Revolution did, in fact, advance something qualitatively new, then, it was neither a reorientation of commerce with an eye toward clientele nor even the deployment of fresh rhetoric—the key terms and phrases essentially stayed the same. What changed, rather, was the preeminence afforded to continued class struggle within the largely enduring retail system.

The Primacy of Class Struggle

Class struggle had, of course, been a topic of interest in the commercial arena before the Cultural Revolution, but prior to the mid-1960s class struggle was mostly discussed as something that had largely been dealt with in the past. The success of the socialist trade sector was itself meant to testify to the progress that had been achieved once the old system was toppled. This, after all, was the gist of "speaking bitterness" (*su ku*) activities, which continued well after land reform. Narratives of heinous past behavior were used to say "look how far we've come" and, effectively, "let's not go back there again." Vigilance against complacency and bourgeois-style corruption was definitely called for, but bona fide class enemies were few and far between in retail before 1964 or so, at which point a salesperson's revolutionary wherewithal became increasingly tied in the official press to the study of Mao Zedong Thought.[78] Until then, continued improvement of the retail sector had been called for in the name of serving the masses even better—with unparalleled customer service and ever-dwindling waste and inefficiency. The frugal (*qinjian*), cost-conscious store, staffed by proletarian, knowledgeable, warm, and patient salespeople in the model of Zhaozhou Pharmacy (Zhaozhou yiyao shangdian) was the early 1960s' ideal.[79] By the time of the Cultural Revolution, however, salespeople were additionally required to root out the class enemies—now understood to be very much active—among their customers and colleagues. Commerce had become a veritable front (*zhanxian*) in an ongoing class war.

It is important to note that the newfound emphasis on class struggle as an ongoing historical force animated both the initial, chaotic years of the Cultural Revolution, when Red Guards ran amok, and the relatively stable period of the 1970s. Indeed, it is during the latter that we see a shift in the understanding of class struggle as a developmental motive force that can be harnessed *by* the retail system rather than simply be wielded *at* offending aspects *of* the retail system. Moreover, while we might expect this more constructive—as opposed to destructive—approach to class struggle in commerce to be associated with the more moderate wing of the party, headed by the likes of the resurgent Zhou Enlai (1898–1976) in 1972 and the newly rehabilitated Deng Xiaoping in 1974 and early 1975, indications are that radicals, including the members of what became known as the Gang of Four, were pushing class struggle in more vociferous, but ultimately equally constrained, terms. This view is clearly reflected in and espoused by the many theatrical and literary works set in retail stores, for example, when moderates were increasingly under attack in late 1975 and 1976.

The best-known Cultural Revolution work set in a retail environment is undoubtedly *Xiangyang Store* (*Xiangyang shangdian*). A work of *pingju* (a local operatic form popular in the northeast), it initially rose to national prominence on October 1, 1973, when a performance by the Beijing Pingju Troupe (Beijing pingju tuan)—better known as the China Pingju Institute (Zhongguo ping yuan)—was broadcast live on national radio.[80] *Xiangyang Store* was then chosen to represent the city of Beijing at the Northern Regional Arts Festival (Huabei diqu wenyi diaoyan) held in the capital in January and February 1974. After it emerged as a festival favorite, the opera was touted in the national press as proof of the positive influence of the model works (yangbanxi) on theatrical development.[81] China Records quickly released a full recording of the opera as a four-disc set.[82] Like each of the model works, *Xiangyang Store* had a pre–Cultural Revolution history: It was first performed in 1963 as a reworking of an even earlier piece from the Great Leap Forward, *A Paean to Life* (*Shenghuo de kaige*). It was only after many rounds of revision—supposedly guided by the shining examples provided by the yangbanxi—and direct input from Minister of Culture Yu Huiyong (1925–77) that the final 1974 version of *Xiangyang Store* emerged, with primary authorship attributed to Guo Qihong (1940–), of later Beijing opera fame, and Hu Sha (1922–2005), the troupe director, in addition to the requisite collective (*jiti*).[83] For those who had seen multiple iterations of the play—people like the model salesman Zhang Binggui—the direction the revisions were taking was clear: towards an ever-increasing emphasis on class struggle and, further, on the appropriate role of retailers in that struggle.[84] It is the 1974 version that I will discuss here.

The play begins on the outskirts of Beijing in the eponymous Xiangyang Store in the late summer of 1963 as the local branch secretary, Wang Yongxiang, informs the store manager and branch committee member, Liu Baozhong, that he will soon have a new employee: Manager Liu's own nineteen-year-old daughter, Liu Chunxiu. While this news is positively received by the store's current workers—they already know and respect Chunxiu for her steadfast proletarian outlook and tireless work ethic—Chunxiu's father is less than thrilled about his daughter's new assignment; he is clearly uncomfortable with having her under his command, blurring the lines between family and politics. From the very beginning, then, Liu Baozhong emerges as a morally confused figure. It quickly becomes clear that class enemies have conspired to take advantage of Liu's personal failings and maneuver him into advocating policies that are favorable to them. When Liu Chunxiu actually arrives, a full day early, at her new post—she is consistently characterized as a "new soldier" (*xin bing*) on the front—she does so at a particularly crucial moment: An argument breaks out between Cui Yuhai, an apathetic young salesclerk who functions as Chunxiu's alter, and a regular customer, Grandpa Li. Grandpa Li, a retired worker, has come to buy goods for himself and for his neighbors in Baiyun Slope, which, as a recent workers' development, does not yet have retail outlets of its own. This creates an opportunity for Xiangyang Store to "serve the people"—in this particular case, "the people" exclusively comprising the proletariat—in an innovative way, namely, by bringing the store to them instead of them having to send a representative to the store. Liu Chunxiu volunteers to push a cart loaded with much-needed products to Baiyun Slope in order to "deliver goods to [the people's] door" (*song huo shang men*), a new service that quickly becomes embroiled in a pitched battle between those committed to the well-being of the masses and those attempting to line their own pockets. After a series of attempts to sabotage Xiangyang Store's new community outreach initiative, for which Liu Chunxiu is initially blamed, the enemies of the people are identified and appropriately punished, Manager Liu and Cai Yuhai recognize the error of their ways, and the forces of revolution are vindicated. The plot ends on October 1—National Day—with Manager Liu himself delivering goods, now touting the extent to which he has learned from the daughter he once disparaged as a disruptive force.

As Liu Chunxiu and Secretary Wang make clear at the end of scene 2, the incendiary nature of the delivery scheme stems from the fact that "it is not purely a matter of customer service," though that would make it a worthwhile endeavor in and of itself. It is, rather, a matter of filling an official retail vacuum so that unpalatable actors cannot flourish—thus the high stakes of the class struggle that quickly engulfs the store. "Father," Chunxiu says, "I know that certain people have recently been popping up on the slope, and evidence of speculation [*touji daoba*] has surfaced off and on."[85] The store's experiment with mobile retail is therefore actually a class offensive against those who would unduly profit from Baiyun Slope's geographic isolation, and sure enough, we soon find out exactly who the enemies are and the lengths to which they will go to protect their interests. Pan Youcai, himself an employee of Xiangyang Store, turns out to be something of a capitalist mastermind. He steals goods from the store—technically, he has Manager Liu sign off on the transfer of goods to a fictitious factory—and gives them to his relative in Baiyun Slope, Fu Mantang, to sell to locals, who, on top of everything else, are cheated out of their hard-earned money in the bargain. Granny Zhao buys a jin of sugar, for example, that turns out to be short two liang.[86] Pan Youcai's attempts to stymie official delivery services has everything to do with protecting his own side hustle both from competition and, perhaps even more importantly, from discovery. Having the outgoing and observant Liu Chunxiu anywhere near Baiyun Slope is a liability, and so Pan Youcai does everything in his power to get her out of there. He loosens the wheels on one of the carts, causing it to tip over, ruining half the merchandise and injuring Chunxiu's hand. He replaces the store's missing sugar with baking soda and has Fu Mantang stage a scene in which he "discovers" that Chunxiu has sold him the latter in the name of the former. Pan Youcai then floods the store with complaint letters about the baking soda "mix up," which turns out to be widespread, and manipulates his hapless manager into demanding that Liu Chunxiu transfer to another store altogether. Pan Youcai is not messing around.

That Chunxiu successfully beats back all of these attacks should come as no great surprise given the theatrical conventions of the mid-1970s. She behaves just as a hero should by all accounts behave. When her cart is broken and her hand injured, for example, she carries products on her back, trudging through rain and mud. She is indefatigable in her pursuits, much like the figures depicted on M-1022, the album discussed at the beginning of this chapter. But what, ultimately, is her work in pursuit of? To the extent that class struggle is the dramatic impetus for the play's narrative as well as the chief means through which a retailer becomes a warrior, what does victory for Liu Chunxiu look like? If *Xiangyang Store*'s epilogue, set during National Day celebrations, is any indication, victory means vanquishing class enemies and resolving ideological problems. This much, perhaps, is obvious. Pan Youcai and Fu Mantang are nowhere in sight; Cui Yuhai has shed his apathy for trade; and Liu Baozhong has abandoned his misgivings about his daughter and her unorthodox—from his point of view—ideas. But we should not overlook the fact that, on a more mundane level, victory here also means the continuation of the store's mobile retail services. Indeed, the very last lines of the opera consist of suggestions to improve and expand delivery.[87] As we have seen, the original impetus for the delivery service is the discovery that Baiyun Slope is something of a retail desert, which makes it a target of evildoers like Pan Youcai. Resolving this situation ultimately means distributing goods through the official system so that the masses can have their needs met without having to rely on capitalist elements. In other words, it requires salespeople like Liu Chunxiu to make the goods her prospective customers want available for purchase.

The contents of Chunxiu's cart matter, here, and they are revealed in a rather remarkable medley in scene 3. On her first trip to Baiyun Slope, Chunxiu is mobbed by a group of locals. In a sung back-and-forth, she interacts with no fewer than six customers in rapid succession. Each requests an item or series of items—ranging from a children's comic book to tobacco leaves—and each is promptly told that, yes, the item is in fact available. Chunxiu's cart takes on the quality of a magician's top hat, out of which a seemingly infinite array of goods might be plucked with the right incantation. Grandpa Li, along with two of his neighbors, remarks that the variety of products is so impressive, "it's as though Xidan Department Store and Chaonei Vegetable Market had moved to our town!"[88] (Xidan had been promoted as a model of Cultural Revolution commerce, as mentioned above. For its part, Chaonei was one of Beijing's four major vegetable markets.) Grandpa Li and the others are essentially marveling at the notion that big-city retail and, by extension, the specter of consumer modernity that it represents have been quite literally brought to their doorsteps. Progress for the community at large can be measured in things. Because that modernity must necessarily be socialist, however, Chunxiu's cart is said to carry more than the material emblems of prosperity, important as they are. Grandpa Li again declares, "What the cart brings is not only needle and thread, oil, salt, soy sauce, and vinegar. The salesperson comrade brings us the party's warmth and concern!"[89] In this way, although Liu Chunxiu is not herself a CCP member, she nonetheless is understood to bestow the populace with commodities on the party's behalf. Indeed, as Grandpa Li's insight implies, the salesperson is crucial to properly suturing party beneficence and commodity together.

Serve the People

While extended store hours and delivery were touted during the Mao period as important ways to make shopping more convenient for the working masses who could not run errands while on shift, they were insufficient in and of themselves to guarantee that the right message would be conveyed by this increase in access to goods for purchase.[90] That much, at least, was very much dependent on the way in which these so-called commercial advancements were carried out by people on the ground. It was up to shopworkers to safeguard the ideological integrity of the revolution in the face of commodity consumption. The range of salesperson behaviors that could either facilitate this process or stand in its way fell under the general rubric of customer service. Not coincidentally, the term *customer service* and Mao's directive to "serve the people" both turn on the notion of *fuwu*, which made it that much easier to expand the notion of customer service to include proletarian class responsibilities. On one hand, the category of customer service encompasses customer encounters on the level we might expect. Salespeople are meant to know their wares so that they can accurately respond to potential buyers' questions; they are meant to be responsive to their customers' needs, desires, and critiques as directly expressed in such venues as store suggestion books (*yijian bu*) and public fora or more subtly inferred from customers' actions; and they are meant to be warm and patient, regardless of how much or how little a customer is thinking of purchasing.[91] (Note that salespeople did not work on commission.)

On the other hand, *customer service* also comprises a familiarity with and alertness to the world outside the confines of the retail outlet. Indeed, in a certain sense, a retailer's job is never done—even when there is no merchandise to be bought and sold. *Xiangyang Store*'s Liu Chunxiu, for example, is familiar with the plight of the workers on Baiyun Slope before anyone else in the shop and is able to anticipate and ultimately meet their needs because of it. She is forever seeking opportunities to be of assistance without even being asked: When she overhears Granny Zhao say that she needs chicken gallbladder to mix her medicine, Chunxiu procures some for her from an unknown source, despite the fact that Xiangyang Store does not otherwise carry it. (The opera is somewhat unclear about whether Granny Zhao ever pays for the elusive ingredient or whether Chunxiu provides it to her at no cost.) Chunxiu also makes a point of sweeping Granny Zhao's courtyard, effectively donating her labor to a cause that does not further the distribution of goods, let alone the movement of store inventory.[92] A similar donation of time and energy features in the short story "Pairing Socks" ("Pei wazi"), mentioned in the introduction, which follows a new retail worker as he learns about one of Shanghai Number 1 Department Store's 180 signature services. If and when customers lose or wear out one sock out of a pair, they can bring the remaining sock to the store to have it matched according to color, thread count, thickness, cuff length, pattern, and size. The newly formed pair is then made available for pickup within a few days. As is quickly made clear to the neophyte retailer, this is a tremendously laborious process that at times even requires workers to travel to nearby factories in search of leftovers from past production lines.[93] And all of this is done in order *not* to force the masses to buy from the department store's assortment of new pairs of socks.

This extraordinary service is consistent with efforts to promote not only sales but also repair, replacement, rentals, and reuse. One must be careful, however, not to mistake such endeavors as indicators of a general turn away from a notion of prosperity and modernity heavily reliant on the availability and acquisition of goods. Contrary to Wang Ning's characterization of pre-1978 Chinese society as "ascetic" (*kuxingzhe*), the enemy was not materiality or, more specifically, the dream of material plenty.[94] As we have seen, access to consumer commodities and the party's magnanimity were meant to go hand in hand. Rather, the pursuit of plenty was coupled with a war on waste (*langfei*). Not the ascetic, but the frugal (*qinjian*) were to be commended for wringing the most out of what they already had and what they would go on to possess in the future. The idealized retailer could help with both the acquisition of goods, when appropriate, and their proper consumption, that is, with milking them for all they were worth. That meant repairing, darning, and using things until they were no longer usable; it also required tremendous additional dedication and labor on the part of salespeople that had little to do with the selling of commodities or, in some cases, with the selling of their time. These service innovations, all of which depended on the correct comportment of retailers above and beyond the mere facilitation of monetized exchange, were touted as newborn things, constitutive of socialist commerce and its superiority over capitalist trade.

Still, there were supposed to be limits to retail workers' willingness to go above and beyond their more conventional responsibilities. The customer was not *always* right. More precisely, not all customers had an equal claim to a salesperson's time and energy—or even to their merchandise. One was encouraged to help a worker in whatever way possible, for example, but abetting a class enemy remained to be avoided. To return to the case of *Xiangyang Store*, Liu Chunxiu is perfectly able and more than willing to say no to Fu Mantang when he tries to make trouble for her: She refuses to sell him *er guo tou* (sorghum-based liquor) from her cart in quantities that suggest speculation. When she initially directs him to take it up with the store—she does not have ten bottles with her—Fu responds in a very crafty way. "Aren't you guys always talking about serving the people 'completely' [*wanquan*] and 'to the utmost' [*chedi*]? It seems to me you should send this young comrade [Cui Yuhai] to fetch some for me!... You have to satisfy your customers [*zuo dao guke manyi*]!"[95] Chunxiu sees through this ploy. She must assert a difference between the kind of delivery she offers, the kind of delivery Fu demands for himself, and, above all, Fu's speculative motives. As Chunxiu pushes against his requests, Fu begins to reveal his underlying assumptions about how commerce works. Not only does he insist on being treated in a certain way ("You're salespeople, and I'm a customer. You should speak to me courteously!"), but he also maintains that his own behavior is irrelevant ("When somebody wants to buy something, you have to provide it to them. It's called business [*maimai*].")[96] What Fu Mantang does not seem to recognize—at his own peril, in the end—is that socialist commerce is not at all meant to be business, in his sense. It is class struggle, and he is the enemy. Serving him would therefore amount to an affront to the masses, not a righteous act of revolution.

Cynically, one might point out that the class enemy exception to the rule of extraordinary customer service provided retailers with a wonderful excuse to refrain from doing anything other than the bare minimum. Consider this account of subpar responsiveness to a customer's needs: "During the Cultural Revolution a man in his fifties entered a department store in Shanghai. Browsing the goods he asked for the store assistant's help. She treated him brusquely and in an off-hand way. He pointed to the slogan above the counter: '*wei renmin fuwu*' (serve the people), a mantra omnipresent at that time and indicated that her behaviour fell short of this revolutionary ideal. Unabashed she retorted, 'how do I know that you're "the people"?'"[97] When the man—who presumably is not an evildoer on the order of Fu Mantang—attempts recourse to the notion of service, just as Fu does in the opera, the man is met with contempt. How is the shop assistant to know whether he is truly deserving of anything else? There is laziness at play here, to be sure, but it is of a very particular sort: an unwillingness to engage in the kind of investigative work and moral discernment righteous class struggle requires. As a model retail worker, by contrast, not only would Liu Chunxiu have attempted to determine whether this poor man was worthy of class love (and service) or class hatred, she would have come to the correct conclusion by definition.

It does not follow, however, that the man in question, having been found an upstanding proletarian, would necessarily have gotten exactly what he wanted. Rather, in an ideal context he would have been granted that which he *should* have wanted in the first place, according to the salesperson. If that did not precisely align with his original wishes, he would have been shown the error of his ways. We see this approach, for example, when Mother He tries to purchase what she deems necessities for her son's wedding banquet in *Delivering Goods on the Road* (*Song huo lushang*), a short Hunanese *huaguxi* opera nationally promoted at much the same time as *Xiangyang Store*. Despite being a peasant in good class standing, she hopes to engage in an ideologically problematic form of consumption, a form of consumption that needs to be policed and educated out of her. That task falls to the local cooperative's leader, Fang Xiuchun, who over the course of the short play manages to convince Mother He to give her son a no-frills, new-style wedding—not because she cannot afford to go all out, but because it is better not to do so. Fang Xiuchun even persuades Mother He to return the items she has already acquired for the occasion.[98] Fang's chief role becomes not to *sell*, but rather to *teach* Mother He how to correctly channel and calibrate her desire in keeping with the prevailing norms of frugal restraint. At the same time, Fang Xiuchun is also positioned as a pedagogue vis-à-vis her new colleague, Xiao Lan, who mistakenly sells Mother He everything she initially wants. The idealized retailer is, in this sense, charged not only with managing scarce goods but additionally with helping those around her manage their desires separate and apart from such petty issues as availability and affordability. This is very much central to the definition of service she is meant to provide; indeed, the whole notion of socialist commerce as radically different—qua developmental/historical advancement—from its capitalist analog depends on it.

As I conclude, it is worth emphasizing that this is fundamentally about desire (and distinction) and not, as we might expect, about usefulness and need. The case of the wedding banquet makes this quite clear, as it would be easy to argue that *any* ceremony at all is inherently excessive. Again, the goal is not abnegation for its own sake so much as it is establishing new social norms of appropriate consumption in such a celebratory circumstance. To wit, Fang Xiuchun ultimately teaches Mother He how to substitute one kind of ritual for another, thereby channeling her desire in a more acceptable direction. Mother He *can* purchase these things; she is simply not supposed to want to. This, then, is the ideal of socialist retail: endless commodities on offer, catering to a clientele with boundless purchasing power who nonetheless chooses to buy only that which is politically acceptable and ideologically correct. Both supply and possible, ultimately denied, demand in this scenario operate as emblems of successful modernization, whereas the consumer's actual purchase aligns with the priorities of socialist construction as an economic and ideological project. The salesperson, serving the people from her shop, is effectively the key to conjuring an approximation of this scene day in and day out. By dint of her extraordinary dedication to customer service, often in ways that are touted as being counter to the capitalist profit motive, she guarantees that her clients' desires are properly directed and that, in the end, the right choice is made. Part teacher and part foot soldier, she mediates and polices the desire her wares instill, all in the name of the party and the masses. In this sense, she resides at the nexus of the competing exigencies of modernization, revolution, and materiality—that is, of newborn socialist things.

3 Productivist Display

> Going down these streets, with their bright, clean windows and extraordinary, well-conceived displays one after the other, is like visiting an exhibition that, through artistic means, reflects commodity production, industrialization levels, the rapid improvement of people's lives, and the face of development since 1949. The display of the products of labor in shopwindows is noble and valuable. Much like putting a painting in a frame, it allows us to enjoy, appreciate, and love the fruits of our diligent labor all the more.
> —Yuan Yunfu, "Chuchuang de gousi"

Over the course of three days in late May 1960, Beijing's Wangfujing shopping district was given a serious facelift. The capital was about to host the roughly six thousand participants of the National Conference of Outstanding Workers in Culture and Education (Quan guo wen jiao qun ying hui), the heroes of the Great Leap Forward come to be feted in the Great Hall of the People.[1] In honor of these visitors, according to press characterizations, the students and faculty of the Central Academy of Craft and Design (Zhongyang gongyi meishu xueyuan) took it upon themselves to re-dress over 160 shopwindows in under seventy-two hours.[2] Like the individuals they sought to emulate, the window designers, many of whom had no experience in the field, pushed themselves to the limit, accomplishing a mammoth task with few resources and little time. The entire exercise amounted to an ode to labor in the face of daunting odds: Not only did the objects displayed in the store windows testify, by their mere existence, to the factory and agricultural labor that produced them—much as this chapter's epigraph suggests—but, as creative undertakings, the 160-plus displays also spoke to the practical value of artistic labor.

One way to interpret this massive undertaking, in fact, is as an effort, on the part of the Central Academy as an institution and design as a field, to justify its continued existence and value to the revolutionary project. With write-ups in the specialized periodicals *Art* (*Meishu*) and (the Central Academy's own) *Art and Design* (*Zhuangshi*), it seems likely that the stunt was targeted, at least in part, at earning recognition for window design as a worthwhile *artistic* activity, both inside and outside the academy. Indeed, one student who participated in the remaking of Wangfujing is pointedly quoted in one of these stories as saying: "I used to think there was nothing to this art form [window design]. I had no idea it required such expertise [*xuewen*]."[3] The implication is that, in the words of Yuan Yunfu (1933–2017), a faculty member at the Central Academy, effective window displays rely on artistic means (*yishu shouduan*) to do their work. They require attention, on the part of the designer, to composition and color, among other things, much as a well-executed painting exerts from its creator.[4] Not just anyone can put a display together on the fly; it takes talent and training—talent and training deserving of the *art* mantle.

Even as would-be designers were jockeying for position in the art world, however, more fundamental ideological pressures on their work remained. Window design meant involving oneself in the politically suspect world of socialist commerce, for these windows were associated with a utilitarian purpose: to visually entice passersby to purchase commodities. In other words, they were meant to spark desire, desire that bordered uncomfortably, one could argue, on commodity fetishism. Art or not, window design generally fell under the problematic heading of advertising (*guanggao*). As Karl Gerth has demonstrated, the question of how to deploy advertising in an appropriately socialist manner garnered great interest in the PRC in the 1950s.[5] And China was not alone in this; the entirety of the socialist world was dealing with these issues, at times even doing so in concert. The PRC Ministry of Commerce sent a representative to two international gatherings on the topic, for example, in Prague (1957) and in Bucharest (1960).[6] The Prague conference, which drew heavily on Soviet, Czechoslovakian, and East German experience, was particularly influential on Chinese domestic practice, followed up as it was by national conferences in Beijing (1958) and Shanghai (1959). The latter, like the Prague event on which it was modeled, featured a display window exhibition comprising over forty windows on Nanjing and Huaihai roads, Shanghai's major shopping thoroughfares.[7] Yuan Yunfu's characterization of these streets as an exhibition space, made some months before, was, in this instance, made quite literal.

What is it that we are meant to see in figure 3.1 or any other such display? Artistry, skill, and political correctness, to be sure, but mostly—mostly—proletarian labor. In a nutshell, the successful socialist store window is

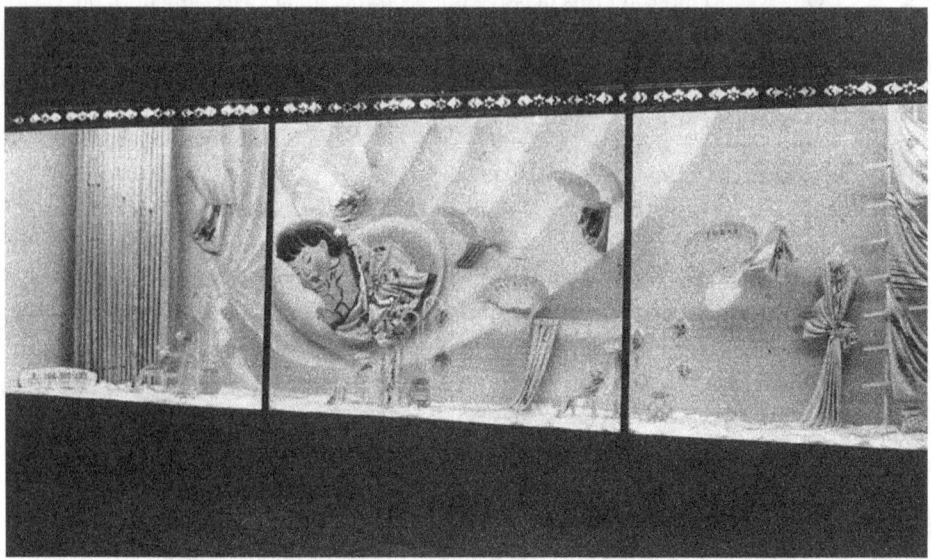

Figure 3.1 Shanghai contribution to the National Conference on Advertising, Window Dressing, and Commodity Display held in Shanghai in August 1959. From *Art and Design*, no. 8 (1959): 39.

intended to skirt the perils of unchecked desire by casting commodities (*shangpin*) destined for exchange and consumption as mere products of labor (*chanpin*). This is the crux of what I am here calling *productivist display*, which seeks to achieve through visual representation what the idealized socialist retailer accomplishes through overt pedagogy and heroic customer service.[8] Both are called on to disarm desire while also mediating the push and pull of industrial and ideological progress found at the heart of the newborn socialist thing; indeed, they typically worked in tandem to do so. Productivist display, however, additionally draws our attention to the question of materiality and its limits, to the thingness—or lack thereof—of the newborn socialist thing. What makes a thing socialist? Does it then still remain a thing?

This chapter explores these issues through the framework of productivism. I begin with the problem of plenty and its treatment in the productivist mode of display. This treatment relies on a particular understanding of production, which I then turn to in the context of the porcelain industry of Jingdezhen, Jiangxi Province, after 1949. The CCP's effort to modernize the porcelain industry resulted in the creation and consolidation of enormous factories, including one devoted to porcelain sculpture (*cisu* or *cidiao*), which were in turn critical to molding Jingdezhen's laborers into a veritable proletariat. I consider the development of Cultural Revolution statuettes as an attempt to reinvent both the art form and its mode of production. This is followed by an examination of the value afforded to decoration and display in the productivist mode, and I end the chapter by returning to department store window displays and the commodity fetish.

Too Much of a Good Thing

Despite the association of socialism with shortage in the popular imagination, a lack of consumer goods across the board was never itself a goal of the party-state system enacted in the PRC or, for that matter, in the Soviet Union and its satellites. As historian of the Stalinist period Sheila Fitzpatrick puts it, "While the Soviet regime may be said to have discouraged consumerism by keeping goods scarce, it was not ideologically on the side of asceticism. On the contrary, future socialism was always conceived in terms of plenty: according to the regime's Socialist Realist perception of the world, the meagre supply of goods in the present was only a harbinger of the abundance to come."[9] In other words, the system for allocating goods may well have been designed in the interests of fulfilling the needs/desires of a chosen elite (the *nomenklatura* in the USSR and the Eastern Bloc and those with access to special supply outlets in the PRC)—and the party-state may well have used its ability to control the flow of goods to its own advantage—but any resulting lack for the general populace was understood as something that needed to be overcome rather than praised.[10] Consider that while communism was imagined as commodity free—unlike socialism, which had to negotiate the commodity's continued existence—it was most assuredly not imagined to be free of things or indeed of the creature comforts currently available to the elite.[11] Rather, communism would involve such general prosperity and abundance that restricted, present-day luxuries would become commonplace to the benefit of all. Far from ascetic, communism was regularly conjured in China as elsewhere as, in the words of Helena Goscilo, a "Cornucopia-Utopia," as an age of plenty.[12]

Even as shortages of some consumer goods occurred within the various socialist systems, moreover, other goods already existed in superabundance. These were the goods that, despite being produced in accordance with the party-state's economic plan and its expectations of consumer demand, found themselves unwanted and rather superfluous. Without a flexible price mechanism responsive to fluctuations in supply and demand to go on, economic planners allocated resources and set production quotas based on rationalized (purportedly scientific) systems of knowledge about the masses' needs and wants.[13] As we saw in chapter 2, a critical part of the retailer's job was to get to know her customers. The reasons for this were twofold. On the one hand, the better the retailer understood her clientele, the better she could serve them, both in the sense of attending to their material requirements and in the sense of educating them in the proper ways of socialist consumption. On the other hand, retailers were in the best position to glean information about the vicissitudes of consumer demand and make predictions about its evolution. As one source puts it, retailers were "the eyes and ears of industrial production" (*gongye shengchan de ermu*).[14] When run up the flagpole to the planning bureaus, shop floor assessments of (prescriptive) consumer behavior could, it was thought, mitigate against miscalculations in the crafting of the plan. The better the information, the better the plan and the fewer the unexpected outcomes, whether shortage or surfeit. The particular form of plenty that led to stockpiles of unwanted goods and what Serguei Oushakine has dubbed a "storage economy," unlike the abundance of the communist cornucopia-utopia, *was* meant to be eradicated through evermore scientific planning.[15] Indeed, plenitude for all could not be achieved unless and until the inefficiencies of the storage economy were eliminated.

In the Soviet case, Oushakine argues, the emphasis on rational planning translated into, among other things, efforts to map out and codify the world of available commodities in minute detail. "Since needs are rationally limited, the number of products that could satisfy these needs by definition is finite. The easiest way to deal with the problem [of stockpiling] was to supply industry with an exhaustive nomenclature of desirable goods. Overstocking, in other words, was associated with the imprecise cartography of production rather than with the fluid nature of desire."[16] Taxonomy, as a form of scientific (scientistic?) knowledge, was meant to rescue the shortage/storage economy by providing a comprehensive grounding for data collection and economic forecasting.[17] One of the most impressive examples of the Soviet drive to taxonomize is found in the nine-volume *Commodity Dictionary* (*Tovarnyy slovar'*), published from 1956 to 1961 by Torgizdat press. The work was ostensibly meant to educate and guide all those involved in the formation and management of the object world it meticulously categorized. It aimed at being exhaustive. For example, "the entry on 'sausage items' went on for seventy-four pages (of very small print), portraying a paradise populated by the following sausage subgroups in the order of their appearance: boiled sausages, camel sausages, dietary sausages, poultry sausages (chicken, turkey, duck, and goose included), deer sausages, horse sausages, smoked-and-boiled sausages, blood sausages, rabbit sausages, liver sausages, half-smoked sausages, fish sausages, raw-smoked sausages, and stuffed sausages."[18] That's a lot of sausage.

Indeed, it seems to me that, despite the apparent goal of such a catalog to provide a better grasp of the material possibilities afforded Soviet citizens, the sheer size of the endeavor—nine volumes, containing some eight thousand entries, comprising over twenty thousand commodities—is positively overwhelming. As "a bible of Soviet materiality, the *Dictionary* is an astonishing piece of evidence of a social attempt to catalogue as meticulously as possible real elements of imaginary Soviet consumption," but it is also, in its own way, an exercise in the fantasy of plenitude and an exploration of the power wielded by such a fantasy.[19] This becomes particularly evident in *Commodity Dictionary*'s use of lavish color illustrations (see, for example, figure 3.2). One is promptly "carried away," to use Rachel Bowlby's phrase, by what amounts to the visual anticipation of the cornucopia-utopia to come in the name of documenting the material richness and variety of present production.[20]

In contrast to the Soviet drive to systematize consumption, powered by a need to overcome the limitations of individual, unscientific actors, which arguably found its apotheosis in *Commodity Dictionary*, the emphasis of the PRC commercial sector, since its inception, appears to have centered much more squarely on the importance of people in making the economic plan function correctly.[21] When considered from the perspective of the threat posed by the commodity form and commodity fetishism to the socialist project—a threat thought to be significantly more acute in China than it ever was in the USSR—the former tack seems to encourage an awe of the system of goods as a whole in order to avoid the possibility of a singular infatuation with any one of its components.[22] This is perhaps one advantage of taking this approach, but there is little to guarantee that this misdirection will actually work. The latter strategy, on the other hand, looks to individual retail personnel (and, ultimately, to consumers themselves) to be the ideological guarantors of the spirit as well as the letter of the plan. This is not to say that product information of the kind featured in *Commodity Dictionary* was unavailable to those who might need it in the retail sector. Trade publications regularly carried surveys of new offerings, pairing them with instructions on proper handling and storage methods. From bean paste to condoms to X-ray film, nearly all conceivable product classes were subject to this kind of industry coverage at one time or another.[23]

This somewhat piecemeal approach to documenting the object world—to my knowledge, nothing on the order of *Commodity Dictionary* and its purported completeness was ever attempted in the PRC—was complemented, however, by displays of the actual goods in question, targeting retail workers. For example, wholesalers and warehouses were called on to establish sample rooms (*yangpin shi*) for the purpose of exhibiting both their current and anticipated inventory. Workers charged with purchasing for retail outlets (department stores, specialized shops, etc.) from these wholesalers and warehouses would be invited to visit the relevant sample room before placing their seasonal

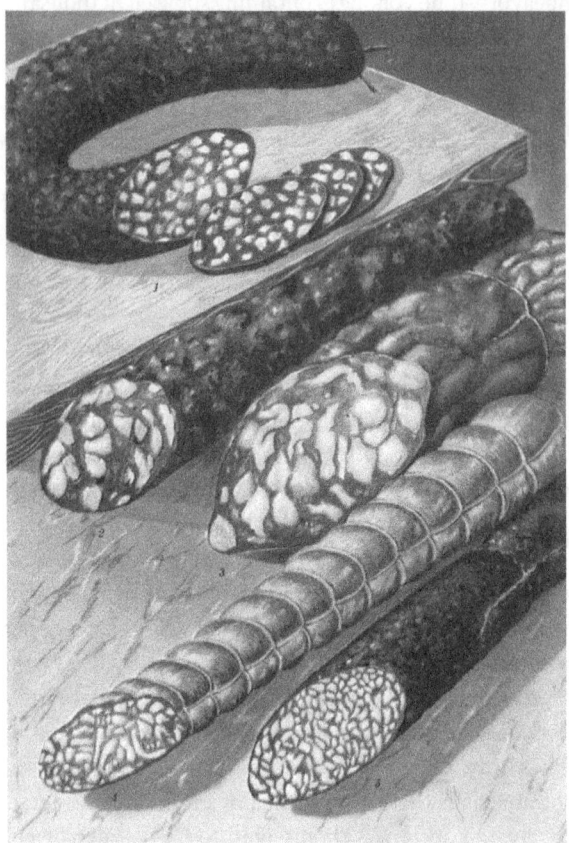

Figure 3.2 Sausages. From *Tovarnyy slovar'* (*Commodity Dictionary*), 3:880.

orders. Given the nature of the Chinese commercial system, even at its most economically liberal moments, sample rooms were not about persuading retailers to buy from one wholesaler over another. Shopping around was not really an option for the wholesalers' clientele; there were too few places for institutional buyers to go within the official system.[24] Rather, the idea behind the sample room was to educate purchasers about the choices they did have *within* the confines of the plan. In the words of Zi Qun of the Hunan General Goods Corporation (Hunan sheng baihuo gongsi), "A so-called 'sample room' is a place where an enterprise [*qiye*] can display [*chenlie*] the various commodities under its control in an orderly fashion so that purchasers [*caigouyuan*] can see all of these commodities in person. These purchasers' assessments and choices will allow the allocation and supply of commodities to most effectively meet demand."[25] Armed with knowledge about end users' needs and wants—gleaned, in theory, from service encounters with customers on the shop floor—retail personnel, it was thought, if also presented with the right information from the supply side, were in the best position to minimize economic miscalculations. In this sense, the sample room was envisioned as an important contact zone for supply and demand.

Such displays arguably put the Soviet impulse to taxonomize into action, but in order to ensure that purchasers ultimately made correct decisions, sample rooms deployed a combination of techniques. On the one hand, the displays were logically organized by type and use (the bar soaps next to the bar soap cases, the toothbrushes next to the toothpastes, etc.) and clearly labeled, each commodity identified by name alongside its product number, brand, major specifications, place of production, price, and availability. Overstocked items were to be placed in prominent locations (*mingxian de difang*) so as to try to increase their sale and free up warehouse space. On the other hand, sample rooms were also expected to be manned by dedicated service staff (*yewu yuan*) with three main responsibilities: "1. to introduce and promote commodities to purchasers and help them make their selections; 2. to promptly answer purchasers' questions regarding commodities, their specifications, quality, characteristics, and order procedures; and 3. to display, manage, and maintain the cleanliness and hygiene of the samples."[26] It goes without saying that sample room workers also needed a "high political consciousness" in addition to a "strong sense of responsibility and a deep knowledge of commodities."[27] In short, sample rooms relied on service in addition to carefully codified display.

In truth, the display tactics described here were utilized in retail as well, for store windows were also meant to convey important information. A mid-1964 *Trade Work* article identifies eight different ways to highlight a store's merchandise by means of interior displays: atop shelving units; in wall-mounted cases; in glass display cases; surrounding pillars; on the bottom shelf of glass counters; on countertops; in stand-alone groups, including pyramids; and on racks.[28] All of these techniques are meant to be used in tandem indoors, while outward-facing window displays address potential customers on the street in much the same terms. In every case, one must concern oneself with clarity. The easiest way to help a customer make an informed purchase is to make the commodities on offer—and their prices—visible. To that end, consider the primacy of clear and rational organization in the two major how-to guides of the Mao era for designing shopwindows.[29] Both take aim at the same enemy: the indiscriminate piling (*dui*) of commodities with little regard for the merchandise's intended use, seasonal propriety, or probable consumers. The cornucopia-utopia—even in aspirational form—cannot be allowed to spill forth willy-nilly. It must instead be carefully managed, as through a series of oft-refreshed but relatively sparse displays, each timely and logically coherent, complete with informational labels.

It is not the methods of display, but rather the collision of (potentially unruly or transgressive) consumer desire with actual displayed objects that ultimately accounts for the differences between the wholesale sample room and the retail outlet. Both rely on similar techniques, in combination with service personnel, to highlight merchandise and facilitate exchange, but only the retailer need court and then wrangle actual desire. In the sample room, desire remains inferred and hypothetical; in the store, it is made tangibly real. Thus the greater attention paid to aesthetics in the latter case: "A store's interior commodity displays must be neat, plentiful [*fengman*], eye-catching, and pleasing to look at. They must aid consumers in choosing what to purchase and retail workers in selling their wares, while making consumers entering the store feel that the commodities are everywhere extraordinary, richly colorful, and lively. They must ignite people's spirits [*huanfa renmen de jingshen*]."[30] The beguiling potential of plenty is invoked by the totality of tidy, scientific acts of display despite the fact that that potential is never meant to be fulfilled, for obvious ideological reasons. To the extent that sample rooms also comprised displays of plenty in this sense, they could largely avoid this predicament by virtue of their apparent proximity to the source of their featured commodities and their apparent distance from consumers. They were evidence of the increasing success of modern, socialist production writ large. Public-facing invocations of plenty, including those found in shopwindows and on store shelves, tried to make the same play, sidestepping the dangers of the desire they conjured by likewise hiding behind production. In other words, productivist commodity displays supposedly weren't about facilitating consumption per se at all. Consumption was rather subsumed under production, thereby rendering it politically acceptable.

Producing the Proletariat

Before examining the immediate concerns of display in the context of consumption qua production any further, it behooves us to take a harder look at the realm of production as such. The means, methods, and structures of labor were far from stagnant or uniform in the Mao period. Tremendous changes took place in the forms of recognized and remunerated labor, to say nothing of the creation of new social institutions such as the work unit and the commune.[31] But not all labor practices were legible as production (*shengchan*), and therefore as fodder for a productivist aesthetic, at all times. Consider that something as central to production as the factory—what it should be, how it should be run, and its ideological justification—was still open to significantly divergent interpretations as late as 1975. Indeed, Alessandro Russo argues that defining the factory was one of the key points of contention between Mao Zedong and Deng Xiaoping just prior to Deng's second fall from grace in the winter of 1975–76.[32] All of this suggests that we not presuppose a sphere of economic activity that manifestly belongs under the banner of production. To that end, I turn now to porcelain and some of the changes undertaken in porcelain manufacturing in Jingdezhen—China's porcelain capital (*cidu*)—after 1949 in order to explore how that industry remade itself according to a particular vision of proletarian production.

Jingdezhen in the Mao era is part of a larger story involving the pursuit of the mechanized assembly line and its quintessentially modern allure, an allure we might well trace back to Taylorism's deep and enduring impact on republican China and Soviet Russia in the late 1910s and 1920s.[33] As a rural industry, moreover, changes in porcelain making in Jingdezhen speak to the peculiar challenges faced by workers in the relatively small sphere of nonagricultural economic activity, including handicrafts, in the countryside.[34] There appear to have been significant parallels in the pressures exerted on porcelain manufacturing and papermaking to "proletarianize," for instance.[35] In this sense, Jingdezhen is representative of discursive and economic development trends that are much bigger than porcelain. It is also the case, however, that the (re)casting of porcelain manufacturing as production was key to the reinvention of decorative porcelain as a politically acceptable component of the Cultural Revolution media environment. This is therefore a story of productivist rebirth as well.

Jingdezhen's reputation as China's leader in porcelain is indisputable. While other provinces, including Shandong, Fujian, Hunan, and Guangdong, boast rich and distinctive ceramic traditions of their own,[36] the Jingdezhen area of Jiangxi has had a largely unchallenged claim on high-end porcelain since at least the Ming dynasty (1368–1644), when its kilns began supplying the capital with ceramics.[37] It held the status of *guanyao* (official kiln) during the Qing dynasty (1644–1911), producing inventive and technologically challenging pieces to satisfy the emperors' insatiable appetite for porcelain. Qianlong's reign (1735–96) is particularly associated with the development of new, illusionist aesthetics made possible by advancements in kiln and glaze technologies devised at Jingdezhen.[38] From blue-and-white (*qinghua*) pattern ware, still so sought after, to high-fire glazes mimicking Tang dynasty stoneware, Jingdezhen is synonymous with porcelain—in late imperial China, throughout the twentieth century, and today.[39] Add to this porcelain's significance to a narrative of Chinese national distinction, and it should come as no surprise that the CCP took a great interest in creating a new, revolutionary Jingdezhen when it came to power in 1949.[40]

This interest took a number of forms, including a shift in the historiography of porcelain, which now emphasized the heavy reliance of pre-1949 workshops on unskilled manual labor in order to extract raw materials. Treating and properly maintaining feldspathic china stone (*cishi*), kaolin clay (*Gaoling tu*), water, and timber supplies was in fact extremely labor intensive. A 1962 history of the industry, crafted by the municipal propaganda bureau, for example, recasts the members of this workforce as a proto-proletariat, trapped in a feudal system not unlike indentured servitude.[41] The CCP's entry into Jingdezhen is therefore described in this volume as the coming of class consciousness to a group of hitherto oppressed laborers that thereby allowed the otherwise inchoate proletariat of Jingdezhen to let loose its fetters and reach maturity.[42] This new historical orthodoxy allowed Jingdezhen to position itself as a centuries-old proletarian town avant la lettre with a working-class heritage that could be constitutive of revolutionary cachet. Jingdezhen also had an additional claim to a special revolutionary position: From June 1930 to September 1933, Jingdezhen operated under the auspices of the CCP's Northeast Jiangxi Soviet. During this time it appears to have boasted some trade unions.[43] After 1949 this early party history was drawn on to counteract porcelain's associations with luxury, the bourgeoisie, and the ruling elite. If porcelain was made by proletarian workers—and had been, in a sense, for centuries—then it lost some of its political ambivalence.

The construction of an actual proletariat required more than a rewriting of local history, however. It also meant the development of new, appropriately modern and revolutionary institutions and labor structures. Porcelain manufacturing increasingly left the realm of the handicraft workshop and was ushered into the realm of the massive, nationalized factory with a concerted effort that began even before the official birth of the People's Republic. In August 1949 the county-level CCP committee took over the Jiangxi Porcelain Company (Jiangxi ciye gongsi), located on the premises of what had been the imperial workshops during the Qing dynasty (on present-day Shengli Road). On April 1, 1950, the Jingdezhen Jianguo Porcelain Company (Jingdezhen shi jianguo ciye gongsi) was officially established; after incorporating a number of other, smaller facilities throughout 1951, it was renamed the Jingdezhen Jianguo Porcelain Factory (Jingdezhen shi jianguo cichang) in 1952. As the word *jianguo* (literally, "establish the nation") suggests, this factory was New China's first centralized foray into the business of making porcelain—but it was only the beginning. More nationally funded factories were developed throughout the 1950s, eventually earning the group designation of the ten great porcelain factories of Jingdezhen (*Jingdezhen shi da cichang*), a phrase still in circulation despite the expansion of ever-more manufacturing facilities.[44] These factories might well be understood as the PRC equivalent of the imperial kilns—a play by the party-state to monopolize high-end porcelain—an interpretation reinforced by the Jianguo factory's physical location and the prestige afforded to it as a result. In fact, Maris Boyd Gillette argues that the CCP takeover of the industry was largely a story of continuity: "When it comes to porcelain manufacture, the Party under Mao Zedong built on and extended key imperial policies rather than rejecting them."[45] This is the case even in terms of the division and organization of labor.

As suggested above, the Jianguo factory and its brethren are manifestations of a much larger process of industrial growth and consolidation. According to official statistics, in 1950 a combined average of 15,900 people worked in Jingdezhen's 2,492 porcelain manufacturers—1,651 of which were individually run workshops. By 1957 this total workforce had grown to 28,849, but the number of porcelain-making units had shrunk to a measly fifty-seven—thirty-two of which employed only a combined fifty-three people. In other words, in 1957, 99.9 percent of workers in the porcelain industry were employed by only twenty-five entities, all of which benefited from some level of state investment.[46] These increasingly homogeneous working conditions were key to forging erstwhile laborers into socialist proletarian worker subjects. More precisely, these large factories constituted crucial environments for the production of a classically recognizable proletariat right alongside porcelain vases. And Jingdezhen seems to have been uncommonly well disposed toward this kind of reorganization, since the town's rise to prominence as early as the fourteenth century was in large part fueled by its rather distinctive labor structures.

> The key technologies for making ceramics, such as throwing, trimming, and moulding, were developed centuries before Jingdezhen appeared as a production site. What Jingdezhen contributed to the history of ceramics technology was organization. The city pioneered labour specialization, where an individual performed only one aspect of manufacturing in a kind of handicraft assembly-line process. Many ceramists worked on a single vessel en route to the finished product: as locals put it, "72 hands to finish a pot." This method meant that producers could create wares of high quality at a consistent rate. Jingdezhen ceramists became extraordinarily skilled at the tasks they performed—but they produced as specialists, not as studio potters. If Jingdezhen ever had a studio tradition, it was over by the fourteenth century. Making porcelain in Jingdezhen was and remains a collective endeavour.[47]

In other words, one might reasonably argue that, to the extent that the PRC factories' labor structures were new, they were new in terms of degree and scale rather than kind. Different processes were integrated under one factory, for example, that might previously have been the purview of separate clans or guilds. But the division of tasks among a large group of people, each with their own specialty, had long been the Jingdezhen way, allowing the site to produce on an impressive scale well before the advent of twentieth-century scientific organization and management techniques.[48]

The consolidation of the new factories was not simply a matter of reshuffling the labor force, however. These work units also claimed to have brought about fundamental changes in the way porcelain was made, specifically, with the much-lauded introduction of new machinery in the factory setting.[49] Modernizing Jingdezhen's defining industry was consistently equated with increased mechanization, automation, and the standardization such changes permitted (*ciye shengchan zou jixiehua zidonghua de daolu*). Other centers of ceramic production were subject to the same trends. There were to be no more small batches of pug clay or hand-molded tableware; the large nationalized factories, in particular, promoted themselves as modern sites of *mechanized* mass production. Despite such grand claims, the actual implementation of new technologies appears to have been much slower and more partial than the official rhetoric might suggest. As an indication of just how slowly changes took root, "only 5.4 per cent of the industry [in Jingdezhen] was mechanized by the end of 1957."[50] Yueyang County Ceramics Factory (Yueyang xian cichang) in nearby Hunan Province was touted for its mechanization as late as 1975, suggesting that it was still considered quite an achievement.[51] (See figure 3.3.) More importantly, perhaps, the language of mechanization encompassed a whole range of new practices, some more closely associated with machines than others. Automation, for example, could mean something on the order of employing hand-operated jigger-jolly machines to shape flat and hollow wares, which still relied heavily on human labor,[52] whereas a shift from stick-spun potter's wheels to foot-pedal wheels could be promoted as half-mechanized even though both were used by ceramists to throw by hand.[53] Some technical advances made in the 1950s were the product of foreign expertise—Soviet advisors shared information on mechanized slip-casting, for instance—but many were attributed to factory workers themselves, who were encouraged to compete in coming up with the best new ideas. "Cadres displayed the results of one [such competition] at a public exhibition in October 1954: new carts for hauling china stone, foot-pedal potter's wheels, plaster-of-Paris moulds to standardize the size of round wares, trimming knives, banding wheels, vehicles for loading kiln wood, and several new production methods, including painting surface decoration with two brushes, two-handed glazing, a technique for stoking kiln fires, strategies for stacking greenware in kilns."[54] While many of these innovations may seem minor, taken together under the banner of the modern factory they speak

Figure 3.3 Yueyang County Ceramics Factory, Hunan. From *China Pictorial*, no. 9 (1975): 36. Photo by Tang Dabai, Chen Mingjie, and Li Yi.

to a system whose goal, if not its reality, was to produce as many identical, machine-made articles as possible. To the extent that they were actually involved, machines were operated by members of the proletariat, themselves cogs in the new machinery of revolution. There would be little chance of mistaking these workers for craftspeople, given their limited, tactile interaction with the porcelain-in-progress.[55] The less they touched it—the more they interacted with the machines instead—the more this idealized workforce became the same as that of any other industry, engaging in labor practices that were legible as production. Porcelain, by extension, was put on a par with other materials, like plastic or steel.

The emphasis on (increasingly mechanized) mass manufacture continued throughout the Mao period but is most clearly reflected in the official statistical record of the 1950s. In 1952, the city of Jingdezhen and its surrounding county produced 90,220,870 porcelain consumer items (*riyong ci*).[56] By 1957, thanks in part to changes in industrial processes and the expansion/consolidation of factory facilities, this total number had ballooned to 275,872,120, a 205 percent increase.[57] Based on the limited data available, this appears to have been peak production, at least in terms of the aggregate number of porcelain pieces. In 1958, despite or perhaps because of the Great Leap Forward (one presumes that consumer porcelains were not the priority), this total was down to 237,572,400.[58] In 1974 the number had decreased to 216,851,700.[59] This further dip—which was turned around by 1977[60]—is at least partially attributable to unrest in the industry in the early years of the Cultural Revolution and the fact that seven of Jingdezhen's ceramic factories were re-tasked shortly thereafter to produce other goods, "including munitions, cars, broadcast equipment, electrical supplies, screws, and textiles."[61] By autumn 1972, when Jingdezhen was declared an "open city" (*kaifang chengshi*) accessible to foreign visitors, the industry was back to running relatively smoothly.[62] This turmoil makes the amount of porcelain consistently produced by Jingdezhen's factories all the more astounding. And to think, they were still nowhere near meeting domestic demand for basic tableware.[63]

Unfortunately, impressive as these numbers are, they tell us very little about the quality and specific kinds of consumer items produced. As to the former, we must rely on the three-tier classification system employed in the official record of the 1950s, whereby porcelain is designated as coarse (*cu*), fine (*xi*), or common (*putong*). Despite the apparent effort to increase the quantity of porcelains across the board—with the additional aim, I would suggest, to combat the material's elitist associations through mass production—high-end porcelains remained the single most important focus of the industry in Jingdezhen. In 1958, for example, a year for which we have data for each of the three classifications, 54.76 percent of consumer porcelain production was dedicated to fine pieces.[64] While Cultural Revolution–era statistics do not include such information, we do know that 44.34 percent of consumer porcelain produced in 1974 was slated for export.[65] (Export ceramics was a tremendously important source of foreign currency for the PRC.) A similar export ratio of 49.20 percent was reported in 1977.[66] Insofar as we can assume that exported porcelain, directed at the international market, was of the finest quality available and that the proportion of high-end porcelain remained relatively steady, then we must conclude that almost all of the porcelain intended for domestic consumption was of the coarse and common varieties.[67] As to discerning what these consumer porcelains actually were—plates versus vases versus Mao badges, and so on—the statistical record remains somewhat helpful in that production numbers are broken down by major factory. Since each factory had its specialty, we can roughly estimate the kind and number of each sort of item.[68]

This brings us to the interesting case of the Jingdezhen Porcelain Sculpture Factory (Jingdezhen diaosu cichang), which provides an important window into the ongoing contradictions at the heart of the project to remake the porcelain industry, as I have been describing it. Founded in 1956 through the consolidation of individual workshops, societies devoted to art and sculpture, and experimental manufacturing facilities, it quickly entered the ranks of the ten great porcelain factories of Jingdezhen and benefited from national backing. Indications are that in late 1974 it employed some six hundred workers.[69] Because, as its name suggests, Jingdezhen Porcelain Sculpture Factory specialized in the production of sculpted porcelains, we can safely assume that all of the 324,000 porcelain items Jingdezhen Porcelain Sculpture Factory produced for domestic consumption in 1974 were of this character—that is to say, essentially decorative.[70] From reliefs to figurines, these porcelains were not meant to be used as part of quotidian life—as a tea set might, for example—so much as to be displayed and visually appreciated. On the one hand, the political discomfort caused by this defining sense of excess helps account for Jingdezhen Porcelain Sculpture Factory's higher-than-average export percentage—a staggering 76.04 percent in 1974, for example.[71] The vast majority of its decorative pieces were intended for consumption outside the Chinese socialist system, making them considerably less politically problematic. On the other hand, Jingdezhen Porcelain Sculpture Factory itself as an institution is emblematic of the tension between the drive toward mass production and standardization and the ongoing notion of the individuated artist or master as the ultimate producer of aesthetic value. In other words, the development of Jingdezhen Porcelain Sculpture Factory illustrates the ways in which the new modes of production initiated by the CCP struggled to bring about the fundamental changes in artistic regimes of value to which it implicitly aspired.

The key here is the extent to which, within the very factory environment intended to be the fount of a new, faceless, and nameless proletariat, masters of porcelain sculpture continued to produce singular pieces with which they were identified as individuals. And nowhere is this more clearly in evidence than at Jingdezhen Porcelain Sculpture Factory, since so much of its success in the decorative arts profited—as it were—from both a claim to socialist modernity, by way of its size and institutional structure, and the cultural capital of the artists under its employ. Consider the inextricable link between the history of Jingdezhen Porcelain Sculpture Factory and the oeuvre of the most important porcelain artists of the Mao period. From father-son duo Zeng Longsheng (1901–64) and Zeng Shandong (1926–) to He Shuigen (1925–) and Liu Yuanchang (1939–), Jingdezhen Porcelain Sculpture Factory developed and was home to Jingdezhen's biggest names and talent, including faculty members of the Jingdezhen School of Ceramic Arts and Technology (Jingdezhen taoci jiyi xuexiao), a forerunner to today's Ceramics Institute (Taoci xueyuan), founded in 1955. Furthermore, it should come as no surprise that these same figures were crucial to the reinvention of porcelain sculpture as an aesthetic form appropriate to socialism in addition to simply being—at least nominally—produced in a factory. Indeed, one suspects that this aesthetic reinvention would have been considerably more difficult without the gravitas of the artists involved in that process.

Porcelain Remade

It is customary to begin accounts of the history of ceramic sculpture in Jingdezhen with a reference to *Notes on the Southern Kilns* (*Nan yao biji*), a text dating from the mid-eighteenth century. In it, the unnamed author indicates that ceramic figurines of lions and elephants were produced in Jingdezhen in the early seventh century. Excavated artifacts seem to confirm the notion that carved ceramics existed during the Tang dynasty (618–907), at the very latest, with sculpted porcelains, including porcelain figurines, emerging and taking off during the Song dynasty (960–1279). The popularity of these pieces increased during the Yuan dynasty (1271–1368), with the advent of blue-and-white patterning. By the Ming dynasty, the possibilities for color application to sculpted works had increased significantly, allowing for the creation of much more intricate and varied detailing. The subject matter of porcelain sculptures during the Ming and Qing was increasingly tied to the representation of Buddhist figures and other gods and goddesses. The bodhisattva Guanyin was a particular favorite and continued to fascinate artists well into the PRC era, even as religious iconography became politically problematic.[72]

Ceramic sculptures (*taoci diaosu*), of which porcelain sculptures are a subset, may be classified in a number of ways, including in accord with a defining technique or characteristic.[73] Traditionally, there have been three basic technical categories: *fudiao* essentially comprise reliefs, not to be confused with engravings, or *diaoke*, in which designs are recessed on a surface rather than raised; *niediao* are pinched or hand-rolled and often involve the combination of small pieces prior to firing; and *loudiao* are characterized by openwork. Each of these techniques may be used in isolation or in combination with others, in which case they correspond less to a type of sculpture than a form of ornamentation. The *linglong* wares for which Jingdezhen is famous, for example, necessitate the technique of loudiao in order to achieve their characteristic open pattern. An additional distinction is made between those pieces, like reliefs, that are intended to be viewed from a single direction—in other words, they concern themselves with a single viewing surface—as opposed to those pieces that are intended to be viewed from all angles. The latter are often referred to as sculptures in the round, or *yuandiao* in Chinese.[74] It is in this last category that I am most interested here.

More precisely, I am interested in what are known in the European context as porcelain figurines or statuettes. Viewable from 360 degrees, they can stand independently and are classic examples of yuandiao. Historically the making of figurines has gravitated toward the representation of people and animals. During the late imperial period, as indicated above, porcelain sculptures of this sort were increasingly associated with the Buddhist pantheon of deities and other supernatural entities. After 1949, of course, such subject matter became increasingly problematic, tied as it was to the putative realm of superstition. Even so, some of the most persistent motifs were recuperated as folk, as opposed to religious, iconography. This attempt at recouping traditional tropes helps explain something like Zeng Longsheng's *The Heavenly Maiden Scattering Flowers* (*Tiannü sanhua*), for example. Zeng had long been known for his porcelain sculptures of spirits and historical figures, and in honor of the PRC's tenth anniversary in 1959, Zeng was instructed to produce a work on the theme of the heavenly maiden for the Jiangxi room in the new Great Hall of the People in Beijing.

At 1.34 meters tall, *Heavenly Maiden* required technical innovations in porcelain firing, but the aesthetics of the piece are very much in keeping with a classically inspired, Buddhist-inflected work. The heavenly maiden is thin, willowy, and awash in movement, dressed in flowing, green skirts and adorned with rippling red ribbons. She stands on a base of stylized clouds, a sign of her celestial domain. Despite the heavenly maiden's fixity in space, the buffeting clouds that surround her evoke the motion of waves and eddies, much like her vestments. Indeed, it is this overwhelming sense of movement—used to convey the ephemerality of the other-worldly—in a by definition static medium that marks *Heavenly Maiden* as a masterpiece in the traditional mode. One is meant to appraise *Heavenly Maiden*'s value as art by virtue of its successful execution of a particular theme as well as a particular aesthetic, very much in keeping with pre-1949 expectations. In this sense, *Heavenly Maiden* is a testament to an enduring mode of porcelain sculpture—one that remained central to the form until the chaotic first few years of the Cultural Revolution.

This is not to suggest that this aesthetic lineage disappeared during the Cultural Revolution period altogether. Zeng Shandong's *Sword Dance* (*Jian wu*), completed in the early 1970s, is a prime example of the continued interest in movement and flowing lines. Even so, there is little doubt that the dominant aesthetic mode operative from 1966 to 1976 was much more closely aligned with the concerns of what we might call—somewhat anachronistically—socialist realism, the highly influential style imported to the PRC from the Soviet Union in the 1950s.[75] Officially, the Cultural Revolution is the age of revolutionary realism and revolutionary romanticism, but by invoking the notion of a socialist realist project in porcelain sculpture, I want to link some of the pieces most emblematic of the Cultural Revolution—the representation of yangbanxi characters, for example—to the emphasis on realist aesthetics in the 1950s. It is during the course of this decade that historical, literary, and folk characters as well as designated models of revolutionary behavior began to usurp the central position of bodhisattvas and immortals as sculpture subjects. Moreover, when these more politically appropriate figures were fixed in porcelain, they tended to be represented as sturdy and rooted rather than as willowy and in motion.

In this regard, one might point to He Nianqi's (dates unknown) 1958 *Girl with a Veil* (*Pisha shaonü*) as a particularly important breakthrough (see figure 3.4). The bust of a peasant girl wearing a headscarf, the piece was understood as evidence of the successful effort to modernize Jingdezhen. This is in part a function, perhaps, of its origin story: A directive was issued by the relevant committee that Jingdezhen needed to produce something on the theme of "a nude with a veil."[76] He Nianqi's response to this directive is notable in at least two respects. First, there is the adaptation of the theme. Instead of a full nude, we are presented with a bust that is very much clothed. The veil reveals nothing; it covers. It has become a sign of well-kept country innocence rather than alluring transparency. Second, the technical execution of the veil or headscarf is remarkable in its verisimilitude. Whereas something like Zeng Longsheng's *Heavenly Maiden* is clearly concerned with using textiles to indicate movement, this headscarf is static. The investment here is in realist aesthetics, more specifically, an internationally informed realist aesthetics. The piece was conceived as a response to a French work and was later touted both inside and outside of China as proof of Jingdezhen's continued excellence in porcelain. In this sense, *Girl with a Veil* speaks to the fact that porcelain sculpture in the PRC developed as part of an international, as well as historical, conversation.

It is primarily the influence of this international push and pull that helps account for both the kinds of figurines produced during the Cultural Revolution and their complex political valences. While some of the elitist associations of porcelain sculpture as a centuries-old traditional art form could be countered, at least in part, through the emphasis on mechanized mass production and the proletarian worker, the very Marxist discourse that facilitated this reorientation was itself deeply suspicious of bourgeois consumption and, crucially, its problematics of taste. As Karen Kettering makes clear, few exemplars of bourgeois domestic trash (*domashniy khlam*) were targeted with as much vitriol in the Soviet Union of the late 1920s and early 1930s as decorative ceramics.[77] Porcelain statuettes, all too commonly invoking, by proletarian

Figure 3.4 He Nianqi's *Pisha shaonü* (*Girl with a Veil*), 1958. From Yu and Liang, *Jingdezhen chuantong taoci diaosu* (*Traditional Ceramic Sculpture in Jingdezhen*), 15.

standards, "such 'tasteless' subjects as unclad bathing beauties, sweet kittens, butterflies, miniature elephants, or charming pairs of lovers," seem to have been particularly offensive manifestations of bourgeois decoration sensibilities.[78] The turn toward realist aesthetics brought this set of associations front and center in China as well. On the one hand, porcelain sculpture was a highly regarded art form that could be made to serve the revolution. On the other hand, the shape that service took came heavily laden with its own political baggage, some imported from abroad and some very much home grown. The result in the Cultural Revolution decade was something of an oddity: the politically apropos figurine (see figure 3.5).

In the words of Frank J. Cosentino, an American familiar with the ceramic industry who visited Jingdezhen Porcelain Sculpture Factory in late 1974, most of the statuettes geared toward the domestic market were "purchased by the government and placed in museums, schools, civic centers and other Chinese institutions. The figures are generally romanticized—handsome, muscular men; beautiful women; healthy, cherubic children. Subjects are military figures of both sexes, the 'barefoot' nurses [doctors] who carry medicine to the outlying provinces; peasants of all types performing all kinds of useful work, soldiers of the people, scenes from Tachai and Taching, etc."[79]

Figure 3.5 Statuette of the peasant girl Xi'er depicting the model ballet *The White-Haired Girl*, 26 centimeters. Part of an eleven-piece set in the collection of the Jianchuan Museum Cluster, Anren, Sichuan Province.

The focus on institutional purchasers suggests avoidance of porcelain figurines in the home. Perhaps more significantly for our purposes, Cosentino also remarks that Jingdezhen Porcelain Sculpture Factory's export catalog did not include such pieces, which were made of a lower quality clay.[80] Further details about domestically available porcelain figurines are difficult to pin down, if only because, on a national level, they appear to have been produced in a relatively unsystematic manner. This has understandably created difficulties for contemporary porcelain appraisers who, in the almost total absence of maker's marks, are often forced to determine a piece's authenticity simply by its quality, or more precisely, by its lack thereof. The finer the execution of a figure's hands, for example, the greater the likelihood that it is a fake, the idea being that much of what was produced during the Cultural Revolution was the work of individuals with limited training.[81] Whether this was in fact the case—recognized artists were often pressed into service, their specialized skills sometimes trumping questionable class backgrounds—the fact remains that there is much about the porcelain figurines of this era that we do not know, including the full range of pieces made.[82]

What is clear, however, is that porcelain sculpture, as practiced at Jingdezhen Porcelain Sculpture Factory and elsewhere, put the limits of mechanized mass production into high relief. At the end of the day, the factory's output, large as it was (approximately one million total pieces in 1974), was tremendously dependent on work done by hand by individual ceramists. This was in large part a function of process. Again, it is worth quoting Cosentino, an industry insider, at some length:

> The volume of pieces further astounds us when we examine the production techniques. Very little slip casting is done. The most complex slip molds we see are comprised of four pieces; the majority are of two. And the molds are made with no locking notches for precision; so the seams on the greenware pieces sometimes are pronounced.
>
> Most of the models are produced from press molds. A pug clay... is cut and shaped to a size slightly larger than the open mold, then pressed by the top half of the mold to form the sculptural image. Parts of models are done this way, then joined together. Extensive tooling and finishing follows....
>
> Coloring is done both by hand and by aerographing (spraying). One of, or a combination of, four different firing cycles are used, depending on the piece and its colors: low, medium, high and comprehensive. Most pieces go through a comprehensive kiln cycle at average temperatures over an average firing time period.[83]

While the use of simple molds allowed for a certain standardization of a figurine's basic form, detailing and refinements were done by hand, such that each piece, even when born of the same mold, was slightly different from the last. Not only is this very much in keeping with the mass production methods employed across media by pre-modern Chinese manufacturers, it also helps explain the practice of assigning politically sensitive tasks to experts, even if that meant rehabilitating them or overlooking problematic class designations.[84] In the final analysis, often times, too much was up to technical artistic execution to take a chance on an amateur.

This is not to say that Jingdezhen Porcelain Sculpture Factory relied on a studio model by any means; rather, it speaks to the limitations of defining proletarian production in terms of mechanized assembly lines. Indeed, one could convincingly argue, I think, that the biggest changes brought to bear on porcelain sculpture during the Mao period were in the realm of aesthetics, not facture. Taken together, the desire to make Jingdezhen synonymous with a once proto-proletarian—now fully proletarian—industry and the concomitant shift toward (socialist) realism combine to make the Maoist figurine the perfect embodiment of productivist display. At the end of the day, productivism is only tangentially concerned with actual means of production. Productivism, on the contrary, is concerned with an *aesthetics* of production, with making production per se visible and consumable in a very particular way.

The Problem with Display

The issue of visibility brings us back into the realm of Cultural Revolution display (*chenlie*), by which I mean simply the placement and ordering of objects for the purpose of being seen. This definition is intentionally capacious, encompassing aspects of interior decoration, the decorative arts, packaging, design, retail sales, and advertising as well as the institutional exhibitionary practices of the Mao period discussed by Denise Y. Ho.[85] Such a wide-ranging definition allows us to think about things and their relation to vision in a more complex and far-reaching manner. Whereas Ho, for example, is concerned with the politics *on* display in a number of museum settings, I want instead to focus on the politics *of* display writ large. From this perspective, it hardly seems coincidental that Wing On Department Store's Guo Linshuang and his possessions featured so prominently in the tremendously popular Exhibition of Red Guard Achievements (Hongweibing gongxun zhanlanhui) held in Shanghai in October and November 1966. Nor is it surprising that curators of this exhibition—put on by none other than the Shanghai Commerce Bureau—were chastised by a visitor not to "put out everyday items like they are commercial products," that is, as though they were stocking shelves and display windows.[86] These overt instances of overlap and slippage between accepted forms of commercial display and the kinds of display engendered by curated object lessons are a testament to the importance of thinking about the visibility and legibility of things—and the transformative potential of an object being seen in a particular way—within a wider productivist frame.[87]

As we proceed in this direction, it is important to emphasize the situatedness and relationality of display as I am defining it here, for capacious as the term is intended to be, it refers not to a class of objects but rather to structures of visual engagement. So-called decorative objects, including porcelain figurines, are objects that principally operate in a presentational mode. As such, they are helpful in reminding us "that the specifically decorative aspect of the object lies...in surface."[88] More precisely, they remind us of the importance of an object's "topography of sensuous surface," its "surfacescape."[89] Objects that are not strictly decorative have surfacescapes, too, which under the right circumstances can emerge as their most salient characteristic. As Jonathan Hay writes: "Simultaneously object-body and surfacescape, the decorative object invites two modes of experience that interpenetrate and mediate each other. Many artefacts are purely decorative in the sense that their surfacescapes impose themselves as more important in any situation. But in the case of many other artefacts, the primacy of the surfacescape is situational. A chair's utilitarian formal economy may prevail at one moment, whereas at another moment one may pay more attention to its surfacescape of hardwood, selected and polished to reveal the material patterning of the grain."[90] Aspects of industrial design and packaging turn on surfacescape just as surely as a decorative statuette precisely because of the flexibility of objects on display. In the Cultural Revolution it was also quite common for all manner of object surfaces to be colonized by official slogans and iconography. During a brief period in 1968, for example, mango imagery conquered surfacescapes right and left.[91] In highlighting the surfaces they colonized, such practices could push even the most utilitarian objects in the most mundane of circumstances into the realm of display.

Instances of self-conscious and deliberate display, including the construction of museum exhibits and the positioning of goods on the shop floor, relied heavily on the power of non-decorative objects to entice the eye when properly placed. In the latter case, retail displays, understood as a form of advertising, were the subject of much consternation both at home and abroad, as mentioned above. But whereas print advertising waned in China in the 1960s, retail displays continued to exert their influence throughout the Cultural Revolution, central as they were to the architecture of the paradigmatic department store. From Le Bon Marché in Paris to Macy's in New York and Wing On in Shanghai, what set the *grand magasin* or department store apart, as a retail innovation, from its forebears was not only the amount and variety of its merchandise but also the fact that this merchandise could be seen.[92] Shopping emerged as an activity separate from buying, and the display of goods, both indoors in glass encasements and in street-facing windows as inducements for passersby to enter, came to define the department store as such. This was the case in republican Shanghai as it was in the United States; indeed, it appears Wing On drew inspiration for many of its window displays directly from US publications.[93] Much like their Soviet counterparts of the 1920s, the major retail outlets of the Chinese party-state were housed in the very same buildings that had been used to beguile prerevolutionary shoppers.[94] As a result, Shanghai's Nanjing Road and Beijing's Wangfujing area continued to be the country's most important shopping districts throughout the Mao period. All of this, to say nothing of the impact of then head of the Soviet food commissariat Anastas Mikoian's 1936 visit to and admiration for Macy's,[95] situates PRC retail firmly within the global history of the department store and its paradigmatic shopwindow.[96]

We know, moreover, that the architectural features we have come to associate with department stores, including high ceilings, open, easily navigable spaces, and large plate-glass windows, continued to be used to best display advantage even after print advertising was considered too problematic for the times. This is quite clear not only from pictorial photo spreads of productivist plenty and street views (see figure 3.6) but also from the guidance issued to

Figure 3.6 Street view of store, village unidentified. From *China Pictorial*, no. 7 (1972): 17–18.

those charged with arranging commodities in stores. Display windows and cases were understood as necessary and useful in the service of politics, production, consumption (*xiaofei*), and urban beautification (*meihua shirong*). Well executed displays "allow[ed] commodities—especially new products—to reach consumers in a timely manner and inspire new consumer habits. They increase the speed of commodity circulation and spur on the continued development of production. At the same time, stores listen to consumer ideas and transmit them to production units so that they can better improve the quality and variety of their products and meet consumer demand."[97] Display practices appear to have continued unabated throughout the Cultural Revolution. Figures 3.7 and 3.8, which appeared in *China Pictorial* in July and December 1967, suggest that the mechanisms of retail display were adapted to promote Mao Zedong's image, words, and Thought. The original caption for figure 3.8, part of a photospread devoted to Shanghai's the East Is Red—formerly, Wing On—Department Store, all but spells this out: "The store's revolutionary workers have thoroughly criticized the small handful within the party taking the capitalist road for their crime of not permitting the dissemination [*xuanchuan*] of Mao Zedong Thought on the shop floor and have now transformed the store into a space devoted to the promotion

Figure 3.7 Beijing Department Store. From *China Pictorial*, no. 7 (1967): 22–23.

Figure 3.8 The East Is Red (Wing On) Department Store. From *China Pictorial*, no. 12 (1967): 34.

[*xuanchuan*] of Mao Zedong Thought."⁹⁸ It would be easy to mistake this caption and its image as evidence of the usurpation of commodity display by political propaganda, as though the two were entirely separate things. If, on the other hand, we posit that they are not at all separate—that Mao has always been commodity-like, if not a commodity proper, as I suggested in the introduction—then this scene is not one of political fervor in the absence of commodity display and desire, but rather one of their wholesale merger and instrumentalization. This is Mao on display *as* an object of desire.

This reading again raises questions about situational transformation, and here it is perhaps helpful to remember that, in the final analysis, display is as much about (real and imagined) looking as it is about showing.⁹⁹ The act of display itself may have been justified in the name of socialist production, but issues of consumption and the visual stimulation of consumer desire were never wholly left behind. Indeed, one is not possible without the other, for this, I believe, is ultimately the rub: Display a commodity, even if only as an index of the cornucopia-utopia to come, and see that commodity transform into something unwieldy and promiscuous in newly discomfiting ways. Moreover, like the commodity whence it comes, this new something begins to reorganize its surroundings—both spatially and temporally.

Representation

On the face of it, the capitalist commodity in the window seems to act as an ode to consumption as such, suggesting an obliteration of any particular, individual commodity's use value. As an exercise in eliciting desire, the attending properties of the commodity on display become merely incidental to the larger glorification of the act of consumption and, by extension, of exchangeability and exchange value. Put another way: The desire to consume and, presumably, to possess the commodity in the window has more to do with the exchange value of that commodity and, therefore, the very possibility of exchange on which notions of consumption and possession are predicated than the uses to which that commodity might be put. As a result, we might well suggest that the transformation effected through display is, in this case, something akin to a reification of exchange value. However, this explanation itself leaves something to be desired, for in emphasizing the commodity's exchange value, it threatens to overlook the mechanisms through which capitalist consumer desire and attention are directed. These remain unquestionably tied to the material specificity of the commodity in question. There is most assuredly an aesthetic component to display, which remains operative, whatever its intended purpose. There is something altogether too constricting about this account of display under capitalism, then, let alone in the context of socialism, actually existing or otherwise.

Instead, we would do better to take a page from Walter Benjamin, for whom "the key to the new urban phantasmagoria was not so much the commodity-in-the-market as the commodity-on-display, where exchange value no less than use value lost practical meaning, and purely representational value came to the fore." The strictures of Marxist political economy give way to a philosophy of representation whereby "everything desirable, from sex to social status, could be transformed into commodities as fetishes-on-display that held the crowd enthralled even when personal possession was far beyond their reach. Indeed, an unattainably high price tag only enhanced a commodity's symbolic value. Moreover, when newness became a fetish, history itself became a manifestation of the commodity form."[100] The question for us becomes the extent to which Benjamin's insights into the commodity-on-display are helpful in articulating the peculiar goings-on of the socialist shopwindow in addition to those of the Paris arcades.

This is not a minor concern. After all, there is a strong argument to be made in which the act of socialist commodity display takes on a radically different set of (explicit) political valences: Commodity production, rather than commodity consumption, is purportedly the motivation for displays as indirect celebrations of labor. As we have seen in the previous pages, however, the singular emphasis on production, essentially defined in terms of the mechanized assembly line, is maintained with great difficulty, if at all. The ultimate motivation for production remains the improvement of living standards *as measured by consumption.* To the extent that this is the case, the socialist window display constitutes a productivist/developmentalist alibi for consumer desire. As such, two of Benjamin's observations regarding the capitalist commodity-on-display remain particularly relevant, here: First, to the extent that the transformative process of display involves reification, it is, above all, the reification of representational value. And second, this process is inextricably linked to the conceptualization and representation of history, a terrain ostensibly controlled during the Mao period by the CCP.

The initial observation that the commodity-on-display raises questions of representation and representability as much if not more than economics seems especially relevant to the (Chinese) socialist context, that is, where the disconnect between representations of material plenty and the lived experience of scarcity was felt very acutely. The department store display did not necessarily jibe with what was actually available on the shelves—whether one could afford any given commodity or not—such that the overwhelmingly representational nature of commodity display was a well-recognized fact. Consider the minority shoppers on the frontier mentioned in the previous chapter: over and over again they appear on the pages of China's official pictorials browsing elaborate arrays of commodities—commodities that likely never made it outside large urban areas in the absence of photographers. Just as there was a recognized gap between the page and what it purported to represent, so was there a recognized gap between the commodity-on-display and the commodity itself. Representational gaps related to commodities had to be negotiated as a matter of daily life. The Ch'en Jo-hsi (Chen Ruoxi) short story "The Big Fish" ("Da qingyu") evocatively captures this process with its portrayal of a Potemkin village–like market staged for the benefit of foreigners and overflowing with produce. When the story's protagonist attempts to take advantage of the rare opportunity to purchase a fish for dinner, it is confiscated from him as he leaves.[101] The tactics of socialist shopping were myriad, and the successful consumption of commodities was directly tied to knowledge of both the workings of the system and the value of technologies and modes of representation.[102]

That the commodity-on-display should be tied to the production of representational value appears, in the abstract at least, to have little troubled the socialist project in and of itself. Indeed, it was consistently put to official use. Where this quality began to cause problems was in relation to questions of class distinction and time. The mechanisms of class distinction in relation to commodity consumption—representational or otherwise—are well known,[103] and they help account for the persistence of material class differences, even during a period such as the Cultural Revolution.[104] From the CCP perspective, class distinctions indicated the necessity for continued class struggle and revolution. One might well focus one's critical energy on a particular class, classist practice, or material manifestation of class—including bourgeois knickknacks, for example—but to rail against the existence of classes under socialism was not on the official Cultural Revolution agenda. Things became significantly dicier in the related matter of the temporal effects of the commodity-on-display, which clearly butted up against the orthodox Marxist understanding of history and the CCP's role in it. Consider the issue of (women's) fashion, which, as Antonia Finnane and Tina Mai Chen have both indicated, remained a contested field after the Communist takeover in 1949 well up to Mao's death in 1976.[105] Fashion's obsession with the new—which for Benjamin is nonetheless always the same—and the consequent concern with being au courant create a peculiar temporality that, like the commodity that produces it, takes on the mystical properties of the fetish. Peter Osborne's reading of Benjamin articulates this point and is worth quoting at length:

> As objects of fetishization, commodities destined for everyday consumption display two closely related features: one is their apparent self-sufficiency or independence from their processes of production; the other is the appearance of novelty, required to make them attractive in the face of competing products.... In the first case, it is the constitutive power of labour, and hence the social relations of mutual dependence, which is the object of fetishistic disavowal. In the second case, it is both the standardization of the commodity and the corrosive effects of time (aging, death) which are acknowledged only through their negation. In its fetishization of novelty, Benjamin argued, fashion "tirelessly constitutes 'antiquity' anew out of the most recent past." It thus constantly leaves its objects behind as "outmoded," reinforcing their independence, and thus their quality as fetishes, *before they have been exhausted by experience*. In their fetishized but outmoded independence, these objects thus come to subsist, their novelty

sealed up inside them, like time capsules. Signifiers of socialized desire (the desire for the new), they are resistant to the self-negating side of novelty (its invariance), by virtue of their very redundancy. In an extraordinary dialectical reversal, the outmoded becomes the privileged site for the experience of novelty, and hence futurity itself.[106]

But futurity and the future were not meant to be up for grabs; indeed, socialist orthodoxy clearly established that only one future was ultimately possible—communism. Moreover, the road to communist utopia was also broadly mapped out. History would develop along a fixed path, and it was China's good luck to find itself advanced to the transitional stage of socialism—with a little help from the political vanguard, of course. This is precisely the temporal orientation at the heart of the newborn socialist thing, which was essentially understood as a signpost along the singular path forward. Newborn socialist things constituted the officially recognized future in the present, and although revisionism was understood, particularly during the Cultural Revolution, as a real threat to that future—and thus, to historical progress—the eventual accomplishment of the ultimate developmental goal was never itself in doubt, nor was it up for debate. The temporality of the commodity-on-display also posits a notion of progress—each new novelty must be better than the last—but from the perspective of a Marxist understanding of historical stages and the newborn socialist thing, it is progress that leads nowhere. The temporality of fashion—and, I would add, interior decoration—is so troublesome precisely because it lays overt claim to a notion of development while, in fact, maintaining the status quo. Put another way, it contends that spinning one's wheels in the bourgeois muck constitutes forward revolutionary momentum.

This clash of temporalities is not without precedent. As Susan Buck-Morss argues with regard to the Soviet avant-garde of the 1920s, the fight to conceptualize history and its future trajectory had far-reaching consequences, including what amounted to the eventual cooptation of the artistic avant-garde by the political vanguard and the dominance of socialist realism under Stalin.[107] The argument I am making here is not quite so straightforward, if only because the tension between the future augured by newborn socialist things and its eternal deferment appears to have produced a sense of time that was very much analogous to the notional temporality it ostensibly opposed. While the commodity-on-display may not have been acting as an engine of progress, the time of revolution was, arguably, similarly stalled. In this sense, newborn things and commodities, meant to be dialectically opposed, proved uncomfortably similar. It would be up to political economy, as a discipline, to distinguish between them.

4 Illuminating the Commodity Fetish

> As the retired dock worker Ma Hongliang sings in the revolutionary Beijing opera *On the Docks* [*Haigang*]: "In this new society, we dock workers have become the masters and are filled with pride. From birth to old age, in sickness and in death, we have something to rely on. The benevolence [*en*] of the Communist Party and Chairman Mao is vaster than the sky!" These few sentences proclaim the true feelings of the new society's working class, which has been emancipated. They reflect the great superiority of socialist relations of production.
> —*Zhengzhi jingjixue jichu zhishi*

This passage, appearing in the chapter on the socialist distribution of consumer goods (*geren xiaofeipin*) in the Cultural Revolution's most consequential textbook on political economic theory, *Fundamentals of Political Economy* (*Zhengzhi jingjixue jichu zhishi*), is remarkable for its unlikely invocation of a relatively minor opera character. Ma Hongliang is not a particularly well-known figure; he is not the protagonist of *On the Docks*. Moreover, while *On the Docks* itself is set in Mao-period China—the only opera in the original model repertoire with that distinction—one would be hard pressed to argue that the distribution and consumption of goods is the piece's primary focus. It could not be confused with *Xiangyang Store* or other works directly addressing retail, for example. Rather, *On the Docks* concerns itself with labor relations and international solidarity among the revolutionary working peoples of the world. Counterintuitive as it may seem, this emphasis is in fact the key to understanding Ma Hongliang's unexpected appearance in the otherwise dry *Fundamentals*: His primary function in *On the Docks* is to educate the younger generation—represented by the figure of Han Xiaoqiang—about the horrors of the prerevolutionary past, lest those born under the red flag become complacent and lapse into revisionism. Ma sings of past pain such that Han might recognize just how much has changed for those on the docks: The once-denigrated workers are now the masters; the last have become first. Ma purports to be both the product and the guarantor of radical changes in the labor structure and relations of production, precisely the changes on which Cultural Revolution–era theories of the socialist commodity (*shangpin*)—and its differentiation from the capitalist commodity—hinged.

Commodities were a tricky business in the 1960s and 1970s. As we have seen in previous chapters, under the right set of circumstances the CCP had no problem promoting an understanding of modernity and historical development closely tied to the display and ready availability of consumer commodities. Shortages of desirable items were mere momentary hiccups on the road to inexorable, universal plenty rather than emblems of a prescriptive asceticism or (the unthinkable!) systemic failure. Not unlike newborn socialist things in this respect, commodities became, within this particular formulation, harbingers of a better tomorrow. And yet, engaging with said consumer commodities, whether through actual exchange or in representation—that is, acting in some fashion on the purported material benefits of modern Chinese citizenship—remained deeply problematic. Heralding the future via commodities came at the steep cost of their revisionist potentialities. This not only compromised commodities' effectiveness as engines and emblems of progress; it pitted them directly against newborn socialist things, as a general category, in the formation of a developmental dialectic. While commodities persisted—and they would axiomatically persist until the dawn of communism—they constituted a double-edged sword for the socialist project: necessary, sometimes useful, but always dangerous.

Ultimately, if socialism was to be different from (read: better than) capitalism, commodity consumption, both literal and figurative, would have to be thoroughly reimagined; this new vision, moreover, would need to be enacted and enforced. Thus the crucial role of the revolutionary salesperson and the shopwindow as educators, modernizers, and mediators of consumer desire. In addition to actively policing suspicious modes of consumption, retailers were called on to counteract them by showing prospective customers the error of their ways. In this chapter I am concerned with the texts on which a salesperson in this position might rely for her education as a would-be pedagogue, texts like *Fundamentals*. In brief, I want to go beyond the quest for an appropriately socialist modernity and back to Ma Hongliang and the political economic basics, namely, to the theory of the socialist commodity itself.

A commodity, defined in accordance with Marx, is a product acquired through exchange for use by someone other than its producer, characterized by a combination of use value and exchange value wherein the latter is defined in relation to labor time. How could this definition be recouped as *socialist?* Where did the commodity form come from under socialism? Why did it still exist? How did it differ from the commodity form under capitalism? What was the precise nature of the danger it posed for the socialist project? How did one manage until such time as it disappeared? How could the commodity's tendency to bewitch be counteracted? All of these questions and more needed to be addressed by the field of Chinese socialist political economy, and they ultimately were, more or less coherently. My immediate interest, however, is less in detailing these answers for their own sake—though I will do some of that—than in exploring their discursive function, for Ma Hongliang's role as the manifestation of socialism's newness is only part of the story. He also pointedly articulates that newness; he brings production relations to the fore, thereby revealing the commodity's origins. I ultimately want to read Ma's abrupt entrance into *Fundamentals* as emblematic of what political economy as a discipline was itself meant to do in the more general struggle against revisionism: counteract the danger ascribed to the commodity in the Cultural Revolution. Commodities persisted, but the inner workings of the socialist commodity form could at least be stripped of their mystery, the argument went. That is, the production and circulation of socialist political economic texts could themselves be deployed as weapons. In a world where the commodity fetish was recognized as a particularly formidable enemy, political economic theory ended up casting itself as the anti-fetish as a way to demystify and therefore disarm. My contention is that this new role pushed (Marxist) political economy to its very hermeneutic limits.

Reckoning with the Commodity

Although scholarship devoted to the material culture of Chinese socialism is sorely lacking, comparable work pertaining to the Eastern Bloc and the Soviet Union has flourished over the past few decades. Even so, attention to the intellectual historical environment in which interactions between people and things took place in these contexts remains limited. One of the most significant exceptions to this rule is Christina Kiaer's masterful *Imagine No Possessions*. In this fascinating study of Russian constructivism in the early and mid-1920s, Kiaer examines a group of artists' dogged pursuit of "socialist objects"—objects with which one would interact not in terms of possession and commodification, but rather in terms of fellowship and camaraderie. The ultimate goal was an alternative to the relationship between the laborer and the product of her labor, the expropriator and the expropriated, constitutive of the capitalist commodity form as Marx had described it. For the constructivists, the eventual elimination of the commodity, the very cornerstone of the capitalist system the October Revolution promised to overturn, was a task the trained artist's eye could help accomplish. Artists knew how to see in a way that was radically different from the factory engineer, and it was precisely this difference—an understanding of form and aesthetics rather than a detailed knowledge of production processes—which, they argued, made them invaluable in the effort to create a new kind of material culture, one characterized by comradely things.[1]

For their part, factory engineers seem to have found this line of argument less than convincing, and it is, for Kiaer, the fact that the constructivists strove to bring about a socialist world of things and thingly relations while simultaneously dealing with the demands of profit-minded entrepreneurs and pleasure–seeking consumers that sets them apart from many other explicitly political artistic movements. "Constructivism is unique among the politically engaged avant-gardes of the twentieth century because it imagined 'no possessions' both from the perspective of an achieved socialist revolution that made such imagining more than Utopian dreaming and—at the same time—from within the commodity culture of NEP [Lenin's New Economic Policy (1921–circa 1928)] that forced that imagining to contend with the present reality of commodity-desiring human subjects."[2] Whereas the initial period of so-called war communism (1918–21) had been characterized by an anticommodity austerity, justified ideologically by the promise of communism's immanent arrival, NEP sought to pair commodity consumption with historical advancement of a much more incremental sort. It is the tension between these two sets of demands—the revolution and the consumer commodity—that makes the constructivist endeavor so intriguing and Kiaer's analysis of it likewise so compelling.

In truth, however, directing and negotiating consumer desire proved a thorny problem for CCP policy makers, just as it had for their Soviet forbearers. Indeed, what Kiaer sees as a tension constitutive of Russian constructivism's singular place in art history might better be understood as one attempt among many to theorize and contend with a predicament facing the socialist enterprise in general, namely, how to reinvent and recast consumer practices in politically acceptable—if not emancipatory—terms. The constructivists may primarily have been concerned with the aesthetics of the socialist object and the remaking of the everyday, but the problem of the commodity and commodification extended far beyond the question of how any given object looked and the interactions between person and thing facilitated by that look. It touched on the very foundations of what socialism and communism were understood to be. How would a socialist economy be structured? What role should commodities play in it? Such questions were well above the retail clerk's pay grade. As in the first few years of the PRC, Soviet market commodities flourished in the 1920s, which therefore required the artists Kiaer discusses to imagine socialist objects in explicitly commodified terms. But even during the Stalinist period, when nationalized industry and collectivized agriculture dominated the Soviet economy, the issues raised by the commodity under socialism persisted. If anything, the tension inherent in the concept became even more acute as the overtly capitalist policies of the past were left behind and socialism was ostensibly achieved.

To wit, it was not just the initial years of Communist rule—both in the USSR and later in China—that were understood as a transitional period. Rather, socialism writ large was conceptualized as an in-between phase heralding the communist utopia, always somewhere in the offing. This suspended state of almost but not quite creates a temporality peculiar to socialism, the crucial point here being that the socialist project, whether aesthetic or economic, is transitional by definition; it pertains to the interim.[3] And like other liminalities, the particulars of this socialist stage of historical development were not—could not be—mapped out in any detail. Even for the CCP after 1949, which could turn to the example set by the Soviet Union, establishing the delimitations of socialist governance and the structure of the socialist economy required a considerable amount of on-the-job learning. There was no definitive guide for the task at hand. Indeed, the socialist commodity was such a difficult circle to square in part because one of the few things Marx ("Critique of the Gotha Program"),[4] Engels (*Anti-Dühring*),[5] and, later, Karl Kautsky (*The Class Struggle*)[6] had been clear about when it came to the communist economy of the future was precisely that it would be commodity free.[7] The underlying logic went something like this: If the (Marxist) commodity form was characterized by a combination of use value and exchange value—the latter necessitating a system of private ownership—once the means of production were controlled by the proletariat and publicly owned, commodities would be no more. There would be labor products, to be sure, but no commodities and certainly no money. In this one respect, at least, the goalposts were clear. That both commodities and money survived for the time being, even *after* the means of production had been taken over by the state, required explanation and theoretical justification.

This was by no means a straightforward or perfunctory task, and it fell to the field of political economy, or what Cyril Lin, after Francis Seton, has called the "diagnostic" branch of (Chinese) socialist economic study. Diagnostic economics

> comprise highly abstract and somewhat philosophical investigations into the existence, under specific conditions of Chinese socialism, of various economic categories (commodity, money, price) and "laws" posited and

used by Marx to explain the inner structure and workings of pre-socialist economic formations in general and of capitalist commodity production in particular.... Such diagnoses in socialist countries are indispensable in gauging the direction and distance travelled away from capitalism and towards full communism; the nature of the economy charted by these periodic sightings then defines the type of policies, mechanisms and production relations ideologically consistent with the socialist odyssey.[8]

It is not coincidental that the act of "diagnosis" is characterized by a post facto temporality; one typically diagnoses an illness after the patient becomes symptomatic. For all its outward emphasis on a scientific future, political economic theory seems to have catered to shifting policy just as much as, if not more than, policy adapted to theory—within certain limits. This need not necessarily be understood as undercutting the centrality of political economy, given the advocation (especially by Mao) of a dialectical relationship between theory and practice.[9] On the contrary, it should alert us to the field's important discursive function as well as the historical specificity of its knowledge production.

To that end, it is worth reiterating that prior to the October Revolution, no detailed political economic imagining or analysis of Bolshevik socialism existed. In fact, in 1920 Nikolai Bukharin (1888–1938) suggested that Marxist political economy, as a mode of inquiry developed to deal with capitalism, would wither away alongside the commodity.[10] Although Lenin apparently disagreed and Bukharin himself later changed his mind, this initial verdict is indicative of just how new and uncertain this intellectual endeavor really was.[11] And it stayed that way for quite some time. Consider, by way of illustration, that while the call for the first textbook on the political economy of socialism in the Soviet Union was made in 1936, such a volume was still under discussion in 1951 and was not actually published until the fall of 1954. It was only then that the aptly titled *Political Economy: A Textbook* (*Politicheskaya ekonomiya: Uchebnik*), translated from Russian into Chinese, among many other languages, codified existing economic practices.[12] In other words, socialist economies were established as such long before their authoritative theorization was available, during which time commodities continued to circulate. It is no wonder that the two became inextricably linked: Part of the task facing (Chinese) political economists in the 1950s and beyond was to explain the dependence on commodities in such a way that socialism nonetheless constituted a historical advance over the capitalist system it had usurped.

While the socialist commodity looked suspiciously like its capitalist cousin—a situation Russian constructivists had attempted to change through aesthetics—it was up to socialist political economy as a discipline to explain how they differed theoretically, that is, how they could be recuperated as temporary and necessary improvements over the capitalist commodities analyzed by Marx. This caused much rhetorical handwringing among CCP theorists, including Mao. Questions concerning the extent to which socialist commodities could threaten historical development were especially critical to the understanding of socialism espoused—loudly and repeatedly—during the 1970s. Despite the fact that actual commodities remained, in many cases, remarkably difficult to get one's hands on, discourse pertaining to the problem of the commodity—ostensibly unmasking its form and counteracting its allure—was well-nigh ubiquitous, especially in the winter and spring of 1975. Deployed through official popularization efforts, political economy in the Cultural Revolution endeavored to be more than a central pillar of the theory of socialist construction; it also lay claim to the (re)structuring of daily life and revolutionary subjectivities as part of its demystifying and pedagogical mission.

Political Economy in the Cultural Revolution

The precise, theoretical formulation of the socialist commodity espoused during the Cultural Revolution, especially as it emerged after the initial years of chaos in the 1970s, traced its roots not to the Soviet Union of the 1920s so much as to that of the 1950s.[13] Stalin's 1952 *Economic Problems of Socialism in the USSR* (*Ekonomicheskie problemy sotsializma v SSSR*), immediately translated and released by People's Press (Renmin chubanshe) as *Sulian shehuizhuyi jingji wenti*, was a particularly foundational text for political economy in the PRC. This short volume included, among three other works, "Remarks on the Economic Questions Connected with the November 1951 Discussion" (hereafter "Remarks"), which articulated Stalin's views concerning the creation of a textbook on the structure of the Soviet economy. These prescriptive views gave rise to the aforementioned *Political Economy: A Textbook* in 1954, also translated into Chinese with all due haste. (It was published as *Textbook on Political Economy* [*Zhengzhi jingjixue jiaokeshu*] in June 1955.)[14] It was in "Remarks" that Stalin offered his final take on the socialist commodity: The commodity form, as defined by Marx, was necessary under socialism because of the enduring combination of two different forms of public ownership, namely, that of the people (the state) and that of the collective or commune. Economic interactions between the two systems, especially in the realm of individual consumption, required commodity relations but did so in a way that did not fundamentally disprove Marx and Engels, since private ownership of the means of production was dead but the people (the state) did not yet own everything outright. This quickly became the orthodox justification for the continued reliance on commodity production in the PRC until the end of the Cultural Revolution.

This is not to say that the Stalinist approach to socialist political economy writ large was adopted wholesale—far from it. At the height of the Sino-Soviet split in the late 1960s and early 1970s, in particular, there was little incentive for Chinese theorists to align themselves with the putatively revisionist USSR, past or present. With the threat of revisionism abroad (the Soviet Union and its satellites) and at home (capitalist-roaders) keenly felt, it should come as no surprise, for example, that mainstream Cultural Revolution political economy considered the socialist commodity a far greater threat to revolutionary progress than Stalin ever had. The view outlined in "Remarks" was such that the commodity form, divorced as it now was from the buying and selling of labor and capitalist exploitation, could not function as a vehicle for capitalist restoration. The newly emergent Chinese position, by contrast, took commodities to be far less benign, even under socialist conditions; left unchecked, they would dismantle the socialist enterprise from within.

This more alarmist take, which regarded the socialist commodity as something of an insidious—albeit necessary—evil, was closely associated with the so-called Shanghai school of political economics, composed of both academics (mostly at Fudan University) as well as political movers and shakers.[15] The portion of the Shanghai Municipal Party Committee writing group (Shanghai shi wei xiezuo zu) dedicated to economics was particularly active in promoting the Shanghai school's views in the 1970s, often publishing articles in major journals and newspapers using collective pseudonyms, as was common practice. The city of Shanghai was a leftist stronghold throughout the Cultural Revolution. Both Mao and his wife, Jiang Qing, found allies there as they began their assault on the Beijing establishment in the mid-1960s. The Shanghai daily newspaper *Wenhui bao* and the propagandist Yao Wenyuan proved crucial to this endeavor. As factional lines emerged in the chaos, Yao was joined by Zhang Chunqiao and Wang Hongwen, also hailing from Shanghai, in forming a clique with Jiang Qing, which later became known derisively as the Gang of Four. Yao and Zhang were both personally involved in many of the municipal writing group's economics-related activities.

Of these activities, the development of new pedagogical materials explicating the Shanghai school's take on political economy and gearing it toward the general public was paramount. The desire to create a Chinese counterpart to the Soviet textbook of the 1950s had been expressed very early on, and a PRC manual was indeed released in 1961.[16] Needless to say, by the time of the Shanghai school, this initial theorization of Chinese socialism was beyond the ideological bounds; a new, authoritative (non-revisionist) reckoning of socialist political economy was urgently required. This task was undertaken by the Shanghai writing group in the form of two interrelated projects: a volume titled *Political Economy of Socialism* (*Shehuizhuyi zhengzhi jingjixue*), which was never finalized, and the aforementioned *Fundamentals*.[17] Five drafts of the latter were released between 1971 and September 1976, of which the 1973 and 1975 editions were the most influential both at home and abroad.[18] Although similar textbooks were also produced by other groups, nothing proved quite so significant and so closely tied to Cultural Revolution radicals as *Fundamentals*.[19] Indeed, its status was such that, after the Gang of Four's arrest on October 6, 1976—the official close of the Cultural Revolution—*Fundamentals* was held up as an example of the group's efforts to sabotage the overall economy.[20] I turn to it here as *the* paradigmatic statement of Chinese political economic theory in the 1970s.

Fundamentals of Political Economy

Written very much in the shadow of its Soviet counterpart, *Fundamentals* was devised for one main purpose: establishing a new Chinese orthodoxy.[21] This orthodoxy notably envisioned a much more historically dynamic socialism, one that relied on ongoing class struggle and always risked devolving into revisionism and, ultimately, capitalist restoration. (While necessary, the commodity was understood to contribute to this risk of developmental retrogradation.) The sense of continuous historical flux imputed to the socialist stage—in contradistinction to the institutionalized fixity of Stalinism—posed a particular analytical and structural challenge for the textbook's authors: how to construct a work that provides a definitive description and theorization of something that is emphatically *not* static. In the end, the authors' chosen strategy seems to have been taken from Mao himself.

As a result, on the one hand, the crafting of *Fundamentals* was clearly patterned on the Soviet textbook's authoritative format, but, on the other, it also drew a great deal on Mao's critical musings about the canonical Russian effort.[22] And Mao's critique was decidedly pointed. He was concerned not just with the particulars of its content, but, perhaps more importantly, with its underlying methodology. (Indeed, he felt the need to state that the work should still be considered Marxist, despite its flaws.[23]) Mao deemed the text "very poorly written, neither persuasive nor interesting to read."[24] The Soviet textbook was not, it seems, a page-turner. "The book does not deal with problems masterfully, with overall control of its subject. Issues do not stand forth clearly. The composition is not persuasive but is dull and illogical, lacking even formal logic."[25] More significantly, perhaps, Mao also took issue with the fact that the textbook did not "proceed from concrete analysis of the contradictions between the productive forces and the production relations nor the contradiction between the economic base and the superstructure." In this respect, the Soviets stood accused of having deviated from Marxist practice; that is, they had written a work that failed in its attempts to be "systematically scientific."[26] When it came time for the Chinese to write their own textbook of socialist political economy, it would be best to begin from "the issues and arguments at the core" as opposed to a priori definitions.[27] More precisely, Mao believed that mimicking the exact structure of Marx's *Capital*, as the Soviets had done, was a mistake.

> In researching the capitalist economy Marx, too, studied mainly ownership of the means of production under capitalism, examining how distribution of the means of production determined the distribution of commodities. In capitalist society the social nature of production and the private nature of ownership is a fundamental contradiction. Marx began with the commodity and went on to reveal the relations among people behind commodities.... Commodities in socialist society still have duality; nonetheless, thanks to the establishment of public ownership of the means of production and the fact that labor power is no longer a commodity, duality of commodities under socialism is not the same as their duality under capitalism. The relations among people are no longer hidden behind commodity relations. Thus, if socialist economy is studied beginning with the duality of commodities, copying Marx's method, it may well have the opposite effect of confusing the issues, making things harder for people to understand.
>
> In writing a political economy of our own we could also begin with the ownership system. First, we describe the conversion of ownership of the means of production from private to public: how we converted private ownership of bureaucratic capital and the capitalist ownership system into socialist ownership by the whole people; private ownership of the land by the landlords was turned first into private ownership by individual peasants and then into collective ownership under socialism; only then could we describe the contradiction between the two forms of public ownership under socialism and how collective ownership under socialism could make the transition to people's ownership under communism.[28]

The tensions defining the socialist economy—between classes, the city and the country, the nation and the work unit, heavy industry and light industry, production and consumption, and so on—would take center stage, consistent with the Maoist approach to contradiction.

Mao's comments mapped out China's response to the Soviet Union's canonization of political economic orthodoxy, and in the 1970s *Fundamentals* was duly laid out according to Mao's instructions. The socialist commodity therefore makes its appearance in *Fundamentals* rather late (chapter 19, the seventh chapter of the section on socialism), after the production relations of the system have already been established, within the context of explaining socialist exchange in its varied forms. This introduction is quickly followed by a discussion on the nature of money in the PRC and its importance in facilitating such exchange. Chapter 21 picks up on these themes with a consideration of the socialist distribution principle—from each according to his abilities, to each according to his work (*ge jin suo neng, an lao fen pei*)—and a critique of bourgeois right (*zichanjieji faquan*)—the appearance of equality vis-à-vis exchange and money, when the social relations hidden behind them are anything but.[29] The textbook explains the persistence, necessity, and danger of socialist commodities as part and parcel of the process of continuous revolution, fueled by unending and irresolvable contradictions.

What fundamentally set the socialist economy apart from its capitalist counterpart, then, was not the overcoming of contradiction—that would be anathema to the dialectical approach, after all—but, rather, the forthrightness with which contradiction presented itself and was recognized. The structure and approach to political economy presented in *Fundamentals* bears this out, but it can be seen elsewhere as well—in the effort to disentangle the attributes of one system from another and form (*xingshi*) from essence (*benzhi*), for example. In the latter case, the task of the political economist was primarily one of demystification, and so one notes the emergence of a common theme whereby that which seems to mirror the capitalist system is consistently dismissed as deceptive appearance. Similarity is largely superficial, for underneath it all is a radically different system of public ownership—divided into two types, as Stalin decreed—which consequently alters the theoretical underpinnings of apparently stable categories and concepts, including the notions of money and wages. These changes are deemed significant enough to foster historical progress toward communism but not so significant as to foreclose the possibility of capitalism's return.

For example, now that private ownership has been abolished, one cannot sell one's labor to someone else as a commodity, and as a result, wages cease to be the manifestation of the exchange value of that labor. They instead become a means of distribution, according to one's work, of assets which the worker as a member of the proletariat always already owns together with her fellow citizens. Exchange requires two distinct (public or private) owners in order to take place, the argument goes. Property rights must be transferred from one entity to another. When this occurs, as when agricultural communes procure goods produced in nationalized factories, the result is commodification in the Stalinist sense. But when we speak of the circulation of goods *within* an entity—as when nationalized factory workers receive wages from a state which they (nominally) constitute or when commune members receive a portion of their communal farm's surplus harvest—this does not constitute commodity exchange of the sort seen under capitalism. Wages are thereby separated from the notion of labor-as-commodity. Pricing and, by extension, money are rendered independent of exchange value in these situations, though they still operate as important concepts.[30] In other words, all of these entities are declared to be both radically different from and functionally the same as their capitalist kin. The sameness afforded these notions is largely attributed to the nature of exchange and its necessity, whereas their radical difference is predicated on the socialist commodity's roots in the newly formed relations of production, brought about under the dictatorship of the proletariat. To the extent that commodities are defined by relations between persons and not relations between things, the revolutionary upending of the class structure is understood to have reconstituted the heart of the commodity form. Same form, new essence.

It is in this context that Ma Hongliang's unexpected appearance in *Fundamentals*, as quoted in the epigraph that began this chapter, becomes particularly meaningful: Ma testifies to and explains this new essence in powerful ways; he illuminates all that has changed in the relations of production such that we might see through the purportedly superficial similarities of form between the capitalist past and the socialist present. This is precisely the task political economy was meant to undertake writ large vis-à-vis the commodity. While the inner workings of the socialist commodity form could not, by definition, be stripped of their duality, they could most assuredly be stripped of their mystery. As Mao claims above, the "relations among people are no longer hidden behind commodity relations." The (capitalist) jig was up: The relations among people had changed, relations, moreover, now plainly understood—at least by those who "read Marxist-Leninist books" like *Fundamentals*.[31] In short, socialist political economic texts themselves became weapons in the war on the commodity fetish.

Riddle Me This

While the commodity form and its dual nature—a combination of use value and exchange value—may have been deemed adaptable to the socialist enterprise, commodity fetishism was relegated to the list of problems specifically attending capitalism. Indeed, one could go so far as to argue that the socialist project as I have been describing it in this book was predicated on somehow solving the fetishistic riddle, namely, on cultivating politically and developmentally appropriate commodity production that made no attempt to hide itself. Not only did socialist commodities spring from a different system of ownership, they also never purported to be anything other than what they were—products of labor. What Marx famously called "the mysterious character of the commodity-form," whereby "the commodity reflects the social characteristics of men's own labour as objective characteristics of the products of labour themselves," seemingly taking on a life of their own, is now anything but "mysterious."[32] It is spelled out systematically and repeatedly with the help of works like *Fundamentals*. As a result, the sleight of hand on which commodity fetishism is predicated—the misrecognition attending "material [*dinglich*] relations between persons and social relations between things"—could be averted.[33] This was arguably the great gamble of socialist commodity production as a whole—that is, that the socialist commodity could somehow skirt the dangers of commodity fetishism. Weaponizing political economy was to help guarantee that this wager would pay out, that socialist dinette sets (unlike Marx's famous table in *Capital*) would not be permitted to dance "of [their] own free will."[34]

But whereas the structure of the socialist commodity form was relatively easy to explain—thanks in large part to Stalin—its beguiling nature proved to be a considerably thornier, and apparently independent, issue. The "magic and necromancy" associated with commodities were uncommonly resilient; consumer delusion (or more charitably, desire) was not so easily wiped away.[35] In the PRC of the 1970s in particular, while the commodity system as a whole was understood as a necessary and manageable threat to the socialist project, its specific danger inhered, at least in part, from the seductive power of the commodity and monetary exchange, neatly ascribed to "the pernicious influence of commodity fetishism" (*shangpin baiwujiao de liudu*).[36] Like the ever-looming shadow of revisionism and bourgeois right, the pull of the commodity fetish was not set to disappear anytime soon: "Commodity and monetary relations are a necessary kind of social relation, produced during a particular period of human social development. They have not always existed, nor will they always exist. As the proletarian revolution progresses [*shenru*] and the commodity economy disappears, commodity and monetary relations will disappear, and commodity fetishism will also disappear."[37] Until such time as this took place—that is, until the advent of communism—the populace needed a vaccine of sorts against commodity fetishism, a shield with which to fend off the commodity's tendency to trick and enthrall.

How precisely could one go about utilizing political economic theory for this purpose? By attributing knowledge of the commodity form's inner workings and apparent retrograde tendencies with the power to dispel the commodity's beguiling, revisionist proclivities. The best way to move history forward toward a commodity-less future was to popularize and scrutinize the ways in which existing commodities were manifestations of the social relations of today. The more prominent explanations of the commodity form became discursively, the less dangerous actually circulating commodities would be. Such faith in the power of political economic theory helps explain its mass mobilization in 1972[38] and again in 1975, when everyone was called on to "study a little bit of political economy" and instructional materials were developed for that purpose.[39] The Criticize Lin Biao, Criticize Confucius campaign in the intervening years of 1973–74 also regularly deployed political economic lines of argumentation, such that the closing years of the Cultural Revolution were characterized by a heavy discursive emphasis on the political economic education of the broad masses.[40] This is clearly borne out by a spike in the publication of new texts on political economy, mostly issued by Shanghai People's Press, explicitly directed at the lay public—as opposed to university students or party members.[41] These works include the 1974 *Political Economy on the Docks* (*Matou shang de zhengzhi jingjixue*), a short volume coproduced by the Fudan University economics department and a worker writing group.[42] Also included is the 1976 *Political Economy in Front of the Smelting Furnace* (*Lianganglu qian de zhengzhi jingjixue*), written by the theory group of the Shanghai Number 5 Steel Factory with the help of the Fudan economics and philosophy departments.[43] Such collaborations were meant to embody a political economy "freed from the classroom and reading room, [which] increasingly became a potent weapon in the hands of the broad worker-peasant-soldier [masses]."[44]

This pedagogical qua weaponizing impulse was not particularly new, of course, nor was it restricted to political economy and its role in the dismantling of the commodity fetish. On the contrary, we find a similar, general understanding of knowledge, its power, and its dissemination at work in the early years of the revolution in Yan'an (1936–48), the base area that became so crucial to the CCP's mythology and Mao's personal power and cachet. David Apter and Tony Saich have characterized Yan'an as an "instructional republic" constructed through a continuous process of "exegetical bonding" undertaken by its participants through a "logocentric" approach to analyzing and changing the world around them.[45] The particular role of language—with its specific abilities and limitations—in Yan'an and beyond is important here, but the centrality of the word and the text, the reliance on and instrumentalization of articulated theory, throughout the implementation of the Maoist project, is in some ways simply a by-product of a more fundamental "epistemic fantasy," as Roy Bing Chan puts it, in which "knowledge itself" becomes a "phantasmatic object." Tasked with "demystifying bourgeois ideology and feudal superstition," it was "hope[d] that knowledge could transform, via its proper application, into an illuminated, new reality."[46] This hope and belief finds its apotheosis, according to Chan, in the rhetorical emphasis consistently placed on light in "unit[ing] both theory and practice; on one hand it constituted the insight of correct theory, and on the other it illuminated a transfigured reality made possible only through the correct application of said theory."[47] In the context of the functional uses and mass mobilization of political economy, this epistemic fantasy helps further account for the notion that understanding the commodity form could in and of itself counter the backward pull of capitalist restoration. Knowing was, in this sense, very much a form of doing—effectively, a form of revolution.

Doing Things with Words

The continued spread and success of this revolution was heavily dependent on language. It was through language that Maoist knowledge qua truth was to be revealed, absorbed, and transmitted *in order that* it could be united with practice. In this regard, the Chinese socialist project was more preoccupied with hermeneutics and exegesis than Marx ever was. Or, more precisely, Mao and the CCP took it upon themselves to take Marx's political economic reading of the capitalist system—as Bill Brown characterizes *Capital*—to its logical, epistemic conclusion.[48] After all, as Apter and Saich suggest, at base the Yan'an revolutionaries "deliberately and explicitly sought nothing less than to change the world by reinterpreting it."[49] And here the flip side of interpretation is representation. Knowledge is not only excavated and possessed; it must be spoken in order to be understood and the world remade. Thus the importance of the precise ways in which the theory of the socialist commodity was articulated as and through language, namely, considerations of form, genre, and aesthetics.

The paradigmatic articulation of Maoist aesthetics, of course, is found in Mao's "Talks at the Yan'an Forum on Literature and Art" ("Yan'an wenyi zuotanhui") (1942), in which the arts' relationship to politics and the masses is laid out clearly, if somewhat paradoxically. For in as much as writers and artists are called on to learn from the masses, they are also supposed to guide them along. This duality of the writer as both student and teacher is replicated in the conceptualization of the artistic product, including literature, and its relationship to everyday life. "Life as reflected in works of literature and art can and ought to be on a higher plane, more intense, more concentrated, more typical, nearer the ideal, and therefore more universal than actual everyday life. Revolutionary literature and art should create a variety of characters out of real life and help the masses to propel history forward."[50] Literature—and therefore language—is meant to both mimetically reflect and, in Chan's sense, "illuminate" life as well as go beyond it, to *be* life and "more" than life simultaneously. Through the production of the "more intense, more concentrated, more typical...and...more universal," life itself, realist literature's purported referent, is altered and made better. Representation, itself a form of interpretation, becomes revolutionary practice.

To the extent that this formulation of Maoist aesthetics pertains not just to a mode of literary production, but to a discursive system, especially operative after 1949, one is struck by the similarity between it—and the desire it bespeaks—and Evgeny Dobrenko's conceptualization of another mode of political economy: the political economy of Stalinist socialist realism as that which *produces* socialism. To claim that "socialism is indeed the main product of Socialist Realism" inverts the hierarchical relationship between representation and referent.[51] But as we have seen, it is precisely the inversion of this relationship that is called on to serve as a means of historical progress in Mao's (Lenin-inspired) aesthetic articulation. Moreover, it fits neatly within the epistemic fantasy of knowing/interpreting/representing discussed above. As Dobrenko argues in the case of the USSR, "Socialist Realism was a machine for distilling Soviet reality into socialism."[52] It was meant to produce its own referent, to bring about a new *real* through the act of representation. That the product of this socialist realist mechanism (socialism) should be distinct from that which it distills ("reality" or what Dobrenko refers to as "real socialism") is to be expected and in some ways beside the point. It is an epistemic *fantasy*, after all. What is important, for our purposes, is that this process of representational exchange and substitution is, in the Maoist context at least, inextricably tied to conceptions of historical progress at work well beyond the confines of socialist realism per se. One might easily characterize what I have attempted to sketch out in this chapter, following Dobrenko, as the political economy of political economy in the Chinese Cultural Revolution.

I will return to an overtly political economic text, *A commodity's tale*, considered along these lines, but for the moment, I want to further explore the instrumentalized inversion of (linguistic) sign and referent, the remaking of the world through its (re)interpretation/representation, and the consequences of this particular mode of upending reality. One of the best articulations of this process is found in Zhao Shuli's (1906–70) 1955 novel *Sanliwan*, which, itself a work of socialist realism, includes discussions of painting and its role in the production of socialism, in Dobrenko's sense. In the midst of cooperativization in 1952, the village of Sanliwan is embroiled in a number of conflicts, primarily concerning land. One of the key obstacles facing the co-op is the construction of an irrigation canal. It is hoped that work on the canal will begin immediately after the harvest, but some private landowners refuse to have the canal dug on their land. By the end of the novel, everything works out and construction begins as promised, but along the way, three paintings of Sanliwan are commissioned from Comrade Liang to aid in the propaganda effort. When presented with an instance of (overtly propagandistic) representation within a novel devised to serve much the same purpose, one is immediately wont to draw parallels between the painter and the novel's author. Certainly, there is something to be said for an approach in which the paintings and the discussions of them essentially function as metafictional devices. More than that, however, given our interest in the production of socialism, it is worth considering how the characters' confusion when faced with the prospect of representation within the novel's diegesis betrays an underlying conceptualization of how representation works.

The reader is first introduced to a painting of present-day Sanliwan when Comrade Liang asks for criticism of his work just prior to a party meeting. The beginning of the passage is worth quoting at length.

> "Why, that's Sanliwan!" cried Yuyi. As they drew nearer, he went on: "The Upper Flats, the Lower Flats, Lao-wu's Plot, Sandy Creek, Thirty *Mou* Field, Hilt Field, Dragon Neck... it's all there to life!" [*zhen xiang*]
>
> "If you stand a little further off," remarked someone else, "you feel you could walk straight into it!"
>
> "Don't just be complimentary," begged the artist. "Please point out some of the faults."
>
> Still no one had any criticism.
>
> "Comrade Liang!" said Yusheng. "Can you paint things that don't exist yet?" [*Xianzai hai meiyou de dongxi ni neng bu neng hua*]
>
> "Things that don't exist in Sanliwan, or that don't exist in the world?"
>
> "I mean something like the canal." Yusheng pointed at the picture. "It'll start from here in the Upper Flats, pass Sandy Creek, run south by the foot of the cliff, and then branch out to water the Lower Flats. All the waterwheels in the Lower Flats will be bunched by the canal here in the Upper Flats, and the water pumped up here will go through three channels and any number of ditches to the Upper Flats. When both Upper and Lower Flats are irrigated, we shall harvest much richer crops. Can you paint a Sanliwan like that?"
>
> "Of course I can!" was Liang's answer. "A very good idea! We can call that 'A Better Sanliwan' [*Tigaole de Sanliwan*] or 'Sanliwan Tomorrow.'"[53]

This second painting is quickly commissioned as part of the upcoming propaganda campaign surrounding the canal. A third painting is also requested, depicting Sanliwan with tractors, trucks, and new homes, that is, Sanliwan under socialism. When an onlooker asks what the new buildings will look like, someone else replies,

"It's to give the general idea! There may be three cars in the painting, but that won't stop us from having five later, will it? If he paints a field of millet, that doesn't mean we can't plant sesame there afterwards."

"Right!" confirmed the artist. "All I can do is imagine what Sanliwan will be like then, on the basis of what I know about mechanized agriculture. What I leave out or get wrong can be filled in and corrected according to future developments."[54]

What is of greatest interest here are the comments made by the (mostly nameless) viewers of the painting who seem to be unaware of how pictorial representation works, especially with regard to its relationship with its referent. Over and over again the speakers assume a one-to-one correspondence between the painting in front of them and the village they call home. From the praise of the first painting in the language of trompe l'oeil (as that into which one can physically enter) to the questioning of how to represent something that has yet to exist, the naive onlookers assume a connection between the painting and that which is painted; their naivete is couched in terms of the straightforwardly mimetic.

This presumptive mimesis is troubled, however, precisely by the prospect of representing the nonexistent. In this sense, odd as it may at first appear, Yusheng's question is precisely the right one. If representation is subordinate to a referent, what happens when the referent does not (yet) exist? How can we speak of realism when there is no real to reflect? We might answer, as Comrade Liang essentially does, that the referent can be (and is) produced by the act of representation itself. Remarkably, in this passage, the inexperienced viewers seem to be confused as to the terms in which that production takes place. The reassurance offered by some unknown individual that the future of Sanliwan will not be restricted by what Comrade Liang paints, while no doubt meant to be humorous, actually draws our attention to the ways in which the depiction of Sanliwan under socialism *does* affect the village's future, delimiting its possibilities as it produces the future in the present. The third painting produces socialism insofar as it defines its conditions of possibility and creates the expectation of a referent corresponding to the representation.

Indeed, this is precisely the reaction of the viewers of all three paintings when they are unveiled later in the novel. Villagers are convinced that the canal will be beneficial because they interpret the second painting not as what *could* be, but what *should* and therefore *will* be. Likewise, the third painting, when examined by the gardener, Wang Xing, prompts a number of questions about what it will be like then (*dao nei shihou*), namely, when socialism is achieved. Concerned about the location of his water-wheel, his crops, and traffic, Wang Xing's queries are always met with the same laughing, yet categorical, explanation of how it will be under socialism.[55] For all intents and purposes, therefore, to look at both the second and third paintings is to look at Sanliwan's future, at the "road Sanliwan ought to take," and, by the force of the prescriptive mode and the mechanics of socialist realism, to go back to Dobrenko, the path it must inevitably follow.[56]

It goes without saying that Zhao Shuli's novel itself partakes of the political economy of socialist realism, but the socialism it produces is slightly different with regard to its relationship to the (historical) present. Whereas the second and third paintings may be understood as constructing conditions of possibility, within the context of the circulation of the novel, first serialized in *People's Literature* (*Renmin wenxue*) in 1955 and then published as a book in 1958, the future conceptualized in Comrade Liang's paintings was tied to the present at the time of publication. In other words, the novel produced socialism as a promise already fulfilled, and it is precisely in this sense of a future that is already here that we see the double nature of socialist realism as at once tied to that which is and that which should be. Socialist realism closes the distance between the two in such a way that time is collapsed and history is pushed forward.

The point I want to make with this apparent digression is that political economic texts and rhetoric served a similar purpose in the Cultural Revolution as this socialist realist machine. More precisely, both these linguistic operations drew from the same source and relied on the same basic inversionary interpretive moves and epistemic assumptions. What sets the political economy of the later era apart from other textual pursuits, perhaps, is the centrality afforded diagnostic economics within the Marxist approach to historical advancement and a direct reckoning with the pernicious nature of the commodity fetish. No text sums up the difficulty of the latter—all while flirting with the literary, to boot—quite like *A Commodity's Tale*.

In Its Own Words

A commodity's tale (*Shangpin zishu*) first appeared on the pages of *Study and Criticism* (*Xuexi yu pipan*) in the summer of 1975. The journal, which ran from September 1973 to September 1976 for a total of thirty-eight issues, was closely associated with what became known as the Gang of Four and the Shanghai Municipal Party Committee writing group, that is, with the forces behind *Fundamentals*. Published by Shanghai People's Press, like *Fundamentals* and other materials meant to popularize and weaponize political economy, *Study and Criticism* was an important outlet for the aforementioned Shanghai school and its understanding of and approach to the socialist commodity. In this respect, *A Commodity's Tale*, attributed to Jing Chi, a known Shanghai writing group pen name, is a prime example of orthodox Cultural Revolution political economic theory. One might be tempted, in fact, to think of it as something of a more readable, whimsical repackaging of the underlying developmental assumptions of *Fundamentals*. The particular story relayed in *A Commodity's Tale* is straight out of the 1970s historical materialist playbook, delineating the forms of exchange and social relations employed in each successive stage of Chinese history—from the birth of the commodity at the tail end of primitive communism, to the rise of first slave and then feudal economies in the early dynasties, to the capitalist colonial expansion of the Opium War (1839–42), to the dawn of socialist construction and the shrinking role of commodity relations. As we might well expect, the last of these receives the greatest emphasis, with eight of the text's twenty-one chapters devoted to the revisionist danger posed by the socialist commodity's ever-present ability to hatch (*fuhua*) a new bourgeoisie. The text is a product of its time in all these respects. Its jaw-dropping noteworthiness stems from a single fact: Its canonical story is relayed *by a commodity* in the first person.

In a world where commodities are rigorously disavowed mystical powers—where the dissemination of knowledge through language is effectively meant to disarm the commodity fetish—shockingly, this text gives the commodity an officially endorsed voice with which to narrate political economic development. The Chinese title, *Shangpin zishu*, makes the commodity's role as narrator explicit in the compound *zishu* or self-narration. This is a commodity "in its own words"—which puts us in something of a pickle: Although the *zishu* designation turns on the troublesome conceit that commodities can have their own anything, the text as a whole is meant to convince the reader of the danger posed by such ideas to the socialist project. And, to complicate matters still further, this particular commodity is nothing if not aware of its readers' sociopolitical circumstances. Thus the text's short preface:

> I'm called a commodity [*shangpin*]. We are a huge clan [*jiazu*] with tracks spanning the entire world. Each of you readers interacts with me [*yu wo laiwang*] every day. Isn't that so? The fish, meat, and vegetables you buy at the market; the rice and flour you buy at the granary; the clothing and accessories you buy at the department store—each and every one is a member of our clan. But it's easy to miss the forest for the trees.[57] Although you cross paths with me daily, that doesn't necessarily mean you know my lot in life [*shenshi*]. Today, all of China is studying the Marxist theory of the dictatorship of the proletariat, and I have become a topic of discussion. Whether in the study sessions of the work unit and classroom or the leisurely conversations of the street, field, and market, people regularly invoke my name.

> I take this opportunity to give the reader a little account of my life and engage in some self-dissection [*ziwo jiepou*].[58]

This commodity goes under the knife of historical materialism voluntarily as part of the campaign to study the theory of the dictatorship of the proletariat, a theory it wholeheartedly supports.

In sum, the narrator of *A Commodity's Tale* is a Marxist commodity, both in the sense that the anatomy it describes is consistent with the tenets of Marx and in the sense that it is ideologically invested in the success of the socialist project. Indeed, the narrator blithely looks forward to its own demise in the text's afterword. "All things [*wanshi wanwu*] in the universe have their own process of emergence, development, and extinction. I am no different. Of course, I am not a fortune teller; I cannot say precisely when I will disappear. But my life's end cannot be altered."[59] It cannot be altered because Marx has already foretold it; the die has been cast. "I have already recounted my life experience and actions, and although they say one can only pass judgment once the coffin has been sealed, I do not think that is necessarily the case. Because Marxism passed scientific judgment [*dinglun*] on me early on." In the meantime, "if you want to know more about how Marxism assesses my life, I suggest you study a little bit of Marxist political economy. See you in the midst of production and circulation!"[60] It is a stunning send-off for a stunning text—urging the reader to participate in the current campaign while positing that the narrator's voice firmly belongs in the context of the reader's daily life, a life of production, circulation, and (as the preface clearly implies) consumption, even as the commodity's act of public self-dissection is meant to deny the very possibility of this voice. Given the contemporary concern about the commodity form's capitalist-restorationist proclivities, this paradox is remarkably loaded. And yet, neither the work—wholly devoid of paratextual explanatory devices—nor the narrator betray any anxiety about the clear and present danger so obviously at hand. Does the conceit (a talking commodity) not uncut the power of the content (demystifying knowledge)? Worse, what happens if conceit trumps content outright?

These questions go unexpressed, let alone unanswered in *A Commodity's Tale*. The text's strident denunciations of former party leaders Liu Shaoqi and Lin Biao are apparently deemed sufficient to avert any serious misunderstandings. An earlier attempt at commodity narration, by contrast, brims with self-conscious trepidation. Deng Kesheng's (1911–76) *Autobiography of a Commodity* (*Shangpin zizhuan*), which the authors of *A Commodity's Tale* were almost certainly aware of,[61] was first published by Jiangsu People's Press in 1960.[62] Revised editions were also released by the same publisher in 1962 and 1978. Much like *A Commodity's Tale*, the story Deng's commodity relays to the reader is perfectly in keeping with the political economic consensus of its time. *Autobiography* is not particularly concerned with the threat of capitalist restoration, for example. It calls unabashedly for an increase in commodity production and an expanded deployment of the law of value. In this sense, it diverges sharply from the Shanghai school position of the 1970s.[63] The underlying contradiction between *Autobiography*'s first-person narrative and its pedagogical mission, on the other hand, is very much of a piece with *A Commodity's Tale*. But whereas the latter text seems unperturbed by its own paradoxical existence, *Autobiography* shows marked signs of strain. From the start of the opening chapter:

> Dear reader: This is the first time that I—(a commodity) have been able to communicate with you earnestly in my own name. On one hand, I feel greatly honored to do so, but on the other hand, I am extremely uncomfortable [*shifen wei nan*]. I feel honored to have this opportunity to provide you with a little introduction to my background, my character, my uses, my past—in sum, to all that I am—in order that you might know and understand me. I am wholly willing to do this. I am uncomfortable, however, because I am not actually a sentient thing [*genben shi yi ge wuzhi zhi wu*]. I don't speak, nor am I able to speak. How then can I open my mouth to communicate with you? Since the author of this book has deemed that I must speak on my own behalf, I have no choice but to attempt the impossible [*mian wei qi nan*] and tell my own story via the author's pen.
>
> Although I am speaking now, I don't want to deceive you. Allow me first to address my makeup: I am not a person, nor am I a spirit. That I am called "commodity," that I can be produced, is entirely the result of human labor. Thus, you absolutely cannot anthropomorphize me [*rengehua*], still less can you develop superstitions [*mixin*] about me.[64]

The narrator goes on to explain that it is particularly concerned about this because commodity fetishism has historically been a problem that it does not now wish to compound.

In stark contrast to the preface of *A Commodity's Tale*, which, like its ending, makes a point of blurring the narrator's voice and the circulating commodities in the reader's daily life, *Autobiography* repeatedly highlights the constructed nature of its animating narratorial device. A helpful distinction is made, for example, between the narrator and the author, reenacting the principle that commodities—even talking ones—are products of human agency and labor. The 1960 and 1978 editions also feature something of a typographical tic: the clarification "I—(a commodity)" (*wo—[shangpin]*) is strewn throughout *Autobiography* apparently at random—sometimes multiple times in one paragraph, sometimes pages apart—as though out of fear that the work's overarching conceit is on the verge of collapse (or success?). It makes for clunky, anxiety-ridden prose. *A Commodity's Tale* commits to the commodity-narrator concept in a way that *Autobiography* never quite manages. In essence, *A Commodity's Tale* takes *Autobiography* to its formal devil-may-care conclusion.

Historically, talking commodities and the stories they tell have more generally been associated with the unsettling expansion of capitalist consumer culture than with an attempt at this system's de-articulation. A fad for such tales—dubbed "it-narratives" in scholarship on the topic—emerged in late eighteenth-century England, for example, a phenomenon which has garnered increasing critical interest since the early 1990s. Aileen Douglas's pathbreaking article on the it-narrative set the parameters of the dominant approach to narrating objects/commodities, declaring that "it would be difficult to imagine another literary genre more thoroughly determined by the logic of consumerism."[65] The logic of consumerism, after all, had only recently made its way into every nook and cranny of English society, troubling traditional social structures and mores wherever it went. This meant that the circulating commodity could now claim access to the most intimate of spaces—access itself destabilizing for developing notions of privacy, authenticity, and sentiment—and, as a result, the position to relay the best-guarded of secrets. The well-worn guinea or sofa or hackney coach had seen it all and was now eager to recount its journey.

That these discomfiting stories of commodity circulation were themselves circulated in the newly commodified form of the book has not been lost on scholars of the genre. This additional twist has led some, including Lynn Festa and Jonathan Lamb, to read the English it-narrative fad as symptomatic of shifts in what it meant to be an author or to "own" a text in the late eighteenth century.[66] Christina Lupton has recently also drawn attention to the importance afforded writers and paper in it-narratives, highlighting the genre's self-reflexive take on its own materiality.[67] But even this sophisticated line of inquiry seems predicated on a sense of social disruption left in the commodity's wake. By all accounts, there is something new and troubling going on in these works. As Douglas puts it: "The very notion that objects have adventures, and that society is integrated through the transmission of objects from hand to hand, is itself a novel way of thinking. The displacement of the human voice in this later eighteenth-century fiction expresses fear and excitement particular to the times. The fear is that people have become enthralled to things and that objects, therefore, can explain society as it really is; the excitement comes from the unfamiliarity and novelty of the society the objects reveal."[68] For the concerned Marxist bent on demystifying the commodity fetish, the problem is precisely that the excitement seems to inevitably trump the fear.

To be clear, I am not suggesting that *A Commodity's Tale*—or *Autobiography* before it—is a direct descendent of the eighteenth-century English it-narrative. I wish simply to call attention to the fact that in the latter genre, the object's narratorial voice emerges in response to the bewitching potential of society's consumption. A similar move is being made in *A Commodity's Tale*, despite its participation in a very different cultural and material environment; at the end of the day, commodities are no less bewitching for being scarce. In fact, the ever-vigilant Chinese consumer of the 1970s was constantly reminded of the opposite: the fewer commodities there are, the more powerful their would-be hold over the individuals who make them. This is precisely why, at the end of the day, the form of this work appears so counterproductive, especially since it is not a novelistic exploration, but rather an overtly pedagogical rehashing of political economic history. Such things were not meant to be overly exciting. And yet, *A Commodity's Tale* was created by the very same people as *Fundamentals*.

The key to understanding the former lies in one crucial way in which it clearly does diverge from the English it-narrative of the eighteenth century: In *A Commodity's Tale*, we are given a transhistorical account of the commodity form rather than that of a particular object *circulating as* a commodity. It is not the story of a bicycle or a radio; there are no anecdotes of the crimes of a particular person or family. It is, instead, a tale told by an abstraction, the commodity stripped of material specificity. This explains the endless slippage in the text between the singular commodity's "I" and the "we" of the commodity's "clan." Since commodities are exchangeable by definition, the voice of one speaks for all. This level of generalizability is anathema to the classic it-narrative, which follows the thing on its travels as facilitated by commodity exchange rather than the commodity tout court as a conceptual entity. The "it" in question in *A Commodity's Tale* is of a somewhat different order, then, which ultimately suggests a kinship with the longstanding Chinese genre of satirical biography or pseudobiography (*jia zhuan*).[69]

The (transgressive) conceit of the pseudobiography, unlike the it-narrative, is not that an object can speak, but rather, that an object deserves to be spoken about in a manner traditionally reserved for historically significant human actors, as per the model of Sima Qian's (circa 145–85 BCE) *Records of the Grand Historian* (*Shiji*). The issue at stake is the prestige associated with the biographic form, prestige that is used to problematize the superiority of people to things. The objects in pseudobiographies *are* historically significant; that's part of the problem. The earliest known pseudobiography, Han

Yu's (768–824 CE) "Biography of Fur Point" ("Mao Ying zhuan"), speaks to this clearly.[70] While treated as though it were the name of one of the emperor's human advisors, Fur Point is revealed to be a writing brush, more specifically, a writing brush descendent from a long line—an enduring clan, as it were—of writing brushes. For many literati, Han Yu's word games went over the line, venturing into disrespectful territory.[71] Others began emulating him, tracing the inanimate genealogies of the surrounding object world. This move, required by the biographic form being parodied, sets up a slippage, similar to what we see in *A Commodity's Tale*, between a singular exemplar (one particular writing brush) and the category or clan to which it belongs (writing brushes in general).

The many pseudobiographies of money take this blurring to its logical conclusion. Gao Ming's (circa 1305–70) "Biography of Wu Bao" ("Wu Bao zhuan"), one of the earliest texts in this subgenre, is a case in point.[72] In this piece, Wu Bao refers to paper money *in general*, in contradistinction to specie. This is not a biography of a singular paper bill and its individual exploits. It is, rather, an exercise in skewering the societal place afforded to paper money, its circulation, and its accumulation writ large. I have found no attempts at the pseudobiography of the commodity.[73] However, the generic emphasis on money, as a facilitator of trade, raises many of the same issues not only about the gap between a quasi-Platonic ideal and a materially specific object but also about the disjuncture between an abstract notion of equivalent, exchangeable value and materiality as such. In other words, the pseudobiography of money, though ostensibly still turning on the treatment of a class or clan of material objects, traverses much of the same conceptually bumpy terrain as *A Commodity's Tale* precisely because of the peculiar, abstract political economic nature of these objects. I would submit, then, that we think of this subgenre as establishing a formal, literary precedent within Chinese letters, modified and deployed as pseudo-*auto*biography in *A Commodity's Tale* in order to deal with the perceived threat of the commodity to the socialist project, a threat specifically associated with the allure of commodity fetishism. In this regard, this remarkable work should be read as something of a cross—in spirit, if not in actual influence—between the Chinese pseudobiography and the English it-narrative.

At the end of the day, though, when looking for textual antecedents to both *Autobiography* and *A Commodity's Tale*, we need not look much further, perhaps, than Marx. "If commodities could speak," Marx muses in *Capital*, "they would say this: our use-value may interest men, but it does not belong to us as objects. What does belong to us as objects, however, is our value. Our own intercourse as commodities proves it. We relate to each other merely as exchange-values."[74] Marx's speaking commodity is an abstract form, spouting political economy instead of consumer secrets. Indeed, the only secret it can divulge—in light of its conceptual nature—is that of its own structure. What we find in *A Commodity's Tale* is precisely an attempt to have the commodity speak itself—both in the sense of finding a voice of its own and in the sense of producing itself through words—while skirting the dangers of commodity fetishism by dint of abstraction. Just as the broader socialist project tries to rid commodity production of its unsavory associations, this text seeks to preclude commodity fetishism by evacuating it from the object: This is commodity fetishism without the fetish.[75] The great gambit, here, is that what we are left with in the wake of this purge are the social relations once occluded by the material, and these social relations, we are repeatedly told, have irrevocably changed. The new system(s) of ownership have put a putative end to exploitation, for example. The socialist commodity, stripped of materiality with which to hide its now-open secrets, therefore presents itself as an improvement over the capitalist incarnation of the form.

But what this really amounts to is one sleight of hand replacing another: Rather than social relations masquerading as thingly relations, we are given abstraction in lieu of specificity and the materiality of language in place of the materiality of things. Marx himself was not immune to this problem. Consider this famous passage, also from *Capital*'s opening chapter: "The form of wood, for instance, is altered if a table is made out of it. Nevertheless the table continues to be wood, an ordinary, sensuous thing. But as soon as it emerges as a commodity, it changes into a thing which transcends sensuousness. It not only stands with its feet on the ground, but, in relation to all other commodities, it stands on its head, and evolves out of its wooden brain grotesque ideas, far more wonderful than if it were to begin dancing of its own free will."[76] The commodity "transcends sensuousness"; it leaves sensuousness—or materiality—behind, and in this process of transcendence, the logic of capitalism reveals itself. As Brown notes, "Marx presents *Capital* as a hermeneutic enterprise: an extended interpretation of one structural fact, the fact that the commodity is both a thing and not a thing at all, 'its sensuous characteristics... extinguished.'"[77] Within this formulation, Marx almost exclusively focuses on the un-thing-ness of the commodity—on the commodity form as such—its successful shedding of particularity and its reliance on the leveling operations of exchange value. It is in the specter of the dancing table that we glimpse something else: the thingness of the commodity, namely, the failure of the commodity form to transcend a sensuous materiality that will not be denied. Returning to Brown: "Only the table emerges, out of *Capital*, as an object worth imagining or an object worth having, as an object personified while remaining very much an object."[78] The table is therefore symptomatic of that which exists in excess of analysis, of that with which Marx cannot grapple. In this sense, the commodity's failure to fully transcend particularity bespeaks Marx's own fundamental failure to account for materiality in political economic discourse, to unravel the magic of capitalism while nonetheless addressing something beyond its logic.

Political economy's new, weaponized role within the socialist project as pursued in the Cultural Revolution, when talking about how commodity fetishism works was supposed to make it go away, might best be understood as an attempt to grapple with this failure. The question of materiality *in* political economic analysis is transformed into one concerning the material efficacy *of* political economic analysis. Political economic discourse is itself fetishized, thereby becoming a new manifestation of the same problem rather than its solution. This turn of events is beyond the realm of possibility for Cultural Revolution texts, despite the fact that any absolute victory in the war on commodities is necessarily deferred to a communist future.[79] Indeed, the issue as I have discussed it here in my analysis of *A Commodity's Tale* is far too fundamental: Try as we might to abstract, we still live in a world of things, of tables with a penchant for dancing. Strictly speaking, this is not so much a problem of commodities as it is a problem of the relationship between language and things, and as a result, even the supposed harbinger of the commodity relation's long-awaited demise, the newborn socialist thing, was plagued by it as well. If political economy approached the commodity fetish by emphasizing the language side of this equation, other spheres of Cultural Revolution society attempted to make an end run around language, instead tackling the mechanics of embodiment. This is the subject of the next chapter.

5 Remediating the Hero

On the last page of its April 14, 1974, issue, the national newspaper *Liberation Daily* (*Jiefang ribao*) republished a well-known image from 1971. The caption identifies the small black-and-white illustration as a propaganda poster by Shan Lianxiao (dates unknown), who, in accordance with the usual practice of the time, is identified simply as a worker (see figure 5.1). The reason for the image's return to prominence here is found in the figure of the young woman in the upper right-hand corner: With her single, long braid, clenched fist, and red lantern, she is instantly recognizable as Li Tiemei, the quintessential revolutionary successor. As one of the heroes of the model opera *The Red Lantern*, Tiemei was thrust back into prominence in 1974, when the yangbanxi were once again vigorously promoted throughout the official media, this time as powerful weapons in the Criticize Lin Biao, Criticize Confucius campaign.

Despite her iconic status, however, Tiemei is not alone in capturing the viewer's attention. Indeed, backed by a red flag and hovering weightlessly in an ill-defined space, Tiemei is contrasted with the presence of the larger, more grounded, young woman dominating the lower half of the image, identifiable by her armband as a member of the militia. Gazing off toward the same utopian future and holding her left elbow at the same angle, the militia woman is presented as Tiemei's real-life double. Tiemei's fist is offset by a rifle, and whereas Tiemei raises her red lantern, symbol of her revolutionary inheritance, her counterpart wears a Mao badge and clutches a copy of *The Selected Works of Mao Zedong* (*Mao Zedong xuan ji*), complete with a pink bow. It is the interplay between the two women—now exact duplicates, now complementary—that drives this poster, as the eye of the viewer moves

Figure 5.1 "BE THIS KIND OF PERSON," poster by Shan Lianxiao, 1972, 106 by 76 centimeters. Ann Tompkins (Tang Fandi) and Lincoln Cushing Chinese Poster Collection, C. V. Starr East Asian Library, University of California, Berkeley.

along the diagonal they form, an axis additionally delineated by the flag's white pole and the book's edge. A line of text also graces the image's left side: "BE THIS KIND OF PERSON" (*zuo ren yao zuo zheiyang de ren*), it asserts, ostensibly clarifying just who is worthy of emulation in Mao's China.

But if the inclusion of this slogan is meant to put arguments about appropriate role models to rest, it paradoxically raises a whole host of new questions by exploding the poster's otherwise clearly demarcated frame. Many of these questions arise from the ambiguous nature of the demonstrative determiner "this." Just who is imitating whom? Surely the poster is first and foremost addressing the viewer, calling on her to fall into line and act as the young militia woman does. The militia woman is not in and of herself a fixed point or stable entity, however; her importance, rather, derives from her relation to and imitation of Tiemei. And yet Tiemei is not all that self-enclosed a figure either. The poster's tagline is, in fact, the title of one of Li Tiemei's arias in *The Red Lantern*, marking an important step in her journey toward fully assuming the revolutionary mantle. The "this kind of person" she refers to is her (adoptive) father, Li Yuhe, who himself makes repeated references to what a generic revolutionary does and can withstand. In other words, even the heroic figure of Li Yuhe is, in a sense, a mere cipher, an isolated instantiation of a generalized and generalizable revolutionary ideal. In the end, it is Chairman Mao who emerges as the ultimate model: It is his name that Li Yuhe shouts on the execution ground and his likeness and words that rest so close to the militia woman's heart.

This attention to Mao's status (and presence in the poster) as master signifier within the Cultural Revolution's media environment is not to deny the importance or impact of figures like Li Tiemei and Li Yuhe. On the contrary, it is to suggest that the importance of such figures derives precisely from their participation in chains of signification that draw their power from the "Red Sun" himself. They operate as mediators between the individual and the fount of discursive power, Mao. But whereas Mao necessarily remains singularly unmatched in his position of semiotic supremacy—there can be only one Chairman Mao—the yangbanxi heroes are eminently reproducible: the more the merrier.[1] Indeed, this is arguably their main purpose as models of idealized revolutionary behavior. The question becomes how this mass (re)production is supposed to take place. Put another way, what kind of process does one undergo to mold oneself into "this kind of person"? A distinction must be drawn here between emulation, imitation, and mimesis, on the one hand, and becoming, on the other, for it is quite pointedly the latter that this poster asks of the viewer. Don't just play the revolutionary; don't simply mimic her. *Be* her.

This chapter examines a key technology of this mass (re)production of revolutionary models: amateur performance, as carried out in the context of the yangbanxi popularization campaign (*dali puji yangbanxi*), officially begun in July 1970. I focus primarily on the discursive construction of performance as a transformative process through which revolutionaries can be (re)made. Critical to this construction is the attention given to the amateur's body as the technology's relevant medium. This is a technology rooted in a conception of the amateur body as plastic, on the one hand, and a fantasy of perfect identity between appearance and essence, on the other. The greater the attention paid to the standardization of performance, however, the more one detects an underlying anxiety about the absolute correspondence of bodily training and ideological self-fashioning. This anxiety, bound up in the figure of the villain and what I call a Cultural Revolution *hermeneutics of suspicion*, is also evocative of an ever-present spectral figure in Marxist thought: the alienated worker under capitalism. To the extent that the utopian promise of communism is freedom from alienation—of one's labor, of one's body, of one's self—the promise of amateur performance lies not just in the (re)production of heroes, but in a concomitant (re)integration of the subject. But if the products of this technology of amateur performance are idealized for their completeness and stability, paradoxically, the technology itself undermines their very possibility by invoking the notion of the plastic amateur body as one medium among many (porcelain, painting, television, film ... the list goes on). The amateur body is thereby implicated in a broad system of remediation—a constellation very much on the order of the newborn socialist thing—that facilitates a kind of bodily abstraction and detachment. To be an amateur performer not only involves molding oneself into a hero, a model established through prescriptive representations and discourse, but also rendering one's body as alienable.

Amateur Performance

The ideal functioning of amateur performance as a technology of mass (re)production is perhaps best illustrated by "Before and after the Performance" ("Yanchu qianhou"), the short story surrounding the aforementioned image in *Liberation daily*. Narrated by Sister Afang, an amateur portrayer of Li Tiemei in a northeastern propaganda team (*xuantuandui*), the story follows the development of Honghua (literally, "red flower"), as she transitions from avid fan to Li Tiemei performer and ultimately to lead actress and head of her local propaganda team. This evolution is established through flashbacks of Sister Afang and Honghua's first two meetings. Although Sister Afang has been dispatched by her brigade commander to go learn from Honghua's troupe in the story's present, this is a reversal of their original relationship. When the women first meet five years earlier, it is Sister Afang who performs and Honghua who watches with rapt attention. Having walked for miles to see the performance, she is unable to get a ticket and is forced to watch through a window with a crowd of other peasants. Sister Afang is so moved by Honghua's love of the yangbanxi that she has the performance relocated outside, where everyone can have a better view, further insisting on singing herself despite an illness. As Honghua begins her long journey home after the show, she is tellingly heard singing, "Be this kind of person."

When the women meet again two years later, they are both performing as part of a special evening of entertainment for an important visitor. Calamity strikes when Sister Afang realizes that she has misplaced her braid, an integral part of the Li Tiemei costume, the loss of which threatens to derail her performance before it has even begun. Without a second thought, Honghua cuts off her own beloved braids—she has had them for eight years—affixing one to Sister Afang's head and thereby allowing the show to go on. This gesture is understood by everyone involved as a great personal sacrifice for the good of the dissemination of the yangbanxi. Indeed, Honghua says as much in a speech ultimately credited for inspiring Sister Afang's best-ever performance. The story ends in the present with Honghua portraying Jiang Shuiying, the much-lauded heroine of *Song of Dragon River* (*Long jiang song*) on an impromptu stage. The audience, which now includes Sister Afang, is duly impressed, everyone rushing to learn from Honghua on completion of her performance.[2]

Honghua's apparent linear trajectory from student to teacher is combined here with a circularity typical of Maoist discourse in general and Cultural Revolution discourse in particular. Even as Honghua watches from the sidelines—indeed, she finds herself literally on the outside looking in—it is she, not Sister Afang, who has the most ardent revolutionary spirit. It is Honghua who consistently inspires Sister Afang, not the other way around. One might say, therefore, that the story's structure mirrors that of Mao's famous dictum "from the masses, to the masses" (*cong qunzhong zhong lai dao qunzhong zhong qu*). As with the mass line, however, circularity here does not imply stagnation; there must, after all, still be progress. And this is precisely where Honghua's development from spectator to performer *alongside* her increasingly revolutionary behavior becomes so crucial. In Honghua's evolution lies the promise of our own.

The engine of Honghua's development is precisely her performance of Li Tiemei and other yangbanxi heroines. Performance is rendered transformative, with the expectation that one will, in a sense, become the hero one portrays. This attitude is neatly summed up by Honghua's grandfather, who is not at all surprised by his granddaughter's decision to gift her braids for the glory of the yangbanxi. "Yes," he says, "Chairman Mao's propagandists [*xuanchuanyuan*] should act this way!"[3] The underlying logic behind this matter-of-fact expectation is subsequently articulated by a peasant onlooker in the story's present, impressed with Honghua's versatility in embodying her roles. "When she plays a hero, she learns from that hero, and when she learns from that hero, you see it in her actions."[4] This is a simple restating of a common slogan in the discourse surrounding amateur performance: "Play a hero, study a hero, see it in the actions" (*yan yingxiong, xue yingxiong, jian xingdong*).[5] Crucially, the progression delineated by this slogan—and ventriloquized in the story by a discerning audience member—effectively explodes the notion of the stage as a delimited space within which one can and should appropriate the behavior and mannerisms of a hero or heroes. The goal is rather to mold oneself into a hero in everyday life.

To wit, official media outlets cheerfully reported instances in which the transformative promise of yangbanxi amateur performance had apparently been borne out, propagating a new crop of models who traveled effectively between on- and offstage in the process. The propaganda teams of Shanghai's Number 4 Benefit the People Food Products Factory (Yimin shipin si chang; hereafter, Yimin Factory) were some of the most prominent of these models. Articles describing their achievements commonly found their way into the pages of the Shanghai daily *Wenhui bao* as well as the national *People's Daily*. When members of Shanghai Normal University's Chinese department put together a volume lauding the amateur performers of seven worker, peasant, and soldier work units in 1975, Yimin Factory was given pride of place.[6] The exploits of the performers in the collection are varied: increased production, better work-unit morale, the successful reform of problematic persons in the work unit, the creation and development of new works, and so on. Furthermore, in the best tradition of yangbanxi heroes, these model amateurs are said to overcome great difficulties in order to carry out their tasks, such as wading through frigid water and performing in challenging conditions.

Provincial-level newspapers likewise touted local exemplars of real-life heroes forged through performances of the yangbanxi. *Sichuan Daily* (*Sichuan ribao*) offered a most dramatic account of the fruits of this process in the case of one Ma Zilan. As part of its commemoration of the thirty-second anniversary of Mao's "Talks at the Yan'an Forum on Art and Literature," the May 23, 1974, issue of *Sichuan Daily* included a number of articles pertaining to the yangbanxi. A few of these describe the state of yangbanxi popularization in Sichuan proper, including in Dengzhan Commune, where efforts were led by amateur propaganda teams. It is in the seventh brigade's team that we find Ma Zilan, who, after performing a revolutionary heroine onstage, reportedly braved an actual burning building. Climbing onto the roof alongside her male comrades, Ma did not hesitate to put herself in harm's way in order to quell the flames. Indeed, despite being injured when the roof collapsed, she is said to have gone into the fire to save a small child. This harrowing account is promptly juxtaposed with figures concerning the number of commune propaganda team members who have successfully joined the party.[7] The message is clear: The (proper) performance of yangbanxi can propel individuals into the pantheon of revolutionary figures, thereby also becoming worthy of reproduction, whether as firefighters or bureaucrats.

This focus on everyday, real-life heroes aids us in refining the notion of the amateur, for, as Ellen Judd notes, it is rather difficult to pin down. In general, of course, we tend to understand the amateur as one who engages in a particular activity without remuneration in addition to her trade or employment. This understanding is explicit in the Chinese term I have been translating herein as amateur: *yeyu*, literally, "in addition to work."[8] We should note that, throughout the decade from 1966 to 1976, revolution was meant to go hand in hand with increased industrial output, as the slogan "take firm hold of revolution and stimulate production" (*zhua geming cu shengchan*) makes clear. Indeed, from the very beginning of the yangbanxi popularization campaign in 1970, great emphasis was placed on the fact that production was not to be adversely affected.[9] The campaign to popularize the yangbanxi was to take place during the participants' time off. This depiction of the amateur—hardworking machinist by day, opera performer by night—did not always jibe with what was happening on the ground, however. The continued touring required of the Yimin Factory performers, for example, left little time for work on the factory floor, meaning that these individuals were essentially living off their art.[10] It was also common for nominally amateur groups to include or be advised by individuals who had been members of professional troupes up until the Cultural Revolution. Professional opera and song and dance troupes may have disbanded in great numbers after 1966, but in many cases they were simply reinvented in more politically acceptable forms, including those of amateur status. Educated, urban artists sent to the countryside were likewise recast as talented, amateur peasants.[11] The term *amateur* must therefore be understood as incredibly elastic during this period.

This elasticity is fundamentally rooted in political desirability. Whereas the professional operates on the basis of formal training and thus is positioned uncomfortably close to bourgeois priorities and hierarchies, the amateur succeeds by virtue of ideological fervor.[12] This is the amateur's political cachet: motives are clearly borne out by actions. Moreover, the amateur never achieves mastery of her area of interest; the amateur is and forever will be a student of the masses. This is precisely Sister Afang's position with respect to Honghua in "Before and after the Performance." As the latter moves from spectator to performer to teacher, the former's position as eternal student is further cemented. There is always more to learn; one can always be better. Just as the yangbanxi are rendered more and more perfect with every subsequent round of revision, the amateur performer is forever perfecting her art—and through it, herself.

This is the essence of the notion of performance as transformation, a formulation that was ultimately neither restricted to the yangbanxi—although, as the pinnacle of the socialist performing arts, they were understood as the most effective tools with which to bring about the desired transformation—nor applicable only to actual novices. In transforming themselves into offstage heroes alongside firefighting brigade team leaders, professionals, too, could lay claim to amateur status. As Xiaomei Chen points out, a number of the professional performers of the yangbanxi rose to political prominence, becoming not simply the portrayers of model heroes, but "model actors" in their own right.[13] As with amateur performers, "it was believed that by acting out the roles of revolutionary characters—that is, by creating the revolutionary other while rejecting the nonrevolutionary self—the actors would be reformed and shed their bourgeois ideology. In concentrating on every body movement and perfecting every operatic tune, the players of the model operas rechanneled their energies toward a revolutionary ideal."[14] But whereas professionals were relatively few in number, (potential) amateurs were everywhere. The great promise of the specifically *amateur* performance movement was one of scale: heroes could be mass (re)produced. Through performance, China could truly become a nation of Li Yuhes and Jiang Shuiyings.

The Logic of Remediation

This desired transformation required and produced the blurring of distinctions between on- and offstage. In light of this and the importance of performance as an intellectual paradigm in contemporary thought, it is perhaps not surprising that scholars have approached the yangbanxi and their position of prominence in everyday life in the Cultural Revolution from this perspective. Both Xiaomei Chen and Ban Wang, for example, address the "theatricalization" of the Cultural Revolution quotidian, essentially arguing that the disintegration of the stage as a distinctly defined, performative space extended the performative logic of the theater to all corners of society.[15] Life is said to have imitated art or even to have become art tout court.[16] As Teri Silvio has suggested in a different context, however, a "performance paradigm" tends to emphasize issues of identification and constructions of "self" in relation to roles at the expense of questions of materiality and relations between persons and objects.[17] And yet, such questions remain crucial and productive both in discussions of overtly performative occasions (onstage) and the everyday (offstage). Consider that yangbanxi protagonists appeared not just in theater, but in nearly every conceivable medium. They could be seen on both small and big screens; their likenesses found their way onto every surface, from mirrors to plates to biscuit tins; and their voices could be heard endlessly over loudspeaker and radio. This was the environment in which amateur performances of the yangbanxi took place in the 1970s. How did amateurs' bodies and embodied voices fit into this saturated media world? As an analytical frame, performance alone does not seem to get at this question. This is the stuff of remediation.

According to Jay David Bolter and Richard Grusin, at its most basic, remediation is "the representation of one medium in another."[18] We might think of the yangbanxi films as remediations of theater or the *Shajiabang* symphony as a remediation of the opera by the same name in this sense. One quickly finds, however, that the linear progression from one medium to another implied in Bolter and Grusin's most restrictive definition is problematic in the context of the yangbanxi, if not generally. It becomes increasingly difficult to pinpoint the directionality of the remediation process. Is the image of Li Tiemei in Shan Lianxiao's poster a remediation of the stage? Of film? Of television? Of photography? Of comic books? Rather than rely on a narrow understanding of remediation, I would turn to Bolter and Grusin's own expansion of the concept, as when they suggest that, in a sense, "*all* mediation is remediation" because "media need each other in order to function as media at all."[19] Ultimately, remediation operates not as a series of vectors from one medium to another, but as a system of media, perpetually defining themselves in relation to one another. In other words, remediation facilitates connections on a systemic order, much like those required by the newborn socialist thing. To the extent that we can approach the current discussion of amateur performance from this vantage, the most pertinent issue becomes: How were other media invoked in the construction of amateur bodies as a medium in its own right?

One of the key media in this regard is sculpture, conjured most directly, perhaps, in the operatic practice of *liangxiang* (striking a pose) at particularly important moments. At their most emblematic, revolutionary heroes are completely motionless, temporarily transposed into the realm of statuary. As Paul Clark notes, this propensity toward the striking of poses, and the formation of tableaux via this practice, was by no means restricted to the yangbanxi or even to the operatic; it was also a general technique favored by Red Guard performers in the early years of the Cultural Revolution. In at least one instance, the connection between this performative practice and sculpture was rendered explicit. "In late May 1967, rebel factions at the China Musical and Dance Theatre and the China Youth Art Theatre joined forces to present *Rent Collection Courtyard (Shouzuyuan)*. This showed remarkable intertextuality, as the 'Rent Collection Courtyard' was a group of sculptures created in 1965 in Sichuan to illustrate peasant suffering in the 'old society.'"[20] From the point of view of remediation, such a development was not so remarkable at all, merely the natural culmination of a commonly employed media association. Indeed, in an indication of just how interconnected the various prominent media of the Cultural Revolution were—and, therefore, how important a systemic understanding of media and remediation is—the *Rent Collection Courtyard* sculptures were, from the beginning, crafted based on live models striking "sculptural" poses.[21] The work also made its way onto celluloid and, perhaps most unexpectedly, onto vinyl, when the film soundtrack was released as an LP in 1966.

In the case of the pantheon of yangbanxi heroes, it was precisely their stationary poses that traveled among all manner of media. We might understand this phenomenon in terms of what Marc Steinberg calls "dynamic stillness" and the "dynamic immobility of the image." Steinberg's point of interest is anime's media mix, in particular its origins in character merchandizing practices related to *Astro Boy* (*Tetsuwan atomu*). Steinberg argues that "it is precisely the dynamic stillness of the image that allows limited animation to generate movement across media forms.... Stilling the movement of animation allows the anime image to connect with other media forms, expanding in the 1960s toward the Japanese media mix."[22] Steinberg places considerable emphasis on the way in which anime, as a form of limited animation, is the product of both motion and immobility. Anime characters move against stationary backgrounds; frames are regularly repeated. As a result, anime is predicated on a notion of "dynamically immobile" images, which are easily transferrable to other media precisely because of their "fixed" quality.

Steinberg's insights into the functioning of the media mix as it pertains to issues of stillness and intermediality are instructive insofar as they help conceptualize the movement of characters—in this case, revolutionary heroes—across media. In their theatrical form, the yangbanxi are also invested in "dynamic stillness" with their dramatic, ideologically weighty use of liangxiang, most instances of which exhibit the hero or heroes' determination and defiance. If characters are physically stationary when they strike their poses, they are by no means removed from the ongoing tensions and progress of the plot or, for that matter, of history. Rather, their stillness is felt as intensity, intensity that propels the character(s), and the work as a whole, forward once the liangxiang is broken. One might suggest, building on Steinberg, that this intensity also fuels the dynamism of the immobile yangbanxi image as well.

Consider, for example, that liangxiang of this kind were reproduced in the form of porcelain statuettes, at least some of which were made at Jingdezhen

Figure 5.2 Statuettes of yangbanxi heroes, early 1970s (*from left*): Yang Zirong, Wu Qinghua, Yan Weicai, and Li Yuhe, 28–32 centimeters. Weltmuseum Wien.

Porcelain Sculpture Factory, the center of high-end porcelain production discussed in chapter 3 (see figure 5.2). The making of these statuettes requires first the sculpting or molding of the clay and its subsequent vitrification in the kiln.[23] Their production is thus a rather apt metaphor for the idealized transformative process of amateur performance: The body and embodied voice of the amateur performer first assume (or are made to assume) the form of the revolutionary icon; then, through the act of performance—itself a substitute for the crucible of revolution—they undergo a kind of transubstantiation, becoming literally the stuff of heroes.

Indeed, this link between the performance of the yangbanxi and sculpture is rendered even stronger by the consistent use of the word *suzao* when describing the process of crafting revolutionary heroes onstage. As Judd makes clear, the prescriptive performance theory of the Cultural Revolution evolved and was fleshed out over time. It was fully articulated by the mid-1970s, when the notion of the so-called three prominences (*san tuchu*)—emphasize the positive characters over the negative, the heroic among the positive, and the single most heroic among these—was combined with the basic task (*genben renwu*) of socialist art, that is, to suzao "proletarian heroic types/images/characters (*dianxing/xingxiang/renwu*)."[24] We may well be tempted to simply translate suzao as "to create" here, as Judd does, but the Chinese has a decidedly sculptural connotation to it, as it can mean both to mold a substance, especially clay, into a representative figure and, by extension, to portray a character in the theater or craft a character in writing. The successful suzao of heroes in the yangbanxi was said to be one of their most significant achievements; every tool at the creators' disposal had been used in this endeavor, and the importance of the continued optimal suzao of these same heroes became the central concern of discourse on amateur performance. Amateurs had a responsibility to suzao these by definition flawless characters as best as they possibly could.

The Fear of the Misfire

To the extent that amateurs were, in fact, suzao-ing or molding revolutionary icons, the medium at their disposal was ultimately themselves: their bodies, their voices, and, ideally, their entire beings. They were aided in this process by a number of tools, not the least of which were the definitive and endlessly repeated professional performances disseminated over loudspeaker, radio, television, and, finally, film. The *People's Daily* editorial that marked the official beginning of the popularization campaign on July 15, 1970, makes a point of noting the usefulness of such representations along with the written experiential accounts of professionals. "In order to study the revolutionary yangbanxi well, one must diligently study the scripts, performance recordings, and related television documentaries of the revolutionary yangbanxi, as well as introductions to the creation of the revolutionary yangbanxi and essays on the experience of performing them, published in newspapers and periodicals."[25] All manner of scripts and performance manuals—specifying everything from staging and set design to costumes and properties to gestures and dance steps—were churned out at this time. Scores were also published in various formats, the most common of which featured only the vocal line of the main arias, but full scores and instrumental/percussion scores were also available. Even as these materials proliferated in the ensuing years, however, the purported perfection of the officially distributed yangbanxi performances continued to provide the most important models in whose image amateurs were to remake their characters and themselves.

In this context, Central Radio broadcasts were especially key. The yangbanxi figured prominently in revolutionary literature and art programs as well as programs dedicated to various dramatic forms. But above and beyond this, a significant block of programming was dedicated not just to the airing of yangbanxi recordings for entertainment purposes but also for explicitly pedagogical reasons. According to its published seasonal radio schedule, on any given Sunday in the winter of 1971–72, for example, Central Radio II broadcast a full seven hours devoted to teaching yangbanxi arias (*jiao chang geming yangbanxi*).[26] Educational programming of the how-to variety became generally more prominent as the Cultural Revolution progressed, but even in the context of this overarching trend the amount of attention paid to the yangbanxi is exceptional and reflects the importance afforded their popularization.[27] Proper engagement with these broadcasts was itself promoted in accounts of the difficult—but ultimately always fruitful—learning process facilitated over radio. Consider the tale of Dengzhan Commune's Ma Xiaode, whose status as a model learner/amateur performer derived first and foremost from his skills as an active listener.

> In order to promote the yangbanxi well, Ma Xiaode, a member of the third brigade's propaganda team, would spend his free time every day, morning, noon, and night, sitting in front of the radio or broadcast [loudspeaker], singing along word for word or, after watching a yangbanxi film, practicing each individual movement. He often practiced until his mouth and tongue were dry and his waist and legs ached. Sometimes, he would practice late into the night, without any thought of resting. After a period of this kind of diligent study and bitter rehearsal, he was finally able to portray Yang Zirong, Guo Jianguang, Li Yuhe, and other heroic characters quite well, after which he received acclaim from the masses.[28]

There is little doubt that people in Ma Xiaode's position—a rural brigade member—would have had the opportunity to hear the yangbanxi "every day, morning, noon, and night," but as a model amateur performer, Ma is called on to do much more than just hear them. He is impelled to listen in a way that is synonymous with bodily sonic reproduction. To listen, here, is to join in the sounding of revolution discussed in chapter 1 and thereby to pursue the (re)production of the model in and out of oneself.

Singing guides—some specifically for the yangbanxi and some for singing in general, with a preponderance of examples from yangbanxi—supplemented radio programming and provide clues as to that programming's likely pedagogical emphases, including the importance of singing "scientifically." *Introduction to the Fundamentals of Learning How to Sing Revolutionary Modern Beijing Opera* (*Geming xiandai jingju changshi jieshao*), for instance, includes a number of anatomical diagrams illustrating the head's resonant cavities and the correct positioning of the soft palate and tongue in order to produce the desired timbre.[29] (See figure 5.3.) The book presents sound production, resonance, and amplification as biological phenomena subject to bodily control. This indicates a vocal pedagogy deeply invested in the demystification and harnessing of sound as the outcome of a physiological process. That physiological process, moreover, is normalized in such a way as to promote a desirable and consistent standard, especially with regard to pronunciation. While there is an acknowledgment of difference at the onset of the pedagogical endeavor—speakers of some southern dialects may have trouble distinguishing *si* from *shi*, for example—everyone should nonetheless

图六、平舌音、翘舌音及舌面音发音时的舌位图

平 舌 音 z、c、s

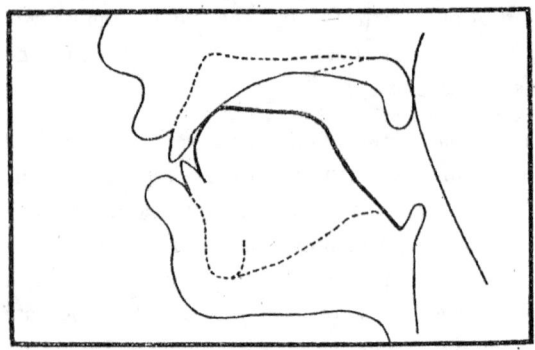

说明：舌尖向前伸，抵住上门牙背后，然后微微
放松，气息从窄缝中摩擦发音。

翘 舌 音 zh、ch、sh、(r)

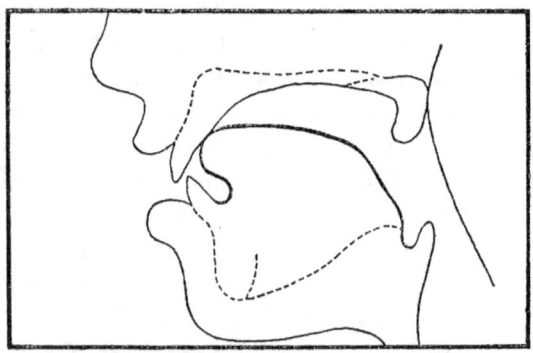

说明：舌尖翘起抵住硬颚最前端（上牙床之后），
然后微微放松，气息从窄缝中摩擦而出。

Figure 5.3 Anatomical diagrams for correct pronunciation. From Xiao, *Geming xiandai jingju xue chang changshi jieshao* (*Introduction to the Fundamentals of Learning How to Sing Revolutionary Modern Beijing Opera*), 24. Courtesy of the Shanghai Library.

be able to reproduce the standard correctly once the training is complete. On top of everything else, the revolutionary hero must be a model for *putonghua*, or, the common language.[30] Maoist ideals must be communicated with perfect *sh*is, *zh*is, and *ch*is.[31] Bodies were thus standardized as the physiological creators of sound and, by extension, the disseminators of a national language. For their part, how-to guides for accompanying instruments, such as the *jinghu*, also worked to standardize instrumentalists' bodily movements, but the accompanist is significantly instructed to pay close attention to the singer's physiological needs in addition to the accompanist's own particularities, a testament to the ultimate primacy granted the vocalist.[32]

This discursive emphasis on the embodied nature of the voice is in keeping with a notion of performance as a transformative technology, which is itself predicated on the assumed plasticity of bodies and individuals.[33] Ban Wang identifies this basic premise as critical to the promulgation of repetitive revolutionary ritual: "The revolutionary rituals appealed to our senses and inner psyches, to our desires, and they worked on the surface of our bodies. They functioned on a cynical premise about individual human beings—on the supposition that the individual's mind and body are malleable, amenable to modeling and shaping by the sensuous medium of a ritual. A person's emotion is capable of being modified and re-educated; one's aesthetic taste and unconscious cravings can be trained, altered, and then pushed in the service of the authoritarian order."[34] Whereas Wang describes ritual as a medium, from the perspective of remediation, it is the malleable individual—who actively molds herself—that is the medium of note here; ritual, like performance, is simply the mechanism through which this molding is carried out. Moreover, the operating assumption is not simply that the mind and body are both plastic, but rather, that the shaping of the latter will necessarily result in the perfectly corresponding shaping of the former, that one can "endlessly reform one's worldview [*shijieguan*] as part of the performance process."[35] This is the logic of labor in thought reform (*sixiang gaizao*) as it is the logic of amateur performance of the yangbanxi: If the body (and voice) are molded in the likeness of a revolutionary paragon, the rest will follow.[36]

The power attributed to the notion of performance as a technology of transformation accounts for the discursive investment in the standardization of that process, but only in part. We might better understand the growing emphasis on the proper way to perform the yangbanxi as indicative, on the one hand, of the precarious position of the model performances' staunchest supporters, that is, Jiang Qing and what would become the Gang of Four, and, on the other hand, a sneaking suspicion that this much-vaunted technology was perhaps not so effective after all. In keeping with the porcelain metaphor, we might call this underlying unease the fear of the misfire—the concern that the transmutation effected in the kiln has gone awry in some way. In the context of amateur performance, the most problematic of misfires are, in fact, not so much imperfectly shaped reproductions of the model heroes (e.g., amateurs singing out of tune) so much as those cases in which vitrification is incomplete: Clay and glaze are not fused and transmuted into porcelain. Despite all hopes and outward appearances, the amateur playing the hero remains just that, an individual *playing* a hero rather than *becoming* one. Appearance (*waibiao*) and essence (*benzhi*), to use two watchwords of Cultural Revolution performance theory, fail to align as they should.[37] That prospect is bad enough, but the greatest difficulty lies in recognizing the misfire if and when it occurs—thus the increasing attention paid to the standardization of performance practice, staging, costuming, properties, and so on. For despite the unsettling notion of a disjuncture between the molding of the body and the concomitant shaping of the individual as a whole, the former remains the preferred way to facilitate the latter. Faced with the possibility of failure, the only recourse here is, paradoxically, to double down on efforts at molding the body correctly, since that can still be at least partially controlled.

But failures we know there were. In a duality that extended beyond the stage and into daily life, appearances could often be deceiving, their disjuncture from essence even leveraged for critique. "A certain tone in singing an aria from one of the model operas, a certain flick of the head in exaggerated parody of one of the central heroes, a clever rewording of a well-known verse could provide an outlet for a largely unspoken but shared sense of the ridiculous."[38] It is no great wonder that the cultural authorities used every tool at their disposal to standardize parodic renditions, exaggerated head flicks, and the like into oblivion. That they did not succeed in doing so should not be surprising: Extreme standardization—or what Alexei Yurchak calls "hypernormalization" in the context of the late Soviet period—has a nasty way of producing new discursive spaces of the very kind it is meant to eradicate.[39] More insidiously for the official transformational project, however, the persistent gap between playing and becoming, the very gap that proved so productive for unofficial and counter discourses, was also embodied in the villains of the yangbanxi repertoire itself.

The Saboteurs in Our Midst

Despite the fact that much if not all of the glory of the yangbanxi was invariably directed at the heroes—and would-be heroes who played them—the performances were not designed to be one-woman or one-man shows. Among the structural tools used to suzao the main heroic character of each work was his or her juxtaposition with other characters, who were dwarfed—sometimes literally—by the comparison. The starkest and therefore most productive contrast was provided by the figure of the class enemy. As Judd explains:

> The negative characters were invariably class enemies, for the most part officers of the Japanese or Nationalist armies or spies. They were few in number, as it was an essential feature of this theory that the positive and heroic

characters must predominate, but their presence was important for both political and dramatic purposes. They were politically necessary because class struggle was at the core of every proletarian drama even if its main line of dramatic conflict lay in the realm of contradictions among the people.... The theory prescribed that the negative characters be created with the primary purpose of revealing the virtues of the hero(in)es, especially the main heroic character. The qualities of the negative characters were of no other interest or purpose in proletarian drama. In order to ensure strong dramatic conflict, the negative characters should be formidably bad, but must not distract attention from the heroic characters, to whom they must give way and whose characterization they must serve to develop.[40]

In the terms of Maoist discourse, we might say that the villain primarily served a dialectical purpose: He—the villain is consistently male—is the antithesis of the hero's thesis; synthesis notably requires them both. But the requisite villain had to be of a rather peculiar type: despicable and cunning enough to put up a good fight yet never so menacing as to throw the triumph of good over evil into any real doubt.

This balance was difficult to achieve but critical to the yangbanxi's propagandistic agenda, lest the works be consistently misread. To wit, one of Jiang Qing's chief criticisms of the version of *Taking Tiger Mountain by Strategy* (*Zhiqu Weihushan*) performed at the conference on Beijing operas on contemporary themes held in the capital in 1964 was precisely that it failed to get the balance right. There had been concerns that the villain of the piece, Vulture (Cuoshandiao), might overshadow the hero, Yang Zirong, from the work's very inception; these fears prompted a series of revisions in Shanghai prior even to the Beijing conference. But Jiang Qing remained dissatisfied with these changes, pointing out that Vulture's scenes were essentially untouched during this process, a fact Jiang attributed to deference to the man playing Vulture, He Yonghua (1922–2006). To truly emphasize the play's heroic characters, Jiang concluded that, despite the actor's talent and skill, the chances for He to shine needed to be excised; Vulture had to become less remarkable in his villainy.[41]

Jiang's preoccupation with Vulture's stature and his position vis-à-vis Yang Zirong is perhaps best understood in the context of the 1958 novel on which the opera was based, Qu Bo's (1923–2002) *Tracks in the Snowy Forest* (*Linhai xue yuan*), and its subsequent film adaptation, both of which appear to have caused worrisome reactions among some readers and viewers. According to Ding Lin, a teacher at Beijing Number 2 Experimental Primary School (Beijing di er shiyan xiaoxue), children were especially vulnerable to Vulture's charms. Ding asserted that children have a "strong propensity toward imitation" (*qianglie de mofangxing*) such that they often reproduce teachers' words and actions as well as fictional character traits in their games and lives.⁴² The child emerges in Ding's account as the malleable learner/viewer/listener par excellence—in other words, as the quintessential amateur performer.⁴³ The playground is the child's stage, as she reenacts what she has seen and heard. But if this is the promise rooted in the figure of the child, Ding Lin reports that in the case of *Tracks in the Snowy Forest* things had gone horribly wrong: Instead of mimicking Yang Zirong as they should, the school's pupils were playing at being the bandits, reproducing their idiosyncratic language and behavior.⁴⁴ The reason? The villains had too many strange tics, tics that both masked the evildoers' reactionary essence and attracted the children's attention. By contrast, the heroes were as bland and uninteresting as could be. In short, the villains were simply too cool, too much fun to play at. The result was ultimately the overshadowing of the protagonist and the inversion of the intended ideological message. This, in a nutshell, is the propagandist's worst nightmare, and though no amount of restructuring and revision could ever completely foreclose this kind of unsanctioned reaction, every attempt was made to restrict the villain's role to essentially that of a foil, a contrastive figure who would not attract any undue attention beyond his dealings with the hero.

This was something of a departure from traditional opera, or at least it was pegged as such by Beijing opera revolutionaries. Gone were the villains one could love to hate; such sentiments were too complex for the understanding of the world promoted by official organs as of the mid-1960s. As one can imagine, this made life difficult for actors who had made a name for themselves playing exactly what was now to be avoided at all costs, namely, memorable, larger-than-life villains. For the famed Yuan Shihai (1916–2002), who was perhaps best known for his portrayal of the infamous historical villain Cao Cao (circa 155–220 CE), learning how to act the villain in a modern opera was essentially a new enterprise, one he finally mastered on his third attempt with *The Red Lantern*'s Captain Hatoyama. As Yuan describes his ultimate breakthrough:

> I [eventually] understood that, when playing a negative character, one should analyze the character's reactionary essence [*benzhi*] from a proletarian perspective; one must possess hatred for the negative character in order to depict [*biaoxianchu*] the negative character's cruel and ruthless reactionary essence. And, most importantly, one must always remember that the purpose of depicting negative characters is to heighten the establishment of the positive characters.
>
> ... Hatoyama is a vicious, cruel character, who has treachery in his heart but thinks himself beyond reproach. He dons a sincere, kind, and worldly

exterior [*waibiao*], but he cannot fully conceal his irascible, empty, and weak nature [*benxing*]. These factors add up to his being a paper tiger. Thus, when I am playing this character, in my heart [*xin li*] I have the following refrain: I must carve out [*kehua*] his "all bark, no bite" [*selineiren*] reactionary essence.[45]

Within the context of Yuan's self-described epiphany, the acknowledgment of Hatoyama's second-tier status vis-à-vis the positive characters comes off as a simple restating of a categorical, official mantra. This is particularly so because of the evident difficulty with which Yuan attempts to explain his creative process. Whereas the relationship between positive and negative characters is provided without any hint of equivocation, the rest of his account lacks such definition; here he ties himself into rhetorical knots.

At issue is the disjuncture between essence (*benzhi*) and outward appearance (*waibiao*). Hatoyama, as a character, is said to be defined by a radical lack of correspondence between the two—which is itself, paradoxically, also described as his essence. He acts one way but is *really* something else: He seems kindly but is vicious; he seems ferocious but is weak. As it turns out, this duality is a trait commonly found in yangbanxi villains; indeed, it is part of what makes them so nefarious. Huang Shiren in *The White-Haired Girl* (*Bai mao nü*) and Nan Batian in *The Red Detachment of Women* (*Hongse niangzi jun*) purport to be good Confucians despite their heinous crimes.[46] The American imperialists in *Raid on the White Tiger Regiment* (*Qixi Baihutuan*) say they want peace on the Korean Peninsula while simultaneously planning their next attack. The villains of the works set during the socialist period are arguably even more two-faced. Huang Guozhong in *Song of Dragon River* (*Longjiang song*) and Qian Shouwei in *On the Docks* (*Haigang*), for example, both reveal themselves to be class enemies hidden in plain sight among the masses. Faced with this kind of foe, for their part the revolutionary heroes further distinguish themselves by not falling for the villains' carefully crafted facades. While everyone else is fooled or even led astray by the enemy in their midst, the hero sees him and his acts of sabotage for what they are—class struggle. The inevitable unveiling of the villain in all his despicableness is one of the hero's chief tasks, and it is made possible by a kind of preternatural discernment, carefully attuned to the underhanded tricks of the wolf in sheep's clothing.

The exceptional ability to see someone for what she *really* is was one of the many things the yangbanxi were supposed to model and teach. This critical skill is described by Tao Youzhi (1935–), a member of the Shanghai Municipal Party Committee writing group, as "penetrating appearance to see essence" (*touguo xianxiang kan benzhi*), which itself is predicated on being able to distinguish between "false appearances" (*jiaxiang*) and "true appearances" (*zhenxiang*). As ever, the key here is the relationship between appearance and essence, when they correspond and when they do not.[47] Tao's attempt at a characteristically dialectical explanation is worth quoting at length.

> Essence and appearance are two different sides of the objective developmental process of things. Essence refers to a thing's nature and internal relations, and appearance is a thing's external form, which we can perceive. Essence cannot be separated from appearance, and appearance cannot be separated from essence. Essence must be reflected via appearance; any appearance is the external manifestation [*biaoxian*] of essence. From this perspective, essence and appearance are mutually related and unified. However, essence and appearance are also distinct, mutually contradictory, and mutually opposed. As essence is stored in a thing's interior, it is relatively stable, but as appearance is revealed on a thing's exterior, it is relatively changeable. That with which people can directly make contact is a thing's appearance. Moreover, appearance may be categorized as true appearance and false appearance. The former directly illustrates some aspect of the thing's essence, while the latter is the distorted and inverted manifestation of essence.[48]

Fang Haizhen, heroine of *On the Docks* and Tao Youzhi's paradigmatic example of a discerning proletarian, is not fooled by these momentary distortions and inversions of the villain Qian Shouwei's capitalist essence. Indeed, Tao goes so far as to suggest that the ability to "penetrate appearance" is, in fact, part and parcel of Fang Haizhen's proletarian "worldview" (*shijieguan*).[49] Thus, taking a revolutionary stand is equated here with a Cultural Revolution *hermeneutics of suspicion*: Although there is a belief in and a desire for a direct correlation between what a person "is" and what that person "appears" to be, one must always be on guard, prepared for those instances in which false appearances might rear their ugly heads.

There proved to be an inordinate number of class enemies hidden in plain sight in the Cultural Revolution. The endless criticism campaigns of senior party officials effectively bore this out. It is most fitting, then, that Tao Youzhi should end his 1974 essay with a discussion of Lin Biao, the Great Helmsman's erstwhile right hand, who was accused of plotting a coup and whose death while fleeing to the Soviet Union in 1971 was a watershed moment for many. Tao draws a connection between Lin Biao and Qian Shouwei: Although they attempted to hide their treacherous inclinations, they were both ultimately found out by perspicacious comrades. The average individual, in molding herself into a Fang Haizhen—through amateur performance, perhaps—is called on to develop this same level of perspicacity, this hermeneutics of suspicion, so that she can ferret out the Qian Shouweis and Lin Biaos in everyday life. But this was easier said than done, if only because, as much as the yangbanxi and officially endorsed readings of them try to persuade us that the shadowy world of the hidden class enemy and his corollary, the undercover hero, might all be neatly squared away, the hermeneutics of suspicion they themselves promote would seem to foreclose that possibility.[50] Appearance and essence are effectively wrenched apart by the repetitive act of interrogating their connection.

In this respect the implications of a widespread hermeneutics of suspicion for the realm of amateur performance are very great indeed. Vigilance against transformative misfires would seem, paradoxically, to guarantee their existence insofar as it maintains a gap between appearance and essence consistent with playing a hero as opposed to becoming one. In truth, the disruptive power of the villain is even more pronounced in this regard by virtue of the modifications to the performance-qua-transformative-technology paradigm his portrayal requires. Whereas the mass (re)production of heroes is an eminently desirable state of affairs, the notion of (re)producing class enemies right alongside them is considerably less so—though it may remain, as we shall see, a dialectical necessity. In the case of the villain, misfires are in fact the goal; the transmutational process is to be intentionally sabotaged. Yuan Shihai's discussion of how to play Hatoyama (quoted at length above) is instructive here insofar as he establishes distance between his essence and that of the Japanese captain. Yuan does not mold or suzao Hatoyama in the medium of his own body, as amateurs are called on to do when portraying heroic figures. Rather, Yuan renders harsh proletarian judgment on Hatoyama even as he plays him. This is not so much a case of performance as a straightforward technology of transformation as it is a real-life invocation of the trope of the undercover revolutionary. If there were a patron saint of villain portrayers it would be *Taking Tiger Mountain by Strategy*'s hero, Yang Zirong, who manages to remain every bit the ardent communist even when he enters the villain's lair in disguise.

Putting these pieces together, this means that a full, amateur staging of a yangbanxi would ideally feature two conceptualizations of performance side by side—as becoming, in the case of the hero, and resolutely *not* becoming, in the case of the villain. The need to discern which was which was not hypothetical, then; it was a tension at the heart of the discourse on amateur performance, confronting individuals on a daily basis. One way of alleviating the tension to some degree was to push the villains offstage as much as possible. Full stagings and even staged excerpts were difficult to perform, requiring considerably more resources than the presentation of a series of triumphant arias, for example, and were, accordingly, the exception rather than the rule. Lacking any rip-roaring arias of their own, villains, therefore, appear to have been given decidedly limited stage time. They are likewise conspicuously absent from official accounts of amateur performances; the figure of the villain is too unsettling to allow onto the pages of *People's Daily* and *Wenhui bao*. Better to whitewash him out of existence.

Try as one might, however, the yangbanxi villain cannot be eradicated, only displaced, for he remains a dialectical necessity: heroes cannot be heroic without adversaries to vanquish. Bumped unceremoniously off the amateur stage, we nonetheless find these villains in the form of a nameless throng of enemies (*diren*) said to oppose the popularization of the yangbanxi at every turn.

> The enemies of the proletariat fear the revolutionary yangbanxi to death and will hate them to their last.... First, they went all out, besieging, cursing, disparaging, and sabotaging; they openly attacked, saying the revolutionary yangbanxi were not good. Their frontal attack was quickly decimated by the high level of political and artistic success of the revolutionary yangbanxi. Later, they tried in vain to weaken the great political educational power and artistic affective potential of the yangbanxi. Some bad people went so far as to use the masses' love of the revolutionary yangbanxi to their advantage, upholding the banner of "performing the revolutionary yangbanxi," in order only to distort, tamper with, and sabotage the revolutionary yangbanxi. This is a tendency in the class struggle on the literary and artistic front that is worthy of our serious attention.[51]

This 1969 *Red Flag* editorial, also reproduced in *People's Daily*, goes on to enumerate some of these attempts at sabotage, the most spectacular of which involve intentionally improper stagings of the works. Despite the nebulous nature of the rank-and-file "bad elements" in society responsible for such performances as described by the official press,[52] their crimes are quite specific: men playing women and vice versa; the reliance on feudal costumes and ornaments even when depicting revolutionaries; the reintroduction of love interests excised from earlier versions; and the use of "makeup, costumes, sets, properties, music, gestures, and choreography to spread the base flavor of capitalism and feudalism, to distort the revolutionary yangbanxi."[53] The perpetrators of these improper acts are the most dangerous of class enemies. They do not attack head on and in plain sight; rather, they infiltrate and corrupt from within. They perform the yangbanxi but do so in such a way as to undermine their status as proletarian models of the arts and a mass technology of (heroic) (re)production. By meddling with precisely those aspects of performance the official discourse is so at pains to standardize, the omnipresent class enemy has the wherewithal to throw the whole system out of whack.

It is nonetheless the case that the class enemy is also crucial to this same system. As unsavory as it would have seemed to the cultural authorities at the time, the (re)production of villains was just as important (if not more so) to the Cultural Revolution enterprise as the (re)production of the heroic masses. The promotion of the yangbanxi as *the* dominant repertoire of the period was often carried out in the name of fighting back against the most high-ranking public enemy at any given time. This was the case when the works first rose to prominence in the years from 1967 to 1969, when former president Liu Shaoqi was the chief target. The surge in writings about the yangbanxi of 1973 and 1974 also coincides neatly with the Criticize Lin Biao, Criticize Confucius campaign, as is the case with Tao Youzhi's essay, discussed above. Finally, in 1976, as the Gang of Four began to attack Deng Xiaoping, defending the yangbanxi was used (unsuccessfully, it would seem) as a rallying point once again.[54] These highly publicized foes notwithstanding, however, just as the amateur performance of the yangbanxi was meant to produce heroes en masse, it had to produce enemies for them to defeat on a similarly large scale. Like their brethren onstage, these enemies had to be adept at hiding their true essence and were necessarily revealed for what they were by a new crop of heroes, fresh from the metaphorical kiln of performance, well versed in the Cultural Revolution hermeneutics of suspicion—until, that is, more enemies were produced out of necessity, repeating the cycle ad infinitum.

What kind of subjectivity reigns in a world filled with endless, potential saboteurs and misfires—that is, in a world where appearance is always threatening to detach itself from essence? What happens to the relationship between the subject and her body, the most obvious manifestation of appearance? In the remainder of this chapter, I want to suggest that the anxiety about distinguishing misfires from successful instances of transformation through performance—and, by extension, hidden class enemies from honest revolutionary heroes—is precisely a function of the amateur performer's relationship to her own body. Detachable appearances all too easily translate into alienated bodies, bodies that ultimately participate in a larger system of (re)mediation. As a medium defined in relation to other media, plastic bodies, molded into heroic characters, become abstract and exchangeable signifiers whose promiscuity is such that the amateur's body does not belong (exclusively) to the amateur. The mass (re)production of heroes also means the mass alienation of amateur bodies.

Unitary Subjects and Promiscuous Characters

From a party organizational perspective, the promise of performance as a technology of transformation was the (re)production, on a national scale, of quintessentially revolutionary heroes in everyday life. Such figures were desirable, I would argue, not just because of their unimpeachable communist credentials and unquestionable (and unquestioning) devotion to Chairman Mao. The supposition that persons and bodies could be molded into perfect alignment also meant that the amateur performer, turned yangbanxi hero, could achieve a kind of wholeness in which her body and being were fully integrated, one into the other. The revolutionary hero embodies this aspiration. *The Red Lantern*'s Li Yuhe is what he does and does what he is: He is always as revolutionary as he seems and never deviates from his nature. Appearance and essence are equated to the point of being synonymous and interchangeable. In short, the yangbanxi hero is everything our porcelain metaphor demands that the hero be: one contiguous and homogeneous substance all the way through. This constitution renders a person's essence visible, that is, accessible and legible, to those in power and precludes the possibility of obfuscation and double-dealing, which constitute the MO of the yangbanxi villain, who lurks where we least expect it. Whereas the villain thrives on the disjuncture between appearance and essence, the hero is the guarantor of their commensurability. The appeal of the idealized amateur is very much in keeping with this idea, that is, the amateur lacks the power (and propensity) to obfuscate that expert training would provide. Rather, she wears her revolutionary fervor on her sleeve in such a way that her naivete also guarantees the correspondence of her essence and appearance. To become the hero through the process of performance, then, not only means transforming oneself into the epitome of revolutionary perfection but also of achieving (or maintaining) a radical unity of being.

I would argue that, in her wholeness, the yangbanxi hero embodies—among other things—one of the great utopian hopes of communism, that is, the (re)integration of the subject, torn to pieces under capitalism. For Marx, of course, the defining experience of the worker in a capitalist society is one of alienation, from one's labor, certainly, as manifested in the commodity form and money, the crystallization of exchange value, but also, by extension, from one's body and self. The worker is alienated from these aspects of her person because they do not belong exclusively to her; they are, rather, implicated in a system of capital far outside her control.[55] Communism promises the rectification of this state of affairs by returning to the individual those parts of herself that previously had been at the mercy of someone (or something) else. To exist in a communist utopia is to be whole (again)—to be human in the fullest sense—in a way that is simply impossible to achieve in a capitalist society. And though no one during the Cultural Revolution claimed to have fully achieved communism—there was, in fact, no end in sight to revolution—yangbanxi heroes nonetheless personified this goal by virtue of their unitary nature.

This claim requires a certain amount of explication, for despite its centrality in Marx's work, the concept of alienation (*yihua*, in Chinese) is conspicuously absent from Mao's writings. It does not appear, for example, in *Quotations of Chairman Mao* (*Mao zhuxi yulu*), better known as the Little Red Book, that most ubiquitous of textual talismans, nor does it appear in the *lao san pian*, the three short texts most commonly circulated and memorized during the Cultural Revolution. Indeed, Mao's lack of concern with alienation is such that it has prompted some to ask whether he was in fact a Marxist at all. As John Bryan Starr points out, however, China's demographic realities prompted Mao and the Communist Party to focus primarily on the plight of the peasantry (the party's power base) rather than that of the small, urban proletariat. This view holds that alienation as a concept was far more relevant to the circumstances of the factory worker than those of the field hand, and since the party's survival was in large part dependent on the latter, alienation fell by the wayside, though Maoism retained the basic characteristics of Marxism as a method, if not as a theory.[56] But even if we accept this line of reasoning, Mao's silence concerning the issue of alienation, in any of its forms, is nonetheless striking.

That being said, one should not confuse this silence with indifference toward the formation of unitary subjects, for while alienation as such may not have been a central issue for Mao, the production of a new (communist) person most assuredly was. Indeed, one might go so far as to argue that this was precisely the point of the Cultural Revolution as an ideological enterprise. The "Sixteen Points" ("Shiliu tiao") decision issued by the central committee on August 8, 1966, as guidelines for the Cultural Revolution, define the movement as, above all, "a new period of socialist revolution" that will "touch people's souls" (*chuji renmen de linghun*).[57] This touch was not to be a gentle caress, but an often violent refashioning of the individual as a whole, body and soul, resulting in the production of the *xinren*, or the "new person," in sync with the new historical age.[58] One of the key technologies at work in this large-scale production was amateur performance, its end goal epitomized by the yangbanxi hero, whose appearance and essence, body and soul are all in line and revolutionary in the extreme. To think of this interest in the unitary in terms of alienation is to suggest that, for all Mao's apparent disregard for the term, the concept nonetheless makes its presence felt in the attention paid to the processes and technologies of subject formation, including amateur performance. The idealized product of these processes and technologies is ultimately a fully (re)integrated, that is, unalienated and inalienable, subject.

But if the body, labor, and self are fused together in the metaphorical kiln of performance, and the subject is therefore made whole (again), the (re)inscription of this new body—which is purportedly coextensive with the individual as an integral unity—in a system of (re)mediation shatters this fantasy of inalienability the moment it is called into being. To the extent that plastic amateur bodies are conceptualized as a medium, that medium is defined as such in relation to others. To return to Bolter and Grusin, "*all* mediation is remediation."[59] Media cannot function in isolation. As we have seen, the characterization of bodies as a medium for yangbanxi heroes is most closely associated with sculpture and, beyond that, porcelain statuettes, but the critical point here is that amateur bodies operate as one medium among many. As a result, whatever sense of particularity is meant to ground the notion of a wholly (re)integrated subject who cannot be equated and exchanged for something or someone else is dramatically undercut. Yoked into a system of (re)mediation, amateur bodies are cast as commensurate with ceramic, vinyl, oil on canvas, and so on. I am not suggesting that these media are actually interchangeable; they each maintain their material specificity to which we must pay appropriate heed. Rather, I am arguing that bodies become thinkable on the same level as these other media and, further, that this conceptual equivalency reproduces that which we see in the capitalist commodity form, that is, the possibility of conceptualizing radically disparate things in terms of a larger overarching notion, like exchange value. Just as the implication of the laborer's body in the capitalist system means that it, in a sense, no longer belongs or is felt to belong to the individual, the implication of the plastic body of the amateur in a system of (re)mediation renders it other; it too becomes alienated from the subject even as performance is intended to bring about its (re)integration.

The enmeshed nature of the yangbanxi in a (re)mediation network makes this broader system of representation, within which the amateur body operates, possible. At the end of the day, however, the transformative technology of performance is also rooted in the abstraction and intermedial promiscuity, in this case, of the character of the revolutionary hero. We have already seen how the dynamic stillness of liangxiang helps propel stationary, sculptural moments in the yangbanxi from one medium to another, but these fixed poses are merely the means through which this dynamism is enacted. The thing that is being moved and reproduced—the whole point of the exercise—is the character, the model into which amateurs are meant to mold themselves. As this intermedial mobility makes clear, the notion of character employed by the yangbanxi is such that they can be dislocated from the confines of plot. Li Yuhe wanders off by himself to grace a vanity mirror, and onstage heroes are called on to carry out new exploits, in sum, to be emplotted anew offstage, as real-life revolutionaries.

In this regard, yangbanxi characters are remarkably similar to those constitutive of anime's media mix, which, as Steinberg notes, operate in excess of any given medium.

> The character is not only materialized in different mediums—celluloid, paper, or plastic—it is also an abstract device that allows for the communication across media forms and media materialities. It is abstract because it is always in excess of its particular material incarnations. The character cannot be reduced to any one of its incarnations but must be thought of both in its material forms and in the ways that it exceeds them. It is this surplus that permits different media and material instances to communicate.
>
> Yet this autonomy from any specific media incarnation does not signal the end to medium specificity; rather, each manifestation of the character foregrounds the distinct properties of the medium in question.... In this respect, the character in its media crossings generates a degree of convergence between media forms around its image, but it also abstracts some of the specificity of each medium and transposes this specificity to other material incarnations.[60]

The character becomes an organizational node within the system of (re)mediation that works to both bring media closer together in communication with one another and expand the system still further, that is, to channel the character's excess into the colonization of ever more media. It is this excess that gives the character the ability to move about the material world, to appear both in a comic book and act as a model for the molding of amateur bodies on the stage. But this excess also means that one incarnation is always haunted by the others. An amateur performer's body transforming (successfully, it is hoped) into a revolutionary hero is never *just* an amateur performer's body. It is, instead, a particular body doubling as an exemplar of an abstraction that can never be fully represented or encapsulated. It is precisely this issue of character excess that accounts for the continued alienation of the amateur performer's body from herself, even as she tries to become an inalienable, unitary subject.

In her study on the "economy of character" of the eighteenth-century English novel, Deidre Lynch speaks to the connection between this excessiveness and the market. She writes of the fear of overly independent characters who do not stay in their intended place, whether within the confines of the novel or without. "The excessiveness that...will subvert the economy of the novel and the ecology of a psychological culture has to do with how characters in England...have propertylike properties. They are objects of merchandising, of commodity tie-ins and spin-offs."[61] At issue is "characters' quality of eerie thing-hood—their quality of being at once 'out there' and 'other-than-us,' the way that, like the commodities in *Capital*, they seem more autonomous, memorable, and real than their makers, our suspicion that their clutter could crowd us out."[62] Characters are unnerving and unsettling in the textual world Lynch examines because they move suspiciously like—and sometimes as—commodities, gallivanting about when we would have them stay put. And just as the commodity reorganizes England's economy in the 1700s, so, too, does this new conception of the excessive character reorient the novel, both in terms of its textual economy and its position vis-à-vis the market, a parallel made concrete in the form of character merchandising, a practice salient to both Lynch's and Steinberg's respective areas of interest.

There is a strong case to be made for understanding the (re)mediation of yangbanxi as a system driven by character merchandising as well. It is the characters, more than anything else, who wend their way from medium to medium, consumer good to consumer good. The same abstracted excessiveness of the character that impels it to migrate in this way, that haunts one representation with the specter of all the rest, also works to inscribe things associated with characters into a system, and therefore an economy, of signification. Comparable but not quite interchangeable, character merchandise of this sort flirts with the exchangeability inherent in the commodity form, if only within the system of (re)mediation itself. The result for the amateur performer is alienation from her own body, which is as much an example of character merchandise as anything else. To the extent that a character's thing-hood has the potential to disrupt, it does so here by turning the amateur body into a thing whose signifying power stems from well outside the individual's control.

Their common promiscuity notwithstanding, however, it is important here to distinguish between the emerging conceptualization of characters in eighteenth-century British fiction as essentially individuals, with inner lives that stretch beyond the confines of the novel, and the approach to characters and characterization in the yangbanxi.[63] For the characters of the yangbanxi are, first and foremost, understood not so much as persons as particular manifestations of generalizable types. We might trace this notion back, once again, to Mao's 1942 "Talks at the Yan'an Forum on Literature and Art" and his explanation, inspired by Lenin, of why the people demand art: "Life as reflected in works of literature and art can and ought to be on a higher plane, more intense, more concentrated, more typical, nearer the ideal, and therefore more universal than actual everyday life."⁶⁴ Characters are not meant to be individuated persons. They are both more and less than that: more because, as exemplars of type, they operate on a higher plane of abstraction and less because this abstraction comes at the cost of particularity and the potential for audience identification. Of course, the classification of characters into types has a long history in China, especially in the realm of the performing arts, where dramatic role types (*sheng* or *mo*, *dan*, etc.) are crucial organizational principles for plays and troupes as well as the deployment of performance conventions. Creating the yangbanxi, especially the operatic pieces of the repertoire, meant grappling with these entrenched role types and reinventing them along sufficiently revolutionary lines. The broad typology that emerged through this process is given voice most famously in the articulation of the so-called three prominences principle, mentioned above. The world of the yangbanxi is essentially Manichean, populated by only three easily recognizable groups: the heroes (*yingxiong*), the villains (*fanmian renwu*), and a select group of characters who demonstrate the capacity for change and growth (*zhuanbian renwu*).

Within this formulation, the hero of any particular yangbanxi is but one example of the proletarian hero type, the sculpting or *suzao* of which was the basic task of socialist artistic production, as we have seen. This leaves the notion of particularity in a rather precarious position, as Fang Yun's treatment of "detail" (*xijie*) makes clear:

> The experience of creating the revolutionary yangbanxi tells us that the use of typical details [*dianxing xijie*] is a powerful artistic method in the sculpting [*suzao*] of the proletarian hero's image [*xingxiang*]. But detail, after all, is detail. It is only a component of a play's overall structure. Only by using the description of detail in service to demonstrating the main issue and sculpting characters, only by adhering to the "three prominences" principle when using detailed description and paying attention to the relations between and among particular details, can we fully make use of the artistic value of the description of detail. There are some authors who do not start from the whole in considering the structural distribution of detail or depart from the main line of contradiction and conflict, attaching all manner of extraneous detail to the heroic character's body. Or they do not distinguish the important from the unimportant, the primary from the secondary, and pad their writing with pretty words. This kind of work resembles a sick tree with a mess of branches and gnarled roots but a short and weak trunk. In this way the contradiction cannot coalesce and the personality [*xingge*] of the heroic character cannot be fully manifested. There are also some plays

that emphasize "stage results" [*wutai xiaoguo*], independently establishing loads of details for "changing characters" [*zhuanbian renwu*] and negative characters or single-mindedly seeking points of interest and spectacle through detail. Thus, the main theme is made insipid and the hero's image is weakened and damaged. These [tendencies] must all be suppressed.[65]

Detail—and, by extension, particularity—is useful only insofar as it helps define the more general type, thus the oxymoronic notion of typical details. By contrast, any element that threatens to take away from the supremacy of the heroic type is rendered dangerously superfluous. And yet, even within the restrictions of this overarching typology, individual heroes are still meant to be compelling as characters, to have personality (*xingge*), for only then can the yangbanxi be truly effective.

This abiding tension is never fully resolved. On the one hand, the typicality of yangbanxi heroes, and thus their intentional generalizability, make them all the more reproducible and intermedially promiscuous. There is no underlying notion here that there can only be one Yang Zirong or Fang Haizhen. There is nothing amiss about the idea of mass (re)producing these figures, since they make no claim of individuality—they are reproducible because they are typical and, conversely, rendered more typical, that is, more abstract, with every instance of (re)production. This emphasis on typicality makes it possible, for example, for a poster attributed to the Central Academy of Craft and Design (circa 1968) to depict two Li Yuhes and two Li Tiemeis within the same frame and for the 1970 National Day parade in Beijing to feature not only yangbanxi floats but also hundreds of people identically dressed as yangbanxi heroes (see figure 5.4). If the repetition of things that should be singular is part of what makes character merchandizing so disruptive to the world Lynch investigates, there are no such expectations here. The more revolutionary heroes there are the better.[66]

On the other hand, however, the abstraction of typicality is always incomplete, for material specificity is never evacuated fully. The hero must ultimately be sculpted out of *something*, and to the extent that amateur bodies are conceptualized as one such *something*, or medium, they in turn circulate as a function of this—albeit always partial—abstraction. In other words, amateur bodies become alienable and, ultimately, consumable within the system of remediation constitutive of the yangbanxi. In the following chapter, I take this argument a step further and suggest that this condition, in which the amateur body is given over, in a sense, to a relational entity, is also shared by the professional. Indeed, it is the professional's body that becomes the most visible terrain on which the tensions between particularity and typicality, medium specificity and abstraction, production and consumption are

Figure 5.4 Mass-producing heroines on the model of *The Red Detachment of Women* in the 1970 National Day parade. From *China Pictorial*, no. 12 (1970): 15.

played out. After all, the production of the revolutionary hero is, more often than not, brought about through the dedicated and repeated consumption of professional performances in all their various (re)mediated forms. Paradoxically, this process, far from achieving the (re)integration of the subject, renders the amateur's body no less an object of consumption than that of the professional star.

6 The Model in the Mirror

At the tail end of 2006, *Time* magazine created something of a stir with its pick for person of the year. Rather than highlight a singular individual who, for good or ill, had made an outsized mark on the planet, as the magazine typically did, it chose instead to honor what it deemed to be an emerging force in the new web economy: You. Not restricted to any one person, this deictic "You" was meant to indicate a legion of independent, solitary, creative actors; it was the "You" of, for, and by YouTube. This "You" was praised "for seizing the reins of the global media, for founding and framing the new digital democracy, for working for nothing and beating the pros at their own game."[1] Although cautioned not to "romanticize all this any more than is strictly necessary," one was clearly meant to feel empowered—and perhaps vindicated—by the notion that one's unremunerated labor qua cat video might well be changing the world.[2] And yet, *Time*'s choice of "You" did not go over well with media critics. Frank Rich, writing for the *New York Times*, spoke for many when he declared it an "editorial pratfall," whose "disingenuous rationale ... was like a big wet kiss from a distant relative who creeps you out."[3] In other words, "You" landed as a painfully obvious gimmick, smacking of "desperation ... to appear relevant and hip."[4] And nothing was quite so gimmicky as *Time*'s cover (figure 6.1): "The magazine's cover stunt, a computer screen of Mylar reflecting the reader's own image, was so hokey that Jon Stewart and Stephen Colbert merely had to display it on camera to score laughs."[5]

It is not my intention to defend, quoting Nora Ephron, such "fantastically cutting-edge and New Media" hokeyness.[6] Nonetheless, I want to suggest that the magazine's decision to pair its use of deixis and apostrophe with a

Figure 6.1 *Time* magazine cover, December 25, 2006.

visual deployment of reflection, of mirroring, is both interesting and deeply relevant to the workings of the Cultural Revolution media environment. One can imagine other ways—old media ways, perhaps, but other ways all the same—of combining rhetorical and pictorial address. James Montgomery Flagg's infamous World War I recruitment poster, in which Uncle Sam gestures at the viewer above the slogan "I WANT YOU FOR U.S. ARMY," is a case in quite literal point (see figure 6.2).[7] What the *Time* cover does, however, by relying on the reflective properties of Mylar, is to insert the viewer into the cover's composition. Looking at the cover, one sees one's own particular face staring out from the frame within the frame: the computer screen/YouTube video. The insertion point is, in this sense, the computer rather than the cover per se. The "You" who is person of the year exists only in cyberspace as a persona facing outward onto real life. Fittingly, then, the Mylar trick worked

Figure 6.2 "I WANT YOU FOR U.S. ARMY," poster by James Montgomery Flagg, 1917, 101.5 by 76 centimeters. LC-DIG-PPMSCA-50554, Prints and Photographs Division, Library of Congress, Washington, DC.

only for those who read the magazine in hard copy; those who perused it digitally had to settle for the word "You" instead of a reflection.

In truth, of course, the old media implicitly snubbed by *Time* have their own share of mirrors and reflective play, often used to tremendous effect. Consider the rise of what Celeste Brusati calls the "still-life self-image" in seventeenth-century Dutch painting, a subgenre characterized by the unexpected appearance of the artist on the reflective surface of an item in an otherwise standard still life. The resulting images trouble facile distinctions between subject and object, person and thing. "Instead of appearing in their pictures as embodied human subjects according to the usual conventions of portraiture, these still-life painters transform themselves into *pictures*, and appear as pictorial images displayed among other representations and products of their art."[8] Consider as well the epistemological and spectatorial complexities afforded by the inclusion of the mirror (in combination with the backside of a canvas) in the Diego Velázquez (1599–1660) masterpiece *Las Meninas* (1656) (see figure 6.3), most famously explored by Michel Foucault.[9]

Figure 6.3 Diego Velázquez, *Las Meninas*, circa 1656, oil on canvas, 3.18 by 2.76 meters. © Museo Nacional del Prado / Art Resource, NY.

Such paintings use mirrors and mirroring as a way of representing spaces, things, and people—most notably, the painter and the viewer—outside the immediate bounds of the pictorial frame. They extend the limits of both representation and representability.

This is not to say that *Time*'s Mylar cover is a poor man's *Las Meninas*, however. Indeed, the two pieces draw on very different logics of viewership in their respective bouts of reflection. The latter invokes a scopic regime of sovereignty by depicting the reflected image of the king and queen of Spain ostensibly posing for the painter seen in the foreground on the left (a self-portrait of Velázquez himself). "That space where the king and his wife hold sway belongs equally well to the artist and to the spectator: in the depths of the mirror there could also appear—there ought to appear—the anonymous face of the passer-by and that of Velázquez."[10] The royals' appearance in the mirror further guarantees their exalted status as both model (for the Velázquez in the frame) and spectator (of the scene unfolding in the painting as well as of the painting itself). If the singular power of the sovereigns is then called into question, it is because what is seen in the mirror comes at the expense of what is not: us. When we look at the painting, are we usurping the position of the monarchs, or are they usurping our own?

On the one hand, it is the ability of *Las Meninas* to provoke such questions that continues to make it so noteworthy some three hundred and fifty years after its inception. On the other hand, one is struck by the limited alternatives (beyond the inclusion of yet another self-portrait) at Velázquez's disposal. In the final analysis, how *does* one paint "the anonymous face of the passer-by"? Can particularity and anonymity ever really be represented in a single, fixed image? The *Time* cover is infinitely more straightforward than *Las Meninas* in part because its much-maligned Mylar allows it to sidestep this question altogether. Anonymity is represented by a changing and changeable reflection—problem solved. Or one problem is solved, at least, while another presents itself: When the reflection in question is our own, what is it that we are meant to see, exactly, when we see ourselves? Can the mirror ensure that we see the right thing? How and at what cost? If *Time*'s recourse to Mylar avoids a host of representational issues, it does so by opening another can of worms when it comes to vision and self-recognition. For, at the risk of repeating myself, it seems clear that the version of ourselves reflected back to us, framed by the computer screen, is intended to be the us of YouTube, not the us of real-life brushing our teeth in the morning. The changeable reflection renders *Time*'s "You" anonymous in the context of its general readership, but it also raises the possibility that we are ourselves changeable as well, that we will see a version of ourselves other than *Time* intended.

I have chosen to begin this chapter with this detour to 2006 because the issues raised by *Time*'s strategic, though perhaps ill-advised, deployment of a changeable reflection are precisely those raised by the unexpected proliferation of mirrors, typically sporting slogans and images on their reflective surfaces, during the Cultural Revolution. My juxtaposition of a US weekly's gimmick and mass-produced objects from a bygone China is meant to be provocative; one would not be wholly off the mark to accuse me of adding gimmicky insult to injury. Still, in my defense, the juxtaposition is meant to facilitate an argument, namely, that the late capitalism of the internet age does not have a monopoly on the dream of individualized media or its unsettling implications for subjectivities, selves, and bodies. As seen in chapter 5, the tension between particularity and reproducibility was rife in the media-saturated world of Cultural Revolution models. Technologies of transformation—amateur performance chief among them—were required to continually reproduce evermore copies of models, taking as their raw material the bodies of the masses. The mirrors of this era are ancillaries to this process but ancillaries of a very peculiar kind: Whereas the notion of performance as a transformative technology turns on the assumption that body and person are one, the mirror reformulates this assumption as a question to be answered with the act of self-recognition. What do I see in the mirror? I see myself. I see myself as model. In brief, I come face to face with my own (re)mediation.

What Does the Hero Look Like?

Lilya Kaganovsky begins her study of male subjectivity under Stalin with a seemingly straightforward question: "What does the socialist realist hero look like?"[11] Kaganovsky's interest is specifically in the dual fantasies of power and weakness at the heart of the new Soviet man (*novyy sovetskiy chelovek*), "that rhetorically constructed figure rising above the Soviet masses to lead them to victory and the bright future of communism."[12] On the one hand, the new Soviet man is characterized by his monumental stature, virility, and strength. On the other hand, beneath this ideal lurks an image of a body spent, broken, and maimed, the remnants of a sacrifice made in the name of historical progress. The superimposition of these two bodily forms—one idealized for its potential, the other esteemed as a sign of promise fulfilled—makes for a complex answer to the question of a hero's looks and points to the value of examining aesthetic tropes we tend otherwise to take for granted. I would therefore put forth a parallel query: What does the Cultural Revolution model look like? Let us begin with the yangbanxi hero.

On the face of it, the answer elicited by this question is quite simple: The yangbanxi hero is tall, muscular, solid, healthy and rosy-cheeked, bright-eyed and smiling, sporting a square jaw and broad shoulders, embodying an aesthetic with so little apparent regard for gender differences that they are often (problematically) said to have been erased.[13] So pervasive is this general aesthetic, in fact, that it is instantly recognizable across media forms and time periods. But whereas the general attributes of the heroic body type may well be indiscriminately reproduced from one yangbanxi character to another, things get significantly more complicated when we attempt to pinpoint that which makes *The Red Lantern*'s Li Yuhe recognizably visually distinct from *Taking Tiger Mountain by Strategy*'s Yang Zirong. Both figures are yangbanxi heroes and therefore models for the general populace, but it would not do to mix up their myriad manifestations with no regard to their integrity as *characters*. Whence that recognizable difference, then?

As I argued in chapter 5, under certain circumstances it was possible for professionals to lay claim to the politically advantageous title of amateur. Like everybody else, they too were permanent students of the masses and engaged in an endless process of self-improvement and transformation spurred on by the performance of revolutionary heroes on stage and screen. The marginalization of training and expertise made for erstwhile professionals who had to rely on new forms and manifestations of cultural capital in order to distinguish themselves. Indeed, dramatically turning one's back on the trappings of bourgeois professionalism and embracing the more egalitarian ethos of the proletarian amateur was arguably one of the best ways for performers to acquire such cultural capital in the late 1960s. To wit, the amateur mantle fell to a great variety of individuals with tremendously divergent backgrounds whose performances differed widely with regard to artistic refinement (an admittedly bourgeois metric, to be sure). Nearly all actors, whether bona fide amateurs or no, held a similar position vis-à-vis the (heroic) character they portrayed: They embodied them—*became* them— onstage with an eye toward being them offstage. There was one set of exceptions to this rule. Those actors who helped develop the yangbanxi or made them famous—Qian Haoliang (Hao Liang) (1934–) as Li Yuhe, Tong Xiangling (1935–) as Yang Zirong, and Yang Chunxia (1943–) as Ke Xiang in *Azalea Mountain* (*Dujuanshan*), to name just three—could boast a slightly more reciprocal relationship with the characters they played. Performing for these actors was not simply a matter of molding their bodies and selves according to the model; rather, they had a hand in forging the model itself. In a sense, *they* were the mold that begat the model in the first place: The original instance of character embodiment was, ultimately and by necessity, predicated on their own image. In short, this small group of actors made the models as much as the models (re)made them.

What, then, does the yangbanxi hero look like? He looks like the actor who first embodied him. And lest this answer be deemed trite, I hasten to add that there is no a priori reason why this should be so. This particular connection between character and actor's body is produced and endlessly reinforced; it is not given. There is no inherent reason why a figural representation of Li Yuhe need look like Qian Haoliang. In the abstract, Li Yuhe can look like anyone; indeed, the notion of amateur performance as a mass technology of transformation is predicated on this possibility. An amateur Ke Xiang need not have Yang Chunxia's distinctive hairstyle to *be* Ke Xiang.[14] And yet, more often than not in practice, the remediation of the yangbanxi hero as a character is also the remediation of the originating actor's body—of both the mold and the model, as it were. It is as though the particularity required to make a yangbanxi hero more than an immaterial type is taken from these individuals' bodies, a particularity that is never truly given back, even as that character then moves from one medium to another.

One might say that character and originating body adhere in such a way that the reproduction of one comes to necessitate the reproduction of the other. The initial, staged moment of adhesion is not the issue, for performance, as we have seen, is ultimately idealized as being: In the moment of performance proper, Qian Haoliang *is* Li Yuhe. But it turns out that, in the case of the professional who develops the role, the reverse is also true: In a very real sense, Li Yuhe is also Qian Haoliang. This identity is perfectly legible—and desirable—during the actual performance. The difficulty arises when Li Yuhe, as a character, begins to move beyond the particularity of one body on one stage. As Li Yuhe flits from medium to medium he takes Qian Haoliang's body with him. We might think of this as a kind of bodysnatching. In essence, Li Yuhe commandeers Qian Haoliang's body and takes it "outside" him. Representations of the hero double as representations of the actor, who becomes abstracted from himself insofar as he is defined by and *as* a system of representation. At this point, Qian Haoliang's body ceases to be his alone. It belongs instead to the system of remediation as a whole. And this is precisely the rub, for while Li Yuhe may have no expectation of singularity, Qian Haoliang does, such that endless repetition and remediation ultimately changes what we mean by "Qian Haoliang" and our understanding of the relation of this proper noun to a body that is at once particular and iterable ad infinitum.

To the extent that this is the case, technologies of yangbanxi remediation also operate as what might be called "technologies of stardom."[15] The invocation of stardom in a socialist context is perhaps counterintuitive. As Krista Van Fleit Hang puts it, "the term 'film star' conjures up associations of luxury, fame and leisure that seem to contradict much of communist ideology." And indeed, "mainland Chinese actors and actresses in the 1950s and 1960s were not referred to as film stars (*dianying mingxing*); like most professionals in the Maoist period they were called workers, more specifically, film workers (*dianying gongzuohe*)."[16] This shift in nomenclature notwithstanding, as Van Fleit Hang herself and others have argued, many technologies of republican-era stardom were consciously replicated after 1949 for the promotion of PRC revolutionary models.[17] "The cultural establishment recognized these [star] images could be harnessed to engage in work that was paradoxically quite similar to that from the Hollywood tradition: using the star image to 'sell.' In this case it was not cigarettes or face cream, it was communist ideology."[18] More important than the parallel deployment of stars or models to persuade is, for our purposes, the fact that both were produced through the same basic technologies of stardom (including various forms of print publicity) and therefore that both have the same fundamental structure. Neither the star nor the model is forged as a singular, integrated subject. The star/model is rather, in the words of Richard Dyer, "a complex configuration of visual, verbal and aural signs."[19] To suggest that yangbanxi remediation produces stars, then, is to suggest that the professional yangbanxi role originator is best considered not as a person, but as a remediated system of signification unto herself as well as a structuring force within the Cultural Revolution media environment writ large.

Mirror, Mirror on the Wall

Turning our attention to the average person, the relevant question is not one of stardom, exactly, but rather of access to the tools of becoming. How does one gain entry to the mediated economy of signification in such a way as to (temporarily) usurp the star's position as embodied model *without* becoming a mere configuration of signs oneself? Performance, in all its myriad amateur forms, would appear to offer one avenue of response. In addition, much like *Time* magazine's use of a changeable reflection on its 2006 person of the year cover, the mirror also offers a solution to the first half of this problem, if only momentarily. More precisely, I want to draw attention to the proliferation of mirrors produced during the Cultural Revolution adorned with representations of yangbanxi heroes, calligraphy, slogans, and other forms of politically potent imagery/discourse. Judging by the collection of mirrors on display at the Jianchuan Museum Cluster's Museum of Red-Era Mirrors (Hongse niandai jingmian guan), which opened in Anren County, Sichuan, in 2009, this type of decoration spanned mirrors of various sizes and quality. The collection is almost entirely composed of wall-hanging mirrors (*gua jing*), though small, rotating tabletop mirrors (with stands), designed to function as part of larger vanity sets, are also on display elsewhere in the museum complex. (These standing tabletop mirrors are particularly notable for having decoration on both the backside as well as the reflective surface.) Such design variations notwithstanding, it is clear from the truly massive number of mirrors held by the Jianchuan Museum Cluster as a whole that the mirror face was an important medium for iconographic reproduction and dissemination in the Cultural Revolution.

It should not be surprising, perhaps, that this was the case; politically charged imagery, broadly conceived, seems to have colonized the surfaces of many—if not most—of the objects that made up the Cultural Revolution–era world of things. As I argued in chapter 3, this process was deeply intertwined with the problematics of display, both in terms of the mechanics of showing off commodities in shopwindows and the productivist reinvention of the decorative arts, including porcelain sculpture. Even in light of these larger trends and issues, however, that the *mirrored* surface should emerge as particularly important seems noteworthy, if only because of the mirror's association with outward appearance. Many of the service industry practices and goods that drew the most ire from Red Guards in the latter half of 1966, after all, were cosmetic in nature. One thinks of the problematic class status afforded lipstick and nail polish, manicures and hair perms, for example, all of which not only tells us something about the intersection of femininity and the bourgeois but also points to a broader class politics of self-presentation more generally.[20] To spend too much time worrying about one's looks—one's appearance rather than one's substantive contribution to the revolution—was behavior associated with the nefarious class enemy, not the righteous proletarian worker. (To be clear, I am not suggesting that workers and peasants were unmindful of sartorial, hygienic, and cosmetic norms, just that such mindfulness was not foregrounded as a hallmark of their class status.)[21]

The story of Chen Xiumei, a middle school student from Guangdong, which appeared in *People's Daily* on May 29, 1973, further speaks to the ideological taint and suspicious nature of protracted mirror gazing, even after the heyday of Red Guard enthusiasm had passed. After repeatedly catching her daughter staring at her reflection, Xiumei's mother becomes concerned that Xiumei is overly enamored with making herself up (*zheime ai daban*), especially for her young age. As it turns out, however, Xiumei's motives are entirely correct and wholly in keeping with the spirit of Lei Feng (1940–62), the famously diligent and conscientious model soldier. Xiumei has been practicing her English in front of the mirror so as to perfect her pronunciation through visual cues.[22] That Xiumei's behavior is ultimately deemed not only acceptable but exemplary speaks to the mirror's ambiguous politics. While the object itself had acquired a certain bourgeois valence, especially when paired with a female or effeminate gazer, under certain circumstances, a reflection could also be put to proletarian use, including, by 1973, for purposes of English-language acquisition. In light of this ambiguity, one might reasonably expect mirrors to have found their way into upstanding revolutionary homes but to have done so in a manner that minimized their presence. Decoration or ornamentation of any kind seems counterintuitive from this perspective. And though we might read the inclusion of a yangbanxi hero on a mirror face as a straightforward effort to rehabilitate an otherwise politically questionable object, more is going on here than initially meets the eye.

In the first instance, mirrors were very discursively rich objects long before acquiring their problematic bourgeois associations in the Mao era. Of most relevance to the current discussion is the fact that mirrors made of plate glass, a material first introduced to China by the French in 1699, were emblems of European technical advancement in the eighteenth and nineteenth centuries.[23] The modern—and in some cases, modernist—valence of both plate glass and plate-glass mirrors continued well into the republican period.[24] Oil painting on glass, including mirrored glass, emerged alongside technical developments in these materials as a new form of decorative art made both for export (chinoiserie) as well as domestic consumption: "Occidenterie," as Kristina Kleutghen puts it.[25] This genre of so-called *bolihua* encompassed French and German practices of reverse-glass gilding and painting (*verre églomisé* and *Hinterglasmalerei*, respectively) in addition to the practice of painting on the glass sheet face.[26] In short, *bolihua* referred to artistic engagements with glass as a material support and medium in a way that quite clearly set the stage for the mirror figures seen in the Cultural Revolution. Despite this fundamental connection, however, it must be said that—based, once again, on the Jianchuan Museum collection—the more recent, mass-produced pieces differ from their predecessors not only with regard to their particular iconography, as one would expect, but also with regard to their status (or lack thereof) as objets d'art. Whereas *bolihua* are first and foremost conceived as *paintings* and only secondarily as table screens or other components of interior design/decoration, Cultural Revolution mirrors primarily operate as *mirrors*, as objects that should be used in order to verify, study, and correct that which is revealed in its depths. (It is in this sense that the figures on these artifacts may be said to "ornament," "decorate," and "adorn," rather than constitute the artifacts as works of art to be appreciated solely or even primarily on aesthetic terms.) More precisely, these kinds of mirrors helped facilitate complex processes of subject (re)formation by virtue of a very carefully constructed scopic regime, traces of which are seen in their distinctive ornamentation.

Mirror gazing, as in the case of Chen Xiumei, could be beneficial to self-improvement projects under the right circumstances, even if such behavior was uncomfortably close to a stereotypically female, bourgeois narcissism and superficiality. But whereas Xiumei's interactions with a physical mirror are meant to standardize her English-language accent thanks to the visibility of her mouth and tongue the object affords, most mirrors appearing in the textual record of this period do so as tools of *ideological* self-improvement. This should not be altogether surprising. Mirrors had long been a topic of poetic rumination and a potent metaphor for self-cultivation, among other things, in the Chinese literary tradition.[27] The mirror is a favorite trope of Western literatures as well, particularly in relation to explorations of trompe l'oeil aesthetics and mise en abyme.[28] It goes without saying that the mirror has also been a historically apt figure for mimetic impulses, up to and including those at work in the realist—and arguably, the socialist realist—novel. The idea that writing both could and should hold a mirror up to society, thereby exposing its ills and instigating change, became something of a critical realist cliché. During the Mao era, however, rhetorical turns to the mirror tended to focus not on the appropriate social role of literature and art, but rather on the need for individual introspection, self-fashioning, and self-knowledge.[29] Repeated calls to "*zhao jingzi*" or "look in the mirror" were paired with directives to "*cha sixiang*" or "search one's thinking" for deficits in revolutionary outlook and remnants of bourgeois influence. Mirrors, in other words, were key players in Maoist discourse concerning the ideological perfectibility of the individual as well as the constant surveillance of the self required to attain such perfection.

Maoist practices of ideological self-censorship and reform are well known, many dating to the Yan'an Rectification movement (Zhengfeng yundong) of the early 1940s.[30] Of these, the most (in)famous is doubtless the foregrounding of *public* acts of criticism and confession. "With the Yan'an Rectification, the party institutionalized a process for re-education that centered around not just reading and discussion of canonical texts but also public criticism (*piping*) and self-criticism (*ziwo piping*). Public criticism entailed public humiliation that psychologically broke down the 'guilty' culprit, forcing him to recognize his sins and write them down or publicly acknowledge them."[31] As Jie Li has persuasively demonstrated, the writing and public performance of self-criticism, which was repeatedly deployed throughout the 1950s and 1960s before culminating in the Cultural Revolution, built on earlier confessional genres in a way that continues to impact discussions of guilt and historical responsibility in the PRC well into the twenty-first century.[32] Unlike, say, the trope of steel tempering (*bai lian cheng gang*), which turns on the notion that (class) struggle is ideologically formative and purifying, the invocation of the mirror as an implement of self-examination—and therefore, inevitably, of self-criticism and self-reproach—turns on making ideological deficiencies visible both to oneself and, by extension, to the party/Mao.[33] In this sense the mirror, as a tool of visualization, gestures toward what Daniela Bleichmar has called—albeit in a very different context—a "visual epistemology," that is, "a way of knowing based on visuality, encompassing both observation and representation."[34] To make deficiencies visible is to make them knowable. Once known, these shortcomings can/must be corrected.

To that end, consider the folksy wisdom, attributed to a Shandong peasant, that appeared in a short piece in *People's Daily* in late 1965: "A mirror is a truly wonderful thing. Throw it just a glance, and you'll know whether or not your face is clean. If there's dirt on your face, you can quickly wash it away. Looking in the mirror is indeed important; it's looking and not washing that's not okay. Even if you look in the mirror several times every day, if you never wash, your face will just keep getting dirtier."[35] Despite this statement's quotidian veneer, the turn to cleanliness and hygiene is exceptionally loaded. Specifically, the emphasis on the need to regularly wash one's face in order to keep it unblemished harkens back to one of Mao's key statements, made at the Seventh Party Congress in April 1945, on the importance of self-criticism as an ideological and political practice. It is worth quoting here at some length.

> Conscientious practice of self-criticism is still another hallmark distinguishing our Party from all other political parties. As we say, dust will accumulate if a room is not cleaned regularly, our faces will get dirty if they are not washed regularly. Our comrades' minds and our Party's work may also collect dust, and also need sweeping and washing. The proverb "Running water is never stale and a door-hinge is never worm-eaten" means that constant motion prevents the inroads of germs and other organisms. To check up regularly on our work and in the process develop a democratic style of work, to fear neither criticism nor self-criticism, and to apply such good popular Chinese maxims as "Say all you know and say it without reserve," "Blame not the speaker but be warned by his words" and "Correct mistakes if you have committed them and guard against them if you have not"—this is the only effective way to prevent all kinds of political dust and germs from contaminating the minds of our comrades and the body of our Party. The reason for the great effectiveness of the rectification movement, the purpose of which was "to learn from past mistakes to avoid future ones and to cure the sickness to save the patient," was that the criticism and self-criticism we carried out were honest and conscientious, and not perfunctory and distorted. As we Chinese Communists, who base all our actions on the highest interests of the broadest masses of the Chinese people and who are fully convinced of the justice of our cause, never balk at any personal sacrifice and are ready at all times to give our lives for the cause, can we be reluctant to discard any idea, viewpoint, opinion or method which is not suited to the needs of the people? Can we be willing to allow political dust and germs to dirty our clean faces or eat into our healthy organism?[36]

The easy slippage between "dust" (*huichen*) and "germs" (*weishengwu*) in these metaphors of psychic housekeeping effectively pathologize bourgeois influence and intra-party dissent.[37] As a result, within this unsettling framework, the Shandong peasant's mirror doubles as a microscope—an implement of visual epistemology, if ever there was one—rendering invisible threats visible in order that they might be properly eliminated.

If, strictly speaking, looking in the mirror was a matter of seeing the heretofore unseen—of visualizing the previously unknown—and acting appropriately in response, then at its most basic, this mode of mirror gazing was also fundamentally comparative in nature. Identifying that which is deficient and extraneous (dirt being essentially "matter out of place") requires a notion of the proper and healthy. As Mary Douglas famously put it, "Where there is dirt there is system."[38] In other words, the mode of visual self-inspection described above and concretized in the form of the mirror implicitly requires a positive standard or model against which to measure oneself and what one sees. This understanding of the mirror as a tool of prescriptive comparison is perhaps most famously articulated in an aphorism attributed to Emperor Taizong (ruled 627–650) in Tang dynastic histories: "If you use bronze as a mirror, you can adjust your robes and cap; if you take the ancients as a mirror, you can understand the mechanisms of rise and fall; if you take other people as a mirror, you can discern the mechanisms of success and failure. I always keep these three mirrors in order to avoid erring."[39] The notion of taking something *as* a mirror (*yi XX wei jing*) has been extraordinarily long-lived, persisting to this day, but aside from its longevity, what is particularly noteworthy for us here is this formulation's implication that the most powerful and profound mirrors are not actually physically reflective surfaces.

In 1962, for example, one Zhang Weici explicitly referenced Taizong and declared that "the proletarian version of 'taking other people as a mirror' guarantees that we will be victorious in all our work." What was this proletarianized process, exactly? "We take the criticism and ideas arising from the broad masses as our 'mirror' in order to discern the 'successes and failures' of socialist revolution and construction."[40] Additional mirrors could be made out of the likes of Norman Bethune (1890–1939), Zhang Side (1915–44), and the Foolish Old Man.[41] But arguably the brightest mirror of all was that created by Mao Zedong Thought.[42] In each of these cases the mirror features as a rhetorical figure for the standard against which continuous ideological self-assessment should be made. A 1971 account of Lüda cadres going to the masses says as much when, after quoting Mao's 1945 discussion of dusting and face washing, the cadres are praised for "taking the vanguard thought of the masses as their 'mirror,' diligently examining themselves by comparison [*duizhao jiancha*], and seeking out the shortcomings [*chaju*] in their own thought. They consciously struggle and reform themselves."[43] To the extent that these non-mirror mirrors are sites of self-reflection, then, it is by displaying the gazer as she ought to be rather than as who she is, so that she can be remade according to that idealized image.

Gateway to Utopia

Given that metaphorical mirrors were meant to serve (prescriptively) as loci of aspirational comparison and unremitting self-improvement, we should approach actual reflective surfaces in similar terms. Cultural Revolution mirrors operated within and produced a scopic regime—a way of seeing/knowing—consonant with the contemporary deployment of the mirror as metaphor. Indeed, it seems likely that discourse and the particularities of person-thing interactions were mutually constitutive. The utopian aspects of mirror gazing are especially noteworthy here, for although Maoist practices of confessional self-(re)formation are typically cast as a form of endless critique and self-censorship, they are predicated on a notion of human perfectibility. In order for the mirror—real or imagined—to facilitate a process of ideological growth, a reflection must be seen and understood as an ideal, a goal to pursue, a model to reproduce. This substitution of the "as if" for the "as is" recalls Evgeny Dobrenko's analysis of the political economy of socialist realism as that which produces socialism by dint of representation.[44] (I made a related argument in chapter 4 about the function of language in Cultural Revolution efforts to diffuse the power of the commodity fetish.) The mirror spatializes this generalizable mode of utopian exchange in a unique and personalized way.

On the one hand, we might attribute this ability to the peculiar status of the mirror object itself as a purveyor of heterotopia, defined as "a kind of enacted utopia in which the real sites, all the other real sites that can be found within a culture, are simultaneously represented, contested, and inverted."[45] As heterotopia, the mirror finds itself, conceptually and culturally, at the center of everything—even, in our case, at the center of the no-place called communism. More to the point, the mirror renders that no-place fleetingly visible, temporarily situating the viewer therein, with tremendous consequences for both real and imagined spaces.

> In the mirror, I see myself there where I am not, in an unreal, virtual space that opens up behind the surface; I am over there, there where I am not, a sort of shadow that gives my own visibility to myself, that enables me to see myself there where I am absent: such is the utopia of the mirror. But it is also a heterotopia in so far as the mirror does exist in reality, where it exerts a sort of counteraction on the position that I occupy. From the standpoint of the mirror I discover my absence from the place where I am since I see myself over there.... The mirror functions as a heterotopia in this respect: it makes this place that I occupy at the moment when I look at myself in the glass at once absolutely real, connected with all the space that surrounds it,

and absolutely unreal, since in order to be perceived it has to pass through this virtual point which is over there.[46]

Chinese trompe l'oeil practices, in which mirrors feature prominently, play with these spatial dynamics, often in the context of interior decoration, by creating unreal spaces that are momentarily taken as real.[47]

The actualization of utopian space is only part of the mirror's magic, however. The difference between the strategically placed perspectival painting or facade and the strategically placed mirror is the insertion of the viewer, by way of reflection, into the unreal space the latter produces. If the mirror acts as a heterotopic gateway to a would-be paradise, it is a very personalized one, tailored, by virtue of its reflective properties, to the individual(s) gazing at, into, and through it at any particular time. It is precisely this aspect of the mirror—the changeability of its reflection—that allows it to represent anonymity so effectively, whether on magazine covers or on living room walls. The key to actually opening the gateway, on the other hand, lies not with the object as such, but with the gazer's ability to recognize the reflection as a version of herself. Without such a moment of recognition, the gazer cannot be transported through the looking glass or undertake the prescribed regimen of self-improvement being demanded of her. In order for the mirror to render me visible to myself, I must register the gaze meeting my eye as my own. It is this eyeline match with myself that ultimately makes the mirror heterotopic as opposed to, say, a straightforward window on utopia: The line between the real and unreal me blurs. Out of this repeated blurring, it is hoped, comes a positive transformation that takes as its end goal the model individual, the idealized socialist hero of the moment. As we have seen, the juxtaposition of self and model was a widely implemented technique meant to facilitate processes of comparison, careful examination, and heightened vigilance of one's thoughts and actions. The remarkable thing about the mirror as a site of such juxtaposition is that the model is ultimately one's unreal self. The model is me, and, arguably, recognition of this fact is what makes everything else possible.

Myself as Model

The consequences of this recognition of the self as model extend well beyond the immediate practices of self-improvement. Specifically, there is another mode of transformation at work here that is pictorial as well as ideological. For all of its ability to unsettle and produce new kinds of space(s), the mirror is also a surface, and mirror gazing therefore involves both the transposition of the self into utopia and the flattening of the physical self from three to two dimensions. The recognition that the figure in the mirror is me also renders me an image, and images exert power differently than bodies. As Brusati contends in her discussion of Netherlandsish still-life self-images, the appearance of self-portraits in canvases primarily depicting objects is bound up with the power that emanates from *being an image* in the seventeenth century, a power typically afforded patrons rather than still life painters.[48] In a time of limited iconography and access to representation—in this case, a time before the age of mechanical reproduction—to be an image was a heady thing, and the reflection was a particularly potent vehicle for image making.

Given our earlier exploration of socialist stardom, it seems especially incumbent upon us likewise to situate mirrors and their imaging effects within the broader Cultural Revolution media environment in addition to the Maoist tradition of ideological self-improvement. From the vantage point of the former, the mirror is more than a heterotopic gateway to a communist-inflected no-place and ideal self. It also emerges as an access point to the complex of representational technologies that make socialist stardom possible. This is not to say that looking at oneself in the mirror could make one a star. Rather, to the extent that being reflected means becoming an image, mirror gazing raises the specter of oneself as a constituent part of the larger, already existing representational system that is the star/model. In chapter 5, I examined the alienating implications of the mass (re)production of models through the transformative process of theatrical performance. Those implications play out in a fully embodied realm both on and off stage. The mirror affords its gazer an image-making process, complementary to the theater, in that it permits her to become formally equivalent to the figural representations of models—and the professional bodies they effectively hijack— endlessly reproduced in newspapers, books, and posters as well as on the surfaces of all manner of material objects, including, fittingly, mirrors. The existence of mirrors featuring the likenesses of models of the kind shown in figure 6.4 brings the formal affinity between the reflection and the visual stuff of stardom into particularly stark relief. Another instance of creating meaning through juxtaposition, the inclusion of figural models on a material support whose reflective properties give it the capacity to make new images of its own suggests that, in this circumstance at least, becoming a model and becoming an image may be much the same thing. More precisely, one might say that becoming an image is a necessary precondition to becoming a model.

The notion of mirror gazing as image making also notably brings us back to the question of how one sees oneself. Images are ultimately made to be seen; they require and beget scopic regimes in the course of being images. It is this simple characteristic that accounts for the so-called pictorial turn in the humanities as "a postlinguistic, postsemiotic rediscovery of the picture

Figure 6.4 Standing mirror with character from *The Red Detachment of Women*, 1970, 19 centimeters. Weltmuseum Wien.

as a complex interplay between visuality, apparatus, institutions, discourse, bodies, and figurality. It is the realization that *spectatorship* (the look, the gaze, the glance, the practices of surveillance, and visual pleasure) may be as deep a problem as various forms of *reading*."[49] In the particular case of Cultural Revolution mirrors, there is little doubt that the gaze of the beholder is prescriptively burdened with aspirational, utopian politics. I submit that the *actualization* of this politics, however, is predicated on the recognition of one's image as oneself and oneself as one's (idealized) image. To frame this would-be equivalence in terms of image is to highlight the specular mechanics that render this moment of recognition both possible and desirable within official Cultural Revolution discourse.

In this context, a mirror with a model decal must be understood as much more than a historical oddity. Rather, a piece like that seen in figure 6.4 encapsulates the dominant scopic regime—as well as, arguably, the media environment of which it is a part—in miniature. To that end, it is significant that the model in the mirror is explicitly doubled here, as is the act of aspirational substitution/becoming it exacts. The version of myself I see reflected back at me—myself as image—is of a very particular kind, itself predicated on a relation of equivalence with the figural model featured in the lower right of the mirror. The doubling and juxtaposition of models on/in the mirror creates a sense of exchangeability, and crucially, because the viewer must volunteer her own likeness to the process in order to make it go, that sense of exchangeability is predicated on the viewer's ability to recognize herself as the mirror would have her be. In other words, in order for the mirror to function in the manner I have been describing, the mirror gazer must learn to see in the prescribed way. Only then can she become her best, model self. Luckily, the model decal constitutes something of a guide for what this model should look like. Indeed, to the extent that mirrors of this kind make images, they are structured in such a way as *to be about* how to see, even as they fulfill their functional purpose, namely, facilitating ideological self-improvement and correctness. That is to say, they are essentially what W. J. T. Mitchell calls "metapictures."

Metapictures are exactly what they sound like: pictures of pictures. In coining the term, Mitchell identifies a number of different types of metapictures.[50] One thing they all have in common is their ability to visualize what it means to be or interact with a picture.[51] As such, metapictures lend themselves uncommonly well to philosophical ruminations on the limits and stakes of representation; they picture theory, as it were. Again, the possibility of a fundamental difference in the workings of images vis-à-vis language helps account for the increased scholarly interest in such concepts as spectatorship and visuality at the turn of the century, and metapictures speak to these concerns directly. Somewhat at odds with their intellectual richness, however, metapictures were also a favorite tool of Maoist iconography in the Cultural Revolution, as Francesca Dal Lago has convincingly shown.[52] They had the advantage, within this latter framework, of demonstrating the manner in which the thorny work of interpretation should be done. In this sense, metapictures function as images complete with their own instruction manual. While this internal interpretive mechanism is by no means all-powerful, it is unquestionably prescriptive and, in the case of our mirrors, has everything to do with the ongoing construction of politically correct, perfectible selves. Since these selves are themselves images and therefore part of the broader media environment, these mirrors in essence show gazers how to *see* as well as how to *be*.

Cultural Revolution mirrors, especially mirrors adorned with models, stand out as particularly potent objects within the era's world of things. They function as personalized gateways to utopia, powered by acts of self-recognition and aspiration; lend their reflectiveness to metaphors of ideological self-censorship; and transform people into images. In this last role, they also become points of entry through which an individual might gain access to the media environment of the age. Indeed, these mirrors offer up the system of mediation in which they participate in miniature. The metapictures they produce allow them this remarkably recursive structure: to gaze into such a mirror appropriately—to see oneself as one should be—is to (re)produce oneself as an image, alongside one's own (fractured) subjectivity, on a par with those of the endlessly reproduced and reproducible star/model. It is, to echo Jie Li's use of Deborah Poole's term, to insert oneself into a "visual economy," if not a more general "media economy," forged in relations of equivalence and exchange: myself as model.[53]

Coda

The Jianchuan Museum Cluster, where I spent some time in the winter and spring of 2013, is a remarkable place. As I have detailed elsewhere, the museum complex is the brainchild of the real estate mogul Fan Jianchuan (1957–).[1] In fact, all of the items displayed in the ever-growing cluster of museums are from Fan's private collection. On the one hand, from this perspective, Fan's museological enterprise is a testament to the importance of individual collector/curators in the construction, preservation, and exhibition of China's recent past.[2] And Fan himself takes this responsibility very seriously. The Jianchuan Museum Cluster's motto makes this quite plain: "To collect lessons for the future; to collect war for peace; to collect disaster for tranquility; to collect folklore for heritage."[3] Fan's collection is thus meant to be for the benefit of all. On the other hand, the clear and close association of the museum complex with a single, singular man also threatens to turn the whole undertaking into a vanity project. The large billboard of Fan overlooking the museum cluster parking lot (as of 2013) does not help matters in this respect. Indeed, the whole thing has a whiff of hero worship about it, a whiff made all the more pungent by the many artifacts on display in the cluster's museums that bear the imprint of Mao's cult of personality. In short, the complex must be regarded, I think, as equal parts selfless dedication to history and ego trip.

This schizophrenic framing notwithstanding, the objects housed and exhibited in the museum cluster are noteworthy in their number, variety, and, often, affective power. Among the museums dedicated to the Red era (*hongse niandai*) (as of this writing, there are eight), two of the most moving exhibits to my mind concern clocks and mirrors, respectively. Both succeed in conveying a sense of disorientation and unease through the strategic arrangement of very large numbers of objects. The clocks displayed in the Museum of Red-Era Badges, Alarm Clocks, and Seals (Hongse niandai zhang zhong yin chenlieguan), for example, are each housed individually in the recesses of a circuitous series of brick walls. Many, if not most, of these recesses are well above the viewer's eye level, making it next to impossible to inspect the clocks housed therein. Indeed, one quickly realizes that the clocks are not meant to be engaged one-by-one at all. There is no information identifying and therefore differentiating the clocks; they are presented in large, orderly groups, only a small subset of which can be closely visually examined; and the sound of the clocks, all of which appear to be actively keeping time, creates an unsettled and unsettling cacophony, a tangled web of clicks and dings. Such "catacomb-like wall display[s]," in the words of Denise Y. Ho and Jie Li, put Fan Jianchuan's general curatorial penchant for "an aesthetic of the mass ornament" to particularly powerful, albeit somewhat clichéd, effect, especially when juxtaposed with other media: "The eerie ticking and chiming of 112 clocks from the Cultural Revolution next to a rotunda lined with violent photographs from the period," for instance, "are meant to serve as 'alarm bells' (jingzhong) against history's repetition."[4] Not only does this mode of display allow Fan to get past party censors, it is also a testament to Fan's commitment to make history speak (rang lishi shuohua) through his collections, as the museum cluster's website proclaims.[5] In other words, it brings the question of history—what it is and what it (ventriloquized through Fan and his collections) wants us to do now—to the fore.

The Museum of Red-Era Mirrors is constructed along the same principles. Room after room features mirrors hanging from every available surface (all of which are white), including, in some cases, from the ceiling. Mirrors are also occasionally embedded in the floor. None of the mirrors is accompanied by any identifying information or details about its production and provenance. It is just mirrors, and it is deeply disorienting. Add to this the labyrinthine architecture of the museum building—small, claustrophobic corridors connect a series of cavernous halls—and the visitor begins to feel as though she is trapped in a carnival funhouse. Given Fan Jianchuan's self-proclaimed interest in issues of historical responsibility, one cannot help but take the exhibit—more of an installation, really—as an implicit critique of linearity. History is not straightforward per this museum; rather, it is confusing and confused. In a literal hall of mirrors, progress loses its meaning, and we are left with multiplicities.

In fact, as a visitor I myself became an array of multiplicities, for the image that followed me in this engineered mise en abyme was my own. On the one hand, in light of the argument I made in chapter 6, we might read this experience as emblematic of how the Cultural Revolution's saturated media environment and its processes of (re)mediation structured audience/consumer subjectivities. That is, we could see in the museum visitor's present experience a shadow of the past. In putting the previous chapters and pages together as I have, one might say that I have attempted to create a similar effect for the reader by virtue of flitting from one kind of mediation to the next with little regard to the boundaries between media or disciplines. Newborn socialist things were always meant to be transgressive in this sense, and so too is the book that now bears their name. To the extent that I have succeeded in channeling this quality through my words, perhaps the reader has had a taste of the historical materialities I have been engaging and their structuring impact on person-thing relations and relationality itself.

On the other hand, to go back to the museumgoer, it seems clear from Fan Jianchuan's stated goals that the act of repeatedly coming face-to-face with one's own image is also meant to prompt a rethinking of the present for its own sake rather than as some vain attempt to recapture or experience some version of the past anew. In other words, we could take history as a mirror so as to better know ourselves. This interpretation has the advantage of being consonant with Fan's aforementioned alarm clocks, warning of the threat posed by a twenty-first-century Cultural Revolution. The Cultural Revolution–as–mirror raises questions of guilt, culpability, and responsibility for those who survived it, but it also raises the specter of return. Could it happen again? What would you do if it did?

I have purposely stayed away from such questions in these pages, choosing instead to focus not on issues of purported distance—as though there were some discrete thing called the Cultural Revolution that is totally separate from us and could return of its own volition—but rather issues of continuity. This was the motivation behind my original invocation of the newborn socialist thing as that which might encompass both the material and the social; the cultural and the political economic; Chinese socialism circa 1970 and Chinese (post-)socialism circa 2020. This is my way of saying that in some very key respects—including and especially the forms of mediation explored in this book—perhaps we have not left the Cultural Revolution as far behind as might otherwise be thought. We might see connections, in fact, in the most unexpected of places.

During the three months I spent in Sichuan Province in 2013, I caught a ride from the capital city of Chengdu to the Jianchuan Museum Cluster more or less once a week. The trip itself was always something of an adventure; we never seemed to wend our way through the city's streets in quite the same way. Only one thing remained constant—one thing, that is, other than the bumper-to-bumper traffic. As we neared the highway that would take us west into the surrounding countryside, a gargantuan edifice—mammoth even by Chinese architectural standards—slowly emerged through the smog. Eventually I discovered that this structure, the New Century Global Center, was set to become, on completion, the largest freestanding building in the world. Then slated to open its doors in September 2013, it was to include, among other things, an indoor beach and wave pool, fourteen IMAX screens, one thousand hotel rooms, and 2.9 million square meters of retail space. At twice the size of the previous record holder in Dubai, the New Century Global Center went on to (briefly) lay claim to being the world's largest shopping center.[6]

A year later I found myself doing research in Wuhan in Hubei Province. As it turned out, my hotel was a mere stone's throw away from another of contemporary China's experiments with the gigantic: The World pedestrian street. At 1,350 meters in length, it proclaims itself to be the longest pedestrian shopping street on Earth.[7] Essentially, though, it is an outdoor mall. Each portion of the street is made in the model of a mock village comprising brand-name stores and fast-food restaurants, each cloaked in architectural facades meant to mimic a given part of old Europe. The Italian section also includes a cathedral, constructed Disneyland style, out of what seems to be an elaborate plastic shell (see figure C.1). Inside, as of spring 2014, were several rows of pews, complete with center aisle, facing a large LED screen playing a wedding photography ad on a loop. The courtyard in front of the church's main entrance was a popular location for such photographs, with many services offering on-site formalwear rentals for the occasion.

It is difficult not to see these structures as symptomatic of the market age in which the People's Republic currently finds itself. Although the apparent obsession with scale arguably has its roots in the party's long-standing interest in monumentality—consider the imposing grandeur of the Great Hall of the People—the New Century Global Center and The World pedestrian street seem to gesture to something even bigger than themselves, something phantasmagoric and redolent of global capitalism. Today's palatial complexes are built in honor of consumption, not the people, and the erstwhile anti-capitalist revolutionary is now called on to worship consumerism at the church of the simulacrum. And yet, to the extent that these mega-malls continue to be couched—by the Chinese Communist Party itself—within a narrative of national development and modernization, even they must be understood within a broader legacy of Chinese socialism, negotiated vis-à-vis and through consumer commodities and the (Marxist) commodity form. We are used to this legacy being cast in terms of a lack triumphantly redressed, a material void finally filled, and, more concretely, once-bare shelves straining

Figure C.1 Faux cathedral in Wuhan, Hubei Province, China. Photograph by the author, May 22, 2014.

under the weight of newly available abundance. I understand the impulse—and presentist imperative—to frame it as such. But doing so, I think, ultimately effaces the complexities of past efforts to remake the material forms by which social relations are made manifest—as well as what we might learn from these (mostly failed) efforts to further our own pursuit of a better world.

That seems an awfully high price to pay for the streamlining of history.

NOTES

Introduction

1. Shanghaishi di yi baihuo shangdian chuangzuozu, *Guitai fengbo*.
2. Established on October 20, 1949, Shanghai Number 1 moved into the Da xin (Sun company) department store's former building on Nanjing Road in 1953.
3. Shanghaishi di yi baihuo shangdian chuangzuozu, "Pei wazi."
4. The discount is implied; it is never made explicit.
5. This was the so-called sales-plus (*yi mai duo dai*) policy undertaken as part of the Criticize Lin, Criticize Confucius campaign (Pi Lin pi Kong) (1973–74).
6. Zhong gong Shanghaishi di yi baihuo shangdian weiyuanhui, "Shangpin jingji shi chansheng zibenzhuyi he zichanjieji de turang," 22. Also mentioned in Shanghaishi Huangpuqu geming weiyuanhui xiezuozu, *Shanghai Waitan Nanjing lu shihua*, 195–96.
7. Sun, "Xinsheng shiwu shi bu ke zhansheng de," 24.
8. Mao Zedong, "On the Correct Handling of Contradictions among the People," Marxists.org, accessed October 21, 2020, https://www.marxists.org/reference/archive/mao/selected-works/volume-5/mswv5_58.htm.
9. I am using Jason McGrath's very useful analytic here. See McGrath, *Postsocialist Modernity*.
10. One suspects this also accounts for the fact that, whereas modernity and postmodernity remain popular critical lenses in PRC scholarship, postsocialism (*hou shehuizhuyi*) has gained little traction. The most notable exceptions to this rule appear to be in the field of film studies.
11. I am deliberately deploying these terms and concepts in a manner reminiscent of Bruno Latour, leading architect of actor-network theory (ANT). Latour has greatly influenced my understanding and theorization of *shiwu* during the socialist period, particularly with regard to thinking about nonhuman actors. As Latour has indicated in some of his more recent work on ANT, however, he ultimately posits the network as a methodology with which to make sense of the world rather than as a preexisting assemblage of humans and nonhumans. By contrast, I am making a largely historical argument about

shiwu: The term was consistently used to refer to both objects and the cultural praxis of which they were a part. In order to properly examine the material culture of the Cultural Revolution, it is imperative that we recognize the capaciousness of this crucial term. For relevant readings on what ultimately became ANT, see Latour, *We Have Never Been Modern*; and Latour, *Reassembling the Social*.

12. Teiwes and Sun, *China's Road to Disaster*.
13. Sun, "Xinsheng shiwu shi bu ke zhansheng de."
14. See, for example, "Wuchanjieji wenhua da geming yunyu chu you yi xinsheng shiwu."
15. Zhou, "Zhichi xinsheng shiwu gonggu wuchanjieji zhuanzheng." My translation.
16. Xu, *Zhengzhi jingjixue mingci jieshi*, 46–47. My translation.
17. Coderre, "Necessary Evil."
18. One notable essay compares the discernment required in this endeavor to that displayed by the legendary horseman Bo Le of the Spring and Autumn period (circa 771–476 BCE). See Yan, "Xinsheng shiwu san ti."
19. The full statement: "Right now our country employs a commodity system. The wage system is also unequal; we have an eight-tier wage system and so on. This can be restrained only by the dictatorship of the proletariat. Thus, if Lin Biao and his ilk were to take power, it would be easy for them to bring about a capitalist system. Therefore, we must read Marxist-Leninist books." "Makesi, Engesi, Liening lun wuchanjieji zhuanzheng." My translation.
20. An edited volume conveniently brings together a number of examples of this (beyond Shanghai Number 1) in one place, though many more can be found in newspaper articles and editorials. See *Zhengque renshi woguo de shangpin zhidu*.
21. Clark, *Chinese Cultural Revolution*, 4.
22. Michaels, *The Gold Standard and the Logic of Naturalism*; Festa, *Sentimental Figures of Empire in Eighteenth-Century Britain and France*; Lamb, *Things Things Say*.
23. Marx, "Fetishism of the Commodity and Its Secret," 166.
24. Dutton, "From Culture Industry to Mao Industry," 165.
25. The difficulty in translating *yangbanxi* lies in the notion of *xi*, which is most commonly used to refer to Chinese operatic genres but here clearly comprises other performance forms as well. For simplicity's sake, I will use the original Chinese term.
26. For more on the origins of the term, see Li Mowry, *Yang-Pan Hsi*.
27. See, most famously, Dai, *Yangbanxi de fengfengyuyu*. The primary concern of much of this work is the reconstruction and demystification of the production history of the yangbanxi, with an emphasis on Jiang Qing's noxious role in their creation. Such research often bears a striking resemblance to the Cultural Revolution memoir, an extraordinarily successful genre since at least the mid-1990s, if not before.
28. This view has waned of late, especially in Chinese film studies, and a number of important publications on the subject have appeared over the past few years, with Paul Clark's aforementioned *Chinese Cultural Revolution* and Barbara Mittler's *Continuous Revolution* chief among them.
29. Nicole Huang's work is perhaps the most notable exception. See, for example, Huang, "Sun-Facing Courtyards"; and Huang, "*Azalea Mountain* and Late Mao Culture."
30. Olsen, *In Defense of Things*.
31. Fehérváry, *Politics in Color and Concrete*, ix.

32. On the one hand, there is the problem of the limited archive, the pitfalls of memory discourse, and the coercive power of the state. On the other hand, one quickly finds oneself in the troublesome territory of measuring propagandistic efficacy.

33. Fehérváry, "Goods and States," 430.

34. Fehérváry, "Goods and States."

35. Ina Merkel's work is particularly influential in this area, explicitly linking the post-socialist popularity of German Democratic Republic "brands" with East German socialist "consumer culture" prior to reunification. See such important works as Merkel, "Consumer Culture in the GDR"; and Merkel, "From Stigma to Cult."

36. Kornai, *Socialist System*.

37. Fehérváry, *Politics in Color and Concrete*, ix.

38. This is precisely what, more often than not, undermined the potential of newborn socialist things to productively amalgamate the material and the social. In practice, it all tended to become discourse.

39. Freedgood, *Ideas in Things*, 28.

40. More than a simple Beatles' reference, I mean to allude here to Miguel Tamen's work, in which friendship is taken as a condition of possibility for interpretation. See Tamen, *Friends of Interpretable Objects*.

41. Freedgood, *Ideas in Things*, 14.

42. Victor Buchli describes a similar predicament in archaeology whereby the superfluity of meaning attending absence in material culture has been the cause of considerable anxiety within the field and a desire to glom onto presence and identifiable structures of being. See Buchli, *Archaeology of Socialism*, 1–22.

43. CCP Central Committee, "Cultural Revolution."

44. As Kevin Latham put it in 2002, "The starting assumption for many debates about the reform period has been that economic liberalization must at the very least have opened up chances for accompanying political liberalization." Latham, "Rethinking Chinese Consumption," 220.

45. Vukovich, *China and Orientalism*.

46. Wu, *Cultural Revolution at the Margins*, 238.

47. Latham, "Rethinking Chinese Consumption," 221.

48. Verdery, *What Was Socialism, and What Comes Next?*, 28.

49. See, for example, Dutton, "From Culture Industry to Mao Industry."

50. Consider a volume whose very title speaks to its underlying historiographic assumptions of rupture: Deborah Davis's *The Consumer Revolution in Urban China*. Yiching Wu also has noted "the prevalent use of such temporally or spatially inflected metaphors as 'U-turn,' 'restoration,' 'retreat,' and 'break'" in scholarly work, all of which imply an attempt not only to disavow the Maoist past but also to unmake the socialist project. Wu, *Cultural Revolution at the Margins*, 226.

51. Latham, "Rethinking Chinese Consumption," 231.

52. Wu, *Cultural Revolution at the Margins*, 227.

Chapter One: The Sonic Imaginary

1. Connor, "Modern Auditory I," 220.

2. Connor, "Modern Auditory I," 207.

3. In this respect, I am following in the footsteps of Corbin, *Village Bells*.

4. See especially chapter 4 of Thompson, *Soundscape of Modernity*. See also Bijsterveld, *Mechanical Sound*.

5. Ma Dayou, *Kexuejia tan 21 shiji*, 27. My translation. Ma Dayou was not alone in drawing a link between factory music and worker productivity. See Jones, "Music in Factories."

6. For Jacques Attali, of course, the naturalization and policing of this distinction is deeply ideological. See Attali, *Noise*.

7. On this point, see also chapter 3.

8. Roth-Ey, *Moscow Prime Time*, 135.

9. For much more on the amateur performance movement, see chapter 5.

10. Huang, "Listening to Films," 190–91. See also Thompson, *Soundscape of Modernity*, 1.

11. Rice, "Soundselves," 8.

12. For a different engagement with Bentham/Foucault and the aesthetics of audio surveillance of the "bugging" variety, see Szendy, *Sur écoute*.

13. Golomstock, *Totalitarian Art*.

14. Barbara Mittler's early work, as well as that of Sheila Melvin and Jindong Cai, for example, consider issues of orchestration, the influence of Soviet composers, the prevalence of Western instruments and instrumental forms, and the extent to which the revolutionary project builds on earlier discussions of colonialism and modernization in music. Lu Guang also catalogs the use of ideologically loaded leitmotifs, such as "The Internationale" and "The East Is Red" (*"Dongfang hong"*), in the yangbanxi and argues that such usage points to an effort to tie the works into a larger system of sonic representation, rooted in repetition. See Lu, "Modern Revolutionary Beijing Opera"; Mittler, *Dangerous Tunes*; and Melvin and Cai, *Rhapsody in Red*.

15. In the interest of full disclosure, I should say that I myself have fallen into this particular trap in the past.

16. Currid, *National Acoustics*, 6.

17. Currid, *National Acoustics*, 13.

18. Currid's notion of "unisonality," for example, with its emphasis on homophony and what can only be called a penchant for the saccharine and monumental (indeed, some might say kitsch), comes immediately to mind.

19. That the two regimes considered themselves to be on opposite ends of the ideological spectrum goes without saying.

20. Currid, *National Acoustics*, 22.

21. Nathan, *Chinese Democracy*, 164.

22. In his essay on radio listening during the Cultural Revolution, Ah Cheng refers to these broadcasts as *ditai* (enemy stations). See Ah, "Ting ditai."

23. Jones, "Quotation Songs," 49–50. The Soviet Union likewise relied on a primarily wired system from the late 1920s until well after the war. See Inkeles, *Public Opinion in Soviet Russia*; Roth-Ey, *Moscow Prime Time*; von Geldern, "Radio Moscow"; and Lovell, *Russia in the Microphone Age*.

24. Nathan, *Chinese Democracy*, 164.

25. Nathan, *Chinese Democracy*, 163.

26. The World Bank estimates the PRC's population at approximately 900 million in 1974. The World Bank, DataBank, "Health Nutrition and Population Statistics: Population Estimates and Projections," accessed May 16, 2020, https://databank.worldbank.org

/reports.aspx?source=Health%20Nutrition%20and%20Population%20Statistics:%20 Population%20estimates%20and%20projections.

27. Alan P. L. Liu examines radio, consumed mainly via this wired network, as one of the communication technologies crucial to the integration of the PRC as a nation as well as the establishment of the CCP's authority after 1949. Liu, *Communications and National Integration in Communist China*, 118–29.

28. "The Walkman provides... the possibility of a barrier, a blockage between 'me' and the world, so that, as in moments of undisturbed sleep, I can disappear as a listener playing music." Chow, *Writing Diaspora*, 162–63.

29. Chow, *Writing Diaspora*, 162–63. By the time of Chow's essay in 1993, the era of the loudspeaker in China was already at an end. Increasingly, the sounds one might strive to keep out were more likely to stem from the din of advertising and construction than uproarious yangbanxi numbers.

30. Chow, *Writing Diaspora*, 162.

31. Birdsall, *Nazi Soundscapes*, 104.

32. Jones, "Quotation Songs," 55.

33. Shanghai renmin guangbo diantai (Shanghai People's Radio), "Guanyu quan guo di jiu ci guangbo gongzuo huiyi youguan guangbo wang gongzuo de zongjie" (Summary of work on the broadcast network per the Ninth National Conference on Broadcasting), document #B92-2-980 (March 1, 1965), 4, Shanghai Municipal Archive, Shanghai.

34. Nathan, *Chinese Democracy*, 163.

35. Shanghai renmin guangbo diantai, document #B92-2-980, 4–5.

36. Deleuze and Guattari, *A Thousand Plateaus*, 310–50.

37. Sterne, "Sounds Like the Mall of America"; Lee, "Technology and the Production of Islamic Space"; Khan, "Acoustics of Muslim Striving"; Larkin, "Techniques of Inattention."

38. Currid, *National Acoustics*; Birdsall, *Nazi Soundscapes*. See, also, among many others, Lovell, *Russia in the Microphone Age*; Liebes, "Acoustic Space"; Douglas, *Listening in*; Bathrick, "Making a National Family with the Radio"; and Askew, *Performing the Nation*.

39. Anderson, *Imagined Communities*.

40. For a statistical analysis of radio schedules from 1967 to 1974, see Hoffer and Rayburn II, "Broadcast Blitz against Revisionism." See also Liu, *Communications and National Integration in Communist China*, 118–29.

41. See, among others, Scannell, "Public Service Broadcasting and Modern Public Life" and *Radio, Television, and Modern Life*. For a slightly different approach to interpreting radio schedules and their effects, see Lacey, "Radio's Vernacular Modernism."

42. Guo, "Jianguo chuqi de Beijing shijian"; Guo, "Zhongguo biaozhun shi zhi kao."

43. Austin, *How to Do Things with Words*.

44. On this point, see "The Famous Mao Slogan."

45. Precious few broadcast recordings are extant, either because such recordings were never produced or because they have since suffered the ravages of time. It is therefore very difficult to systematically assess what people heard beyond the information contained in broadcast schedules, record catalogs, and broadcast guidelines.

46. The importance of topolects was such that municipal and provincial stations often had some limited programming in topolect targeting the countryside as well. See, for example, Gu, "Shanghai diantai de fangyan (huyu) boyin gongzuo."

47. Lu, "Laba yu shijie."

48. Wang, "Hongse guangbozhan," 80. My translation.

49. Nathan, *Chinese Democracy*, 163.

50. The magazine *Radio* (*Wuxiandian*), a publication akin in some ways to *Popular Mechanics*, catered to this group with a section on rural broadcast stations throughout the 1970s.

51. For more on Great China and its place within the history of the gramophone in China, see Jones, *Yellow Music*, 65–67.

52. These records are now remembered as New China's first, despite the fact that they predate the official founding of the PRC on October 1, 1949.

53. International distribution was handled by the China International Bookstore (Zhongguo guoji shudian).

54. If one further distinguishes between leatherette and laminate cases, the total number of models was four, not two.

55. Zhongguo baihuo gongsi Shanghai baihuo caigou gongying zhan (China General Goods Company Shanghai Procurement and Supply Station), "Guanyu shouyao changji jingying fang'an de chubu yijian" (Initial thoughts on hand-crank record player investment), document #B123-6-329-60 (June 1964), Shanghai Municipal Archive, Shanghai.

56. Peony's main domestic competition was the Panda (Xiongmao) line, produced in Nanjing.

57. Production of the East Is Red 101 lasted only a few years. It was surpassed by the Haiyan 713—also a two-speed, hand-crank-operated record player/transistor radio manufactured by the Beijing Radio Factory—in the early 1970s.

58. Note that the document in question defines a multiuse device as a unit combining a transistor radio with some other machine. That is, all 132,750 multiuse devices tallied here contain a radio but not necessarily a turntable. As the most common combination of technologies, however, it seems reasonable to assume that the vast majority of these units were, in fact, of the East Is Red 101 variety. Zhongguo renmin jiefangjun shangye bu junshi daibiao (PLA Ministry of Commerce Military Affairs Representative) and Zhongguo renmin jiefangjun di si jixie gongye bu junshi guanzhi weiyuanhui (Fourth PLA Ministry of Mechanized Industry Military Affairs Standing Committee), "Guanyu xiada 1970 nian shouyinji, kuangyinji, dianshiji, dianchangji shengchan shougou jihua de tongzhi" (Directive regarding the 1970 production and purchasing plans for radios, amplifiers, televisions, and electric record players), document #B123-8-339-130 (March 14, 1970), Shanghai Municipal Archives, Shanghai.

59. Much of China Records's Cultural Revolution catalog was in fact devoted to the yangbanxi, as we would expect given their political and cultural importance. Each of the model performances was released both on ten-inch microgroove vinyl and on seven-inch flexi disc in two forms: a condensed, single greatest hits disc, comprising the most famous arias or scenes, and a multidisc set encompassing the work from first note to last. Despite the continued production of multispeed turntables, these discs were all standard 33⅓ rpm. In addition to these yangbanxi albums, China Records also released recordings of important texts (the so-called *lao san pian* were released in multiple languages, for example), the aforementioned Red Guard quotation songs, new dramatic works, revolutionary songs (*geming gequ*), and exoticized minority musics. The vast majority of these albums were made after the initial unrest of 1966 to 1968, when, like the film and publishing industries, record production experienced a resurgence.

60. Shangye bu baihuoju, *Zhongguo baihuo shangye*, 54–57.

61. See Zhong gong zhongyang (CCP Central Committee), Guo wu yuan (State Council), Zhongyang jun wei (Military Affairs Committee), and Zhongyang wenge xiaozu (Central Cultural Revolution Small Group), "Guanyu jin yi bu shixing jieyue nao geming, kongzhi 'shehui jituan goumaili' jiaqiang zijin, wuzi he wujia guanli de ruogan guiding" (Regulations concerning increased thrift in the making of revolution, controlling "institutional purchasing power," and increasing financial, resource, and price management), document # 261 (August 20, 1967), Chinese Cultural Revolution Database.

62. Chen, "Propagating the Propaganda Film."

63. Lacey, "Radio's Vernacular Modernism," 167. See also Scannell, *Radio, Television, and Modern Life*, 144–78.

64. Bei, "Out of Context," 49.

65. Bei, "Changpian," 42–43. My translation.

66. Eisenberg, *Recording Angel*, 44.

67. Kenney, *Recorded Music in American Life*, 3.

68. Bey, *T.A.Z.*, 130.

69. Bey, *T.A.Z.*, 99; emphasis in the original.

70. Eisenberg, *Recording Angel*, 43–68.

71. Kenney, *Recorded Music in American Life*, 4.

72. One thinks here, too, of Alejandra Bronfman's discussion of radio's role in constructing the Caribbean as a region both near and remote vis-à-vis "the world." See Bronfman, *Isles of Noise*, 37–65.

73. Anders Stephanson suggests that, throughout human history, only the Soviet Union constituted itself in a way that rivaled the "claims to prophecy, messianism, and historical transcendence" at the heart of the notion of America's "manifest destiny." I would add the PRC to the mix as well. Stephanson, *Manifest Destiny*, xiii.

74. Similarly, Stephen Lovell notes that the "bearded *muzhik* in headphones or with receiver was one of the iconic images of the 1920s" meant to epitomize modernity. Lovell, *Russia in the Microphone Age*, 8.

75. Litzinger, *Other Chinas*, 225.

76. Friedman, "Embodying Civility," 689. This situation is likewise addressed by Susan McCarthy: "To the extent [minorities] lose tradition and culture, they lose the identity through which their Chinese membership is bestowed; to the extent they don't modernise, they are inferior citizens." McCarthy, "Ethno-Religious Mobilisation and Citizenship Discourse in the People's Republic of China," 114.

77. For a discussion of minorities' importance in the construction of Han identity, see, among others, Gladney, "Representing Nationality in China."

78. Taussig, *Mimesis and Alterity*, 208.

79. Jones, *Yellow Music*, 53–72.

Chapter Two: Selling Revolution

1. See, for example, Joel Andreas's account of both on the Tsinghua University campus. Andreas, *Rise of the Red Engineers*.

2. This approach was not itself particularly new, but the language deployed to this end after 1968 was considerably more bombastic than that of, say, the early 1960s. In

this, the discursive influence of the Cultural Revolution was keenly felt: Once the stakes of revolution were raised to such lofty heights, it was difficult to bring them back down, even rhetorically.

3. See, for example, Du, "Socialist Modernity in the Wasteland."

4. "Shenbei beiluo shangshan lai" (Going up the mountain, a basket on my back) on *Geming qingnian zhi zai sifang* (Where the motherland needs us most, there is our home), China Records M-1022, 1974, 33⅓ rpm. My translation.

5. Anagnost, *National Past-Times*, 75–97. Calls to improve "trade work" with minority populations from the mid-1960s seem to substantiate this view as well. For example, see Xie, "Jin yibu jiaqiang minzu maoyi gongzuo"; and Yu, "Tigao renshi zuo hao minzu maoyi gongzuo."

6. This, after all, was the rationale behind the requirement that artists experience life (*tiyan shenghuo*). In the case of dancers, see Wilcox, "Dancers Doing Fieldwork."

7. Richman, *Industrial Society in Communist China*, 880.

8. An overly simplified chart can, however, be found in Prybyla, *Chinese Economy*, 223.

9. Lieberthal, "Beijing's Consumer Market," 36.

10. Paulina Bren and Mary Neuburger make a similar point regarding Eastern European socialist regimes (and consumers). Bren and Neuburger, "Introduction," 6–7.

11. I say *arguably* because the Ministry of Commerce did not have a monopoly on all domestic trade. Rice and grain products, for example, were under the purview of the separate Ministry of Grain (Liangshi bu).

12. For a list of corporations from the 1950s and their date of establishment, see Chou, "Wholesaling in Communist China," 258–59.

13. Richman, *Industrial Society in Communist China*; Solinger, *Chinese Business under Socialism*, 33–47.

14. By 1957, 97.3 percent of retail and 100 percent of wholesale commerce was at least partially owned by either the state or a cooperative. Prybyla, *Chinese Economy*, 218–19.

15. Richman, *Industrial Society in Communist China*, 882. See also Prybyla, *Chinese Economy*, 224.

16. For the shifting relationship between cooperatives and communes, see Donnithorne, *China's Economic System*, 291–309.

17. The journal included a running feature, for example, dedicated to the introduction of notable outlets of various kinds to its readership. The feature was called "Every issue, a store" ("Mei qi yi dian").

18. Tsai, "Delicacies for a Privileged Class in a Risk Society." See also Solinger, *Chinese Business under Socialism*, 58n137.

19. For one foreigner's experience with this system, see Klochko, *Soviet Scientist in Red China*, 49–65.

20. This kind of unwanted abundance is addressed further in chapter 3.

21. To that end, consider Smolinski, "Planning without Theory."

22. This was also true of Western wartime economies with similarly long-lasting effects. British rationing of meat, for example, was not fully discontinued until 1954. For the impact of rationing on postwar consumer behavior in Great Britain, see Lyon, Colquhoun, and Kinney, "UK Food Shopping in the 1950s."

23. On the pre-1966 history of (especially urban) grain rationing, see Perkins, *Market Control and Planning in Communist China*, 178–87.

24. Grain rationing resumed briefly in a number of locations in 1995. For the liberalization of grain policy in the 1990s, see Sicular, "Redefining State, Plan and Market," 1024–26.

25. Perkins, *Market Control and Planning in Communist China*, 187–90.

26. Prybyla, *Chinese Economy*, 127–29.

27. On the vicissitudes of memory in this regard, however, see Jin, "Guanyu 'piaozheng shidai' de jiti jiyi."

28. For a detailed look at ration procedures immediately after the Cultural Revolution in 1977, see Chinn, "Basic Commodity Distribution in the People's Republic of China."

29. Solinger, *Chinese Business under Socialism*, 25.

30. Solinger argues that money was systematically marginalized, for example, while Yang emphasizes the role of gifts in forming relationship networks. Solinger, *Chinese Business under Socialism*; Yang, *Gifts, Favors, and Banquets*.

31. Coderre, "Necessary Evil."

32. Braester, "'Big Dying Vat,'" 432.

33. For Nanjing Road's late-Qing and republican-era development, see Cochran, *Inventing Nanjing Road*. See also Huebner, "Architecture and History in Shanghai's Central District," 222–25.

34. On the development of the "big four," see Lien, "From the Retailing Revolution to the Consumer Revolution." On Sincere and Wing On specifically, see Chan, "Personal Styles, Cultural Values and Management."

35. On the early French department store, or *grand magasin*, see Williams, *Dream Worlds*; and Miller, *Bon Marché*. On comparable changes in American retail and consumer culture, see Leach, *Land of Desire*; and Benson, *Counter Cultures*.

36. Lee, *Shanghai Modern*, 15.

37. Yeh, "Guides to a Global Paradise."

38. On the "new" Nanjing Road, see Shanghaishi Huangpuqu geming weiyuanhui xiezuozu, *Shanghai Waitan Nanjing lu shihua*, 191–98.

39. "When the pendulum has swung in the direction of extremism, domestic trade, commerce, and finance have tended to be the first spheres to come under attack. The reason is that these sectors have been regarded as being politically very sensitive because of the large number of bourgeois personnel—capitalists and former private merchants, employees of former private local and foreign firms in China—they have employed and still employ." Richman, *Industrial Society in Communist China*, 883.

40. Mao, "Correcting Mistaken Ideas," Marxists.org, accessed May 30, 2020, https://www.marxists.org/reference/archive/mao/works/red-book/ch24.htm.

41. This scrutiny sometimes took explicit organizational form as when "trade and finance were chosen as the first spheres in 1964 in which special party political departments were established at all levels." Richman, *Industrial Society in Communist China*, 883.

42. Bren and Neuburger, "Introduction," 6.

43. Mao, "Be Concerned with the Well-Being of the Masses, Pay Attention to Methods of Work," Marxists.org, accessed May 30, 2020, https://www.marxists.org/reference/archive/mao/selected-works/volume-1/mswv1_10.htm.

44. On the relationship of the economic experiments in the liberated areas and PRC policy, see Selden, "Mao Zedong and the Political Economy of Chinese Development."

45. Ren, "Zuzhi chengshi renmin de jingji shenghuo shi jianshe shehuizhuyi xin chengshi de yi ge zhongyao fangmian."

46. For the rise of self-service, see Bowlby, *Carried Away*, 30–48, 134–51. For experiments in self-service in the Soviet Union, which began in 1954, see Goldman, "Retailing in the Soviet Union," 14.

47. This is consistent with other socialist countries employing state-run distribution systems for consumer goods. See, for example, Fehérváry, *Politics in Color and Concrete*; and Verdery, *What Was Socialism, and What Comes Next?*

48. "Wo guo shehuizhuyi shangye de fangxiang," 12. My translation.

49. "Wo guo shehuizhuyi shangye de fangxiang," 7. My translation.

50. See chapter 3 for a further discussion of this productivist turn.

51. See, for example, Zhang, "Boxue zhong, quru shen."

52. For more on Zhang Binggui, see notes 54–57. For Yang Jinyu, see Yang, "Wei renmin zhan guitai."

53. See, by way of example, "Geng hao di xuexi Mao Zedong sixiang geng hao di yunyong bianzheng weiwu lun."

54. Zhang, "Wei geming zhan guitai."

55. Zhang, *Zhang Binggui guitai fuwu yishu*.

56. Li, *Zhang Binggui*.

57. Guo and Liu, "New China's Flagship Emporium," 137.

58. See, for example, Gamble, "Consumers with Chinese Characteristics?"

59. See note 39.

60. This was part of the so-called *gai ming feng* (name-changing wind).

61. Guo and Liu, "New China's Flagship Emporium," 120.

62. For a discussion of Wing On's possible replacement names, see "Shanghai Tianjin geming xiao jiang he shangye zhigong."

63. Zhong gong zhongyang (CCP Central Committee), "Guo wu yuan caimao bangongshi, Guojia jingji weiyuanhui guanyu caizheng maoyi he shou gongye fangmian ruogan zhengce wenti de baogao" (State Council Trade Office and National Economic Committee report on questions of trade and handicraft policy), document # 508 (September 23, 1966), Chinese Cultural Revolution Database.

64. Xu, *Wenge shigao*, 361.

65. Zhong gong zhongyang, "Guo wu yuan caimao bangongshi, Guojia jingji weiyuanhui guanyu caizheng maoyi he shou gongye fangmian ruogan zhengce wenti de baogao."

66. Guo and Liu, "New China's Flagship Emporium," 122.

67. "Shanghai Tianjin geming xiao jiang he shangye zhigong."

68. Xu, *Wenge shigao*, 370.

69. Zola, *Au bonheur des dames*; in English, Zola, *Ladies' Delight*. For the store on which Zola based his novel, see Miller, *Bon Marché*.

70. Consider Benson, *Counter Cultures*.

71. Barlow, "Wanting Some" and "Buying In."

72. Zhong gong zhongyang, "Guo wu yuan caimao bangongshi, Guojia jingji weiyuanhui guanyu caizheng maoyi he shou gongye fangmian ruogan zhengce wenti de baogao."

73. For an account of Yao Yilin's experience of the Cultural Revolution, see Yao, *Yao Yilin bai xi tan*, 239–58.

74. "Liu Deng hei dian—'Hei qi hao.'" See also Tsai, "Delicacies for a Privileged Class in a Risk Society," 6.

75. "Cuihui Peng Zhen zai shangye shang de hei judian."

76. "Guangfudao shangdian shi Liu Shaoqi zai cai mao zhanxian shang qinzi shu qi de yi mian hei qi."

77. "Wei gong nong bing fuwu de xin xing shangdian."

78. This is consistent with an important distinction between the initial use of "speaking bitterness" accounts in the 1940s and early 1950s "as a technique of mobilization [and] the 'recalling bitterness (*yiku*)' campaign [which] aimed at reenacting class struggle and reinforcing class awareness by invoking collective memory." Wu, "Recalling Bitterness," 147.

79. A Ministry of Commerce directive promoted this particular model in 1963. See "Zhaozhou yiyao shangdian."

80. Guo, "Wo yu *Xiangyang shangdian*," 52.

81. "Xuexi geming yangbanxi de kexi chengguo."

82. *Xiangyang shangdian* (*Xiangyang Store*), China Records M-2169/2172, 1974, 4 33⅓ rpm discs. A single-disc abridged version was also released as *Pingju* Xiangyang shangdian *zhuyao changduan* (Main scenes from the pingju *Xiangyang Store*), China Records M-2166, 1974, 33⅓ rpm.

83. Guo, "Wo yu *Xiangyang shangdian*."

84. Zhang, "San kan *Xiangyang shangdian*."

85. Guo and Hu, *Xiangyang shangdian*, 14.

86. Guo and Hu, *Xiangyang shangdian*, 43.

87. This implies a sense of space and territorialization not unlike that discussed in chapter 1. Here, victory becomes a question of maintaining some newly acquired territory (Baiyun Slope) served by the official system of commerce (Xiangyang Store).

88. Guo and Hu, *Xiangyang shangdian*, 18.

89. Guo and Hu, *Xiangyang shangdian*, 19.

90. As portrayed, for example, in Shanghaishi di yi baihuo shangdian chuangzuozu, "Er shi si xiaoshi." See also Donnithorne, *China's Economic System*; and Prybyla, *Chinese Economy*, 226.

91. On these official customer feedback mechanisms, see Prybyla, *Chinese Economy*, 224–25.

92. Guo and Hu, *Xiangyang shangdian*, 39–43.

93. Shanghaishi di yi baihuo shangdian chuangzuozu, "Pei wazi."

94. Wang, *Cong kuxingzhe shehui dao xiaofeizhe shehui*.

95. Guo and Hu, *Xiangyang shangdian*, 48.

96. Guo and Hu, *Xiangyang shangdian*, 49.

97. As quoted in Gamble, "Consumers with Chinese Characteristics?," 175.

98. Liu, *Songhuo lushang*.

Chapter Three: Productivist Display

1. The event's formal title was the National Conference of Outstanding Groups and Workers in Education, Culture, Health, Physical Culture, and Journalism (Quan guo jiaoyu he wenhua, weisheng, tiyu, xinwen fangmian shehuizhuyi jianshe xianjin danwei he geren biaozhang da hui), and it was held from June 1 to 11, 1960.

2. Gu, "Wei shangdian pi xin zhuang"; "Feng shou de yi ke."

3. "Feng shou de yi ke," 51. My translation.

4. See, for example, Qiu, "Chuchuang de goutu he secai."

5. Gerth, "Compromising with Consumerism in Socialist China."

6. I refer to the International Conference of Advertising Workers (Chinese: Shehuizhuyi guojia guanggao gongzuozhe huiyi; Russian: Mezhdunarodnaya konferentsiya rabotnikov reklamy), held December 9–21, 1957, in Prague and the All-Socialist Commercial Advertising and Propaganda Conference (Shehuizhuyi guojia shanghui xuanchuan guanggao huiyi), held May 16–19, 1960, in Bucharest.

7. The Shanghai conference actually included materials from the earlier Prague gathering. See "Chuangzao guanggao xin fengge."

8. See chapter 2 for the figure of the socialist retailer.

9. Fitzpatrick, "Good Old Days," 19.

10. This is one of the reasons why Dorothy Solinger argues that the accumulation of goods was more important than money in the commercial bureaucracy. Solinger, *Chinese Business under Socialism*.

11. See chapter 4. See also Coderre, "Necessary Evil."

12. Goscilo, "Luxuriating in Lack," 78.

13. For his part, Leon Smolinski argues that economic planning was actually divorced from any systematic theory. Smolinski, "Planning without Theory."

14. Shanghaishi Huangpuqu geming weiyuanhui xiezuozu, *Shanghai Waitan Nanjing lu shihua*, 197.

15. Oushakine, "'Against the Cult of Things.'"

16. Oushakine, "'Against the Cult of Things,'" 212.

17. This is somewhat reminiscent of the attempt (discussed in chapter 4) to disarm the commodity fetish simply by talking about it.

18. Oushakine, "'Against the Cult of Things,'" 213.

19. Oushakine, "'Against the Cult of Things,'" 213.

20. Bowlby, *Carried Away*.

21. One might reasonably wonder whether this discrepancy reflects the more voluntarist aspects of Chinese Marxism/Maoism. To be fair, however, a greater emphasis on the role of individual retail personnel can also be seen in the USSR of the 1930s. On Soviet retailing prior to 1953, see Goscilo, "Luxuriating in Lack"; Hilton, *Selling to the Masses*; Hessler, *Social History of Soviet Trade*; and Randall, *Soviet Dream World of Retail Trade and Consumption in the 1930s*.

22. Coderre, "Necessary Evil."

23. These items, along with brief articles on sugar, ink, reusable wood packaging, and how to prevent metal fixtures from rusting, appeared in a single two-page spread of *Trade work*. See "Zhigong yuandi."

24. If and when retailers were permitted to acquire goods directly from light-industry factories, these factories were likewise encouraged to set up sample rooms.

25. Zi, "Zenyang banhao yangpinshi," 24. My translation.

26. Zi, "Zenyang banhao yangpinshi," 24. My translation.

27. Zi, "Zenyang banhao yangpinshi," 24. My translation.

28. Chen, "Zenyang chenlie shangpin," 21. My translation.

29. Zhonghua renmin gong he guo shangye bu shangye zuzhi yu yishu ju, *Shangdian chuchuang chenlie yu neibu buzhi*; Shanghaishi guanggao gongsi, *Zenyang buzhi chuchuang*.

30. Chen, "Zenyang chenlie shangpin," 20. My translation.

31. See, among many others, Rofel, *Other Modernities*; and Frazier, *Making of the Chinese Industrial Workplace*.

32. Russo, "How Did the Cultural Revolution End?"

33. See, for example, Bailes, "Alexei Gastev and the Soviet Controversy over Taylorism"; Rogger, "Amerikanizm and the Economic Development of Russia"; Morgan, "Transfer of Taylorist Ideas to China"; and Kelly, "Perceptions of Taylorism." Jake Werner has also recently gone so far as to argue that the Fordist mode of production must be understood as an important point of commonality between the actually existing capitalist and socialist regimes of the 1950s. Werner, "Global Fordism in 1950s Urban China." This is perhaps overstating the case, but certainly the Fordist factory, as a *form*, exerted a tremendous global influence on constructions of modern production.

34. Riskin, "Small Industry and the Chinese Model of Development"; Riskin, "China's Rural Industries"; Schran, "Handicrafts in Communist China."

35. On the latter, see Eyferth, *Eating Rice from Bamboo Roots*.

36. For a general introduction to Chinese ceramics, see Valenstein, *Handbook of Chinese Ceramics*. For a more technical overview, see Kerr and Wood, *Chemistry and Chemical Technology*.

37. For an overview of textual sources concerning the relationship between Jingdezhen and the Ming capital, see Medley, "Ching-Tê Chên and the Problem of the 'Imperial Kilns.'"

38. For a consideration of illusionist aesthetics in painting under Qianlong, see Kleutghen, *Imperial Illusions*.

39. For a much more comprehensive look at the history of Jingdezhen, see Dillon, "History of the Porcelain Industry in Jingdezhen"; and Gillette, *China's Porcelain Capital*. Important historical writings on Jingdezhen are available in translation in Tichane, *Ching-Te-Chen*.

40. For a look at the international circulation of discourse and images related to porcelain production and Jingdezhen in the Qing and beyond, see Huang, "From the Imperial Court to the International Art Market." See also Priyadarshini, *Chinese Porcelain in Colonial Mexico*, 29–61.

41. Zhonggong Jingdezhen shiwei xuanchuanbu, *Cidu jilang*.

42. An earlier history makes a similar argument. See Jiangxisheng qinggongye ting taoci yanjiusuo, *Jingdezhen taoci shigao*.

43. Underground CCP organizing appears to have begun as early as 1928. Dillon, "Fang Zhimin, Jingdezhen and the Northeast Jiangxi Soviet."

44. For much more on the reorganization of this period, see Gillette, *China's Porcelain Capital*, 43–70.

45. By contrast, Gillette contends that the privatization of the industry was far more disruptive. Gillette, *China's Porcelain Capital*, 3.

46. Jingdezhenshi jingji jihua weiyuanhui, *Jingdezhenshi guomin jingji tongji ziliao (1950–1957)*, 23.

47. Gillette, *China's Porcelain Capital*, 16.

48. Jingdezhen was not alone in this. See Ledderose, *Ten Thousand Things*, 75–102.

49. Calls to mechanize Jingdezhen actually long predate 1949, though they gained little traction before the PRC. See, for example, the recommendations made in 1934 by Du Zhongyuan (1897–1943) in Gillette, *China's Porcelain Capital*, 29–35.

50. Gillette, *China's Porcelain Capital*, 56.

51. "Cichang de yi xiang jishu gexin."

52. Frank Cosentino, who was among a group of Americans from the Boehm ceramic studio in Trenton, New Jersey, to visit Jingdezhen in late 1974, reported being astonished by how much of the production process was still done by hand with the aid of such machines. Cosentino, *Boehm Journey to Ching-Te-Chen*.

53. Gillette, *China's Porcelain Capital*, 54.

54. Gillette, *China's Porcelain Capital*, 54.

55. For an account of the mechanization of Red Star Porcelain Factory (Hongxing cichang) and one man's journey to earning the title of engineer (*gongchengshi*), see the story of Zhang Shuigui. Zhonggong Jingdezhen shiwei xuanchuanbu, *Cidu jilang*, 385–95.

56. This category is in contradistinction to porcelain pieces created for industrial or building purposes.

57. Jingdezhenshi jingji jihua weiyuanhui, *Jingdezhenshi guomin jingji tongji ziliao (1950–1957)*, 25.

58. Jingdezhenshi jingji jihua weiyuanhui, *Jingdezhenshi guomin jingji tongji ziliao (1958)*, 25.

59. Jingdezhenshi geming weiyuanhui jihua weiyuanhui, *Jingdezhenshi guomin jingji tongji ziliao (1974)*, 89.

60. The comparable production figure for 1977 is 251,416,500 items. Jingdezhenshi geming weiyuanhui jihua weiyuanhui, *Jingdezhenshi guomin jingji tongji ziliao (1977)*, 107.

61. Gillette, *China's Porcelain Capital*, 67.

62. For an overview of the period from 1966 to 1972 in Jingdezhen, see Gillette, *China's Porcelain Capital*, 63–69.

63. Cosentino, *Boehm Journey to Ching-Te-Chen*, 124.

64. Jingdezhenshi jingji jihua weiyuanhui, *Jingdezhenshi guomin jingji tongji ziliao (1958)*, 26.

65. Jingdezhenshi geming weiyuanhui jihua weiyuanhui, *Jingdezhenshi guomin jingji tongji ziliao (1974)*, 89.

66. Jingdezhenshi geming weiyuanhui jihua weiyuanhui, *Jingdezhenshi guomin jingji tongji ziliao (1977)*, 107.

67. This jibes with Cosentino's account. Cosentino, *Boehm Journey to Ching-Te-Chen*, 102–16.

68. Specializations were established during the Great Leap Forward and persisted through the 1990s. Gillette, *China's Porcelain Capital*, 59.

69. Cosentino, *Boehm Journey to Ching-Te-Chen*, 115.

70. Jingdezhenshi geming weiyuanhui jihua weiyuanhui, *Jingdezhenshi guomin jingji tongji ziliao (1974)*, 90.

71. Jingdezhenshi geming weiyuanhui jihua weiyuanhui, *Jingdezhenshi guomin jingji tongji ziliao (1974)*, 90.

72. For a much more detailed, though still relatively brief, overview of this history, see Yu and Liang, *Jingdezhen chuantong taoci diaosu*, 6–12.

73. As a reminder, all porcelains are by definition ceramics, but all ceramics are not porcelains, *ceramics* being the more capacious term. Porcelain specifically denotes a white, fully vitrified body.

74. For a comprehensive overview of the common classification schema, see Yu and Liang, *Jingdezhen chuantong taoci diaosu*, 71–114.

75. See chapter 4.

76. The exact model was French, though it is unclear which specific work. One suspects something along the lines of Albert Aublet's *Nu avec un voile* (1883). Cao and Chen, *Jingdezhen diaosu ciyi*, 64.

77. Kettering, "'Ever More Cosy and Comfortable,'" 126.

78. Kettering, "'Ever More Cosy and Comfortable,'" 121.

79. Cosentino, *Boehm Journey to Ching-Te-Chen*, 114.

80. Cosentino, *Boehm Journey to Ching-Te-Chen*, 115.

81. Gillette notes a precipitous drop in the number of technical workers in Jingdezhen between 1960 and 1971. Gillette, *China's Porcelain Capital*, 67.

82. Pressing artists into service was a common practice in situations demanding specialized, technical knowledge or uncommon talent. The artists who worked on the so-called 7501 porcelains for Mao's use in 1975, for example, were a who's who of the porcelain industry. This was not the work of amateurs by any stretch of the imagination. For a brief account of this project, see Zeng and Kong, "7501 ci."

83. Cosentino, *Boehm Journey to Ching-Te-Chen*, 115–16.

84. Ledderose, *Ten Thousand Things*, 75–102.

85. Ho, *Curating Revolution*.

86. As quoted in Ho, *Curating Revolution*, 203.

87. For a discussion of the object lesson in the context of this exhibit, see Ho, *Curating Revolution*, 174–210.

88. Hay, *Sensuous Surfaces*, 67.

89. Hay, *Sensuous Surfaces*, 67.

90. Hay, *Sensuous Surfaces*, 68.

91. Murck, "Golden Mangoes"; Murck, *Mao's Golden Mangoes*.

92. For more on these institutions, see chapter 2, note 35.

93. Lien, "From the Retailing Revolution to the Consumer Revolution," 364.

94. Hilton, "Retailing the Revolution," 945–46.

95. Oushakine, "'Against the Cult of Things,'" 198–99.

96. On Soviet display windows under Stalin, see Hetherington, "Dressing the Shop Window of Socialism."

97. Shanghaishi guanggao gongsi, *Zenyang buzhi chuchuang*, 1.

98. *Renmin huabao* (China Pictorial), no. 12 (1967): 34. My translation.

99. For a fantastic genealogy of the modern European and North American shop-window and its shifting mode(s) of visuality, see Bowlby, *Carried Away*, 49–78. See also Friedberg, *Window Shopping*.

100. Buck-Morss, *Dialectics of Seeing*, 81–82.

101. Ch'en, "The Big Fish."

102. This has been an area of increased scholarly interest, especially as it pertains to the experience of socialism in Eastern Europe. Ina Merkel's work on the German Democratic

Republic was crucial in breaking this new ground in the late 1990s. See, for example, Merkel, "Consumer Culture in the GDR." Jos Gamble has endeavored to compare socialist and post-socialist consumer behavior in China in relation to transnational retailers' management and training practices. See Gamble, "Consumers with Chinese Characteristics?" In a very different vein, recollections of the Mao period, including the Cultural Revolution, often describe the lengths to which individuals had to go to acquire commodities. This is a recurring theme, for example, in Zhong, Wang, and Bai, *Some of Us*.

103. See, most famously, Bourdieu, *Distinction*.

104. Much of the history Yiching Wu traces in his recent book is precisely concerned with the persistence of class in its many incarnations. Wu, *Cultural Revolution at the Margins*.

105. Chen, "Dressing for the Party"; Finnane, *Changing Clothes in China*.

106. Osborne, *Politics of Time*, 184; emphasis in the original.

107. Buck-Morss, *Dreamworld and Catastrophe*, 42–69.

Chapter Four: Illuminating the Commodity Fetish

1. This language is taken from Arvatov, "Everyday Life and the Culture of the Thing."

2. Kiaer, *Imagine No Possessions*, 26.

3. On this form of temporality, see especially Buck-Morss, *Dreamworld and Catastrophe*.

4. An initial Chinese translation of "Critique of the Gotha Program" by Li Da (1890–1966) was published in *Xin shidai* (New age) in 1923. The authoritative translation by He Sijing (1896–1968) and Xu Bing (1903–72) was published in 1939 as part of a larger CCP project concerning Marx's writings.

5. Excerpts and analysis of *Anti-Dühring* began appearing in Chinese publications as early as 1920. The first complete translation (from the original German with additional reference to Russian and Japanese versions) was undertaken by Wu Liangping (also known as Wu Liping) (1908–86) and published in 1930. It was the first of many editions. See Huang, "Wu Liangping yiben." For the most relevant passage in English, see Engels, *Anti-Dühring*, 311.

6. *The Class Struggle* was first published in Chinese (translated from an English edition) in 1921. See Ke, *Jieji zhengdou*. On its importance, see Yang, "Zhongguo gongchandang chengli zhi chu Makesizhuyi zhongyiben zhongyao zhuzuo jieshao," 18–19. A new translation (also primarily from English) was published in 1963. See Kao, *Ai'erfute gangling jieshuo*. For the most relevant passages in English, see Kautsky, *The Class Struggle (Erfurt Program)*, 95–104.

7. For analysis of Marx, Engels, and Kautsky on this point, see Szamuely, *First Models*, 23–28.

8. Lin, "Reinstatement of Economics," 6.

9. This is most famously spelled out in Mao's "On Practice," Marxists.org, accessed May 27, 2020, https://www.marxists.org/reference/archive/mao/selected-works/volume-1/mswv1_16.htm.

10. Bukharin, *Economics of the Transformation Period*, 11–12.

11. Bukharin, *Economics of the Transformation Period*, 212–13; Szamuely, *First Models*, 28–29.

12. Akademiya nauk SSSR institut ekonomiki, *Politicheskaya ekonomiya: Uchebnik*.

13. Coderre, "Necessary Evil."

14. Sulian kexueyuan jingji yanjiusuo, *Zhengzhi jingjixue jiaokeshu*.

15. Christensen and Delman, "Theory of Transitional Society"; Christensen, "Shanghai School and Its Rejection."

16. "New Political Economy Textbook"; Yao, *Zhengzhi jingjixue jiaocai*.

17. Christensen and Delman, "Theory of Transitional Society," 7–12

18. 1.69 million copies of the 1973 version were released for domestic use. It was also translated into Korean and Japanese. Chao, *"Wenhua da geming" cidian*, 369–70.

19. See, for example, Shanghai shifan daxue zhengjiao xi and Shanghai dengpao chang lilun xiaozu, *Xuexi shehuizhuyi zhengzhi jingjixue*; and Zhengzhi jingjixue jianghua (shehuizhuyi bufen) bianxiezu, *Zhengzhi jingjixue jianghua*.

20. For a partial list of public critiques of the Shanghai school as it relates to the Gang of Four, see Christensen and Delman, "Theory of Transitional Society," 13–15.

21. The origin and structure of the Soviet textbook is worth noting here. Completed in 1954, its preface makes explicit the direct relationship with the 1951 discussion that gave rise to Stalin's "Remarks"; in essence, the textbook was meant to codify Stalin's pronouncements as incontestable, scientific truth. It attempted to do so in three parts, a structure also adopted by the Chinese *Fundamentals*. The first section is dedicated to precapitalist modes of production while the second concerns itself with capitalism. These portions, which make up nearly half of the 638-page tome, break little new theoretical ground, relying heavily on the writings of Marx and Engels. The latter half of the book is a different story, as it seeks to describe and explain the socialist mode of production in painstaking detail. Here it relies on the principles outlined by Stalin, extending his logic regarding commodities and their relationship to systems of public ownership to similarly delicate questions concerning the meaning of prices and money (chapter 31) and workers' wages (chapter 32) under socialism.

22. Although Mao's comments—made during economic study sessions in the winter of 1959–60—were initially circulated among a relatively small group of party leaders, their inclusion in the Red Guard collection *Long live Mao Zedong Thought* (*Mao Zedong sixiang wansui*), published in 1967 and again in 1969, effectively made them public. Mao, "Sulian *Zhengzhi jingjixu* dushu biji."

23. Mao, *Critique of Soviet Economics*, 106–7.

24. Mao, *Critique of Soviet Economics*, 108.

25. Mao, *Critique of Soviet Economics*, 108.

26. Mao, *Critique of Soviet Economics*, 108.

27. Mao, *Critique of Soviet Economics*, 109.

28. Mao, *Critique of Soviet Economics*, 110–11.

29. The intervening chapter, chapter 20, focuses on the relationship between and among the nation (*guojia*), the collective (*jiti*), and the individual (*geren*).

30. This decoupling of price and exchange is also reproduced and guaranteed by the Soviet Union's centralized pricing mechanism, which, as János Kornai repeatedly notes in his monumental *The Socialist System*, is itself insensitive to shifts in supply and demand in an economic system insensitive to changes in price. This aspect of the Soviet Union's command economy was, of course, adopted throughout the Communist world. Following in the USSR's footsteps, socialism became synonymous with a monetized economy in which prices were fixed from above. See Kornai, *Socialist System*.

31. "Makesi, Engesi, Liening lun wuchanjieji zhuanzheng." My translation.
32. Marx, "Fetishism of the Commodity and Its Secret," 164–65.
33. Marx, "Fetishism of the Commodity and Its Secret," 166.
34. Marx, "Fetishism of the Commodity and Its Secret," 164.
35. Marx, "Fetishism of the Commodity and Its Secret," 169.
36. *Zhengque renshi woguo de shangpin zhidu*, 70–71. My translation.
37. *Zhengque renshi woguo de shangpin zhidu*, 72. My translation.
38. Fang, "Xue yidian zhengzhi jingjixue."
39. Wu, "Xue yidian zhengzhi jingjixue."
40. See, for example, Beijing daxue jingjixi pipanzu, *Kong Qiu jingji sixiang pipan*.
41. A similar push during the Great Leap Forward had focused only on CCP cadres.
42. Shanghai haiwuju Yangcun pu zhuangxiezhan gongren xiezuozu and Fudan daxue jingjixi gongnongbing xueyuan, *Matou shang de zhengzhi jingjixue*.
43. Shang gang wu chang yi chejian gongren lilunzu, *Lian'ganglu qian de zhengzhi jingjixue*.
44. Wu, "Xue yidian zhengzhi jingjixue," 11. My translation.
45. Apter and Saich, *Revolutionary Discourse in Mao's Republic*, 1–30.
46. Chan, *Edge of Knowing*, 124.
47. Chan, *Edge of Knowing*, 124.
48. Brown, "Tyranny of Things," 451.
49. Apter and Saich, *Revolutionary Discourse in Mao's Republic*, 4.
50. Mao, "Talks at the Yan'an Forum on Literature and Art," 470.
51. Dobrenko, *Political Economy of Socialist Realism*, 7.
52. Dobrenko, *Political Economy of Socialist Realism*, 6.
53. Chao, *Sanliwan Village*, 139.
54. Chao, *Sanliwan Village*, 141.
55. Chao, *Sanliwan Village*, 195–96.
56. Chao, *Sanliwan Village*, 140.
57. The original cites a couplet by the Song poet Su Shi (1037–1101), literally rendered: "I cannot know the true face of Mount Lu while I am on the mountain." I have chosen to translate it idiomatically here.
58. Jing, *Shangpin zishu*, 1. My translation.
59. Jing, *Shangpin zishu*, 95. My translation.
60. Jing, *Shangpin zishu*, 96. My translation.
61. Although somewhat marginal to the national debates of the late 1950s and early 1960s on the appropriate role of the law of value in the Chinese economy, Deng was an important figure in Nanjing academic circles. Among many other responsibilities in the provincial party apparatus, Deng headed the Jiangsusheng jingji yanjiusuo (Jiangsu research institute for economics) from 1959 until the early Cultural Revolution, at which point he was denounced for supposedly advocating free markets. *Autobiography* was one of many works Deng wrote in order to popularize political economic theory, something he was known for well before the mass mobilization campaigns to study political economy of 1972 and 1975. For a concise overview of his work in this area, see Shuo, "Zhuming tongsu jingji lilunjia Deng Kesheng."
62. Deng, *Shangpin zizhuan*.

63. The "Editor's Note" to the 1978 edition makes this explicit. Deng, *Shangpin zizhuan*, i.

64. Deng, *Shangpin zizhuan*, 1–2. My translation.

65. Douglas, "Britannia's Rule and the It-Narrator," 68.

66. Festa, *Sentimental Figures of Empire in Eighteenth-Century Britain and France*; Lamb, *Things Things Say*.

67. Lupton, *Knowing Books*. See especially chapter 2.

68. Douglas, "Britannia's Rule and the It-Narrator," 71.

69. This is Herbert Franke's rendering. See Franke, "Literary Parody." An earlier, idiosyncratic antecedent might also be traced to the *Guanzi*. See chapter 1 of Chin, *Savage Exchange*.

70. For both the original Chinese and an English translation, see Nienhauser, "Allegorical Reading."

71. Disrespectful of what or whom, one might ask? Of the human worthies deserving of biographical attention.

72. For both the original Chinese and an English translation, see Franke, "Literary Parody," 27–31. For a look at this subgenre as a form of fetishism, see Zhao, "Zhongguo lishi shang de huobi baiwujiao sixiang."

73. This absence is not surprising given that the popularity of this genre peaked well before Marxism's appearance in China. For a concise history of the pseudobiography, see Franke, "Literary Parody"; Zhang, "Zhongguo gudai 'jia zhuan' wenti fazhanshi shulun."

74. Marx, "Fetishism of the Commodity and Its Secret," 176–77.

75. My thanks to Andrew F. Jones for this pithy formulation.

76. Marx, "Fetishism of the Commodity and Its Secret," 163–64.

77. Brown, "Tyranny of Things," 451.

78. Brown, "Tyranny of Things," 451.

79. Although *A commodity's tale* came under attack after 1976, it was the content rather than the form that was deemed problematic. See Ye, "Ping *Shangpin zishu*."

Chapter Five: Remediating the Hero

A much earlier version of this chapter appeared as "Breaking Bad: Sabotaging the Production of the Hero in the Amateur Performance of *Yangbanxi*," in *Listening to the Cultural Revolution: Music, Politics, and Cultural Continuities*, ed. Paul Clark, Laikwan Pang, and Tsan-Huang Tsai (London: Palgrave Macmillan, 2016), 65–84.

1. On postsocialist Mao-doubling and its implications, see Lee, "Mao's Two Bodies."

2. Shi, "Yanchu qianhou."

3. Shi, "Yanchu qianhou." My translation.

4. Shi, "Yanchu qianhou." My translation.

5. This slogan is sometimes shortened to only the first two terms of the triptych—"play a hero, study a hero"—drawing on the notion of study (*xue*) as itself a kind of embodiment, which has a very long history. Interestingly enough, this abridged saying is also occasionally inverted, becoming instead an adage about proper performance practice: "study a hero to play a hero." In this reversability, we once again find the circularity characteristic of Maoist discourse.

6. Shanghai shifan daxue Zhongwen xi gongnongbing xueyuan diaocha xiaozu, *Yizhi changdao gongchanzhuyi*.

7. Chen, "Yanzhe Mao Zhuxi de geming wenyi luxian shengli qianjin—Ji Dengzhan gongshe."

8. For a discussion of amateur theater in China from 1949 to 1966, see Mackerras, *Amateur Theatre in China*.

9. See, for example, "Zuohao puji geming yangbanxi de gongzuo."

10. See Judd, "China's Amateur Drama."

11. For many examples of this, see Clark, *Chinese Cultural Revolution*.

12. These associations explain the push in 1972 and 1973, when Premier Zhou Enlai was in a relative position of power vis-à-vis Jiang Qing's radical faction, for individuals to be both "red" and "expert" (*you hong you zhuan*).

13. Chen, *Acting the Right Part*, 120.

14. Chen, *Acting the Right Part*, 92.

15. Chen, *Acting the Right Part*, 120–21; Wang, *Sublime Figure of History*, 214.

16. Chen, *Acting the Right Part*, 93.

17. Silvio, "Animation."

18. Bolter and Grusin, *Remediation*, 45.

19. Bolter and Grusin, *Remediation*, 55; emphasis in original.

20. Clark, *Chinese Cultural Revolution*, 194.

21. For more on the work's creation, see Erickson, "The *Rent Collection Courtyard*."

22. Steinberg, *Anime's Media Mix*, 6.

23. Depending on the technique used, color is added under the glaze, prior to the first and only firing; over the glaze, after the initial firing and followed by another or others; or, very occasionally, directly on the biscuit.

24. As translated in Judd, "Prescriptive Dramatic Theory," 95.

25. "Zuohao puji geming yangbanxi de gongzuo." My translation.

26. *Renmin ribao* (*People's Daily*), November 15, 1971, 6.

27. Hoffer and Rayburn, "The Broadcast Blitz against Revisionism."

28. Chen, "Yanzhe Mao Zhuxi de geming wenyi luxian shengli qianjin—Ji Dengzhan gongshe." My translation.

29. Xiao, *Geming xiandai jingju xue chang changshi jieshao*.

30. One is reminded, here, of the similarly standardizing influence of Russian speech in early Soviet sound cinema. See Kaganovsky, "Learning to Speak Soviet," 306–10.

31. The transplantation (*yizhi*) of yangbanxi into regional opera forms did occur; indeed, it was encouraged as a way to interact with the masses more closely. I am speaking here of the standardized *jingju* versions of the operas.

32. Since both of these guides and the yangbanxi vocal scores make use of *jianpu* notation, we would also be justified in including manuals for learning such notation within the discursive sphere concerning amateur performance.

33. This is in keeping with notions of the "new man," both in China and the Soviet Union. See, among others, Chen, *Creating the "New Man."*

34. Wang, *Sublime Figure of History*, 217.

35. "Zuohao puji geming yangbanxi de gongzuo." My translation.

36. For a concise history of thought reform in the PRC, see Smith, "Remoulding Minds in Postsocialist China."

37. See, for example, Tao, "'Yiyang' yu 'bu yiyang.'"

38. Clark, *Chinese Cultural Revolution*, 259.

39. See Yurchak, *Everything Was Forever*. Barbara Mittler also reminds us of the enduring polysemy of propaganda of all sorts during the Cultural Revolution. Mittler, *Continuous Revolution*.

40. Judd, "Prescriptive Dramatic Theory," 100.

41. Jiang, "Tan jingju geming," 1.

42. Ding, "Women de gongtong zeren," 26. My translation.

43. This is in keeping with the understanding of childhood in the 1950s as described in Tillman, *Raising China's Revolutionaries*, 160–209.

44. Ding, "Women de gongtong zeren," 26.

45. Yuan, "Tantan zhengque di duidai biaoyan fanmian renwu," 4. My translation.

46. For a discussion of Chen Qiang (1918–2012), the actor who played these villains in the feature film versions of these works, see Lu, "Villain Stardom in Socialist China."

47. Note that this language and the concerns it is used to articulate are remarkably similar to those found in political economic analyses of the socialist commodity form in which the commodity's largely unchanged appearance is said to mask a radically new essence. For more on this, see chapter 4.

48. Tao, "'Yiyang' yu 'bu yiyang,'" 33–34. My translation.

49. Tao, "'Yiyang' yu 'bu yiyang,'" 35. My translation.

50. Judd, "Prescriptive Dramatic Theory," 112–13.

51. Zhe, "Xuexi geming yangbanxi," 2. My translation.

52. As I have argued elsewhere, the lack of specificity should not necessarily be understood as a failure to deliver a particular propagandistic message. On the contrary, in some cases vagueness can in and of itself be used as a rhetorical tool. In this instance, the enemies of the yangbanxi are potentially so broadly construed as to be anyone and everyone, which is precisely the point. See Coderre, *"Counterattack."*

53. Zhe, "Xuexi geming yangbanxi." My translation.

54. The inaugural March issue of *People's theater* (*Renmin xiju*), for example, includes a series of six articles, all written by professional actors, Yuan Shihai among them, under the title "Resolutely Counterattack the Right-Deviationist Wind to Reverse Correct Verdicts in the World of Literature and Art." Repeatedly, the authors assert Deng Xiaoping's opposition to the yangbanxi and all that they represent. See "Jianjue huiji wenyijie youqing fan'an feng."

55. For a comprehensive discussion of alienation in Marx, see Ollman, *Alienation*.

56. Starr, "On Mao's Self-Image as a Marxist Thinker."

57. "Zhongguo gongchandang zhongyang weiyuanhui guanyu wuchanjieji wenhua da geming de jueding."

58. This is in keeping with Yinghong Chen's analysis. Chen, *Creating the "New Man."*

59. Bolter and Grusin, *Remediation*, 55.

60. Steinberg, *Anime's Media Mix*, 84.

61. Lynch, *Economy of Character*, 18.

62. Lynch, *Economy of Character*, 18.

63. As a result of this understanding of characters as people, Alex Woloch, for example, can speak of the ethical implications of devoting narratological attention to the protagonist at the expense of minor characters in the realist novel. Woloch, *One vs. the Many*.

64. Mao, "Talks at the Yan'an Forum on Literature and Art," 470.

65. Fang Yun was a pen name used by a writing group in Shanghai said to be under the direction of the then minister of culture, Yu Huiyong, to promote the yangbanxi and other works in the official press in the waning years of the Cultural Revolution. Chu Lan is Fang Yun's Beijing counterpart. Fang, *Geming yangbanxi xuexi zhaji*, 79. My translation.

66. For a similar argument about proliferating models, see Pang, *Art of Cloning*.

Chapter Six: The Model in the Mirror

1. Grossman, "You—Yes, You—Are Time's Person of the Year."
2. Grossman, "You—Yes, You—Are Time's Person of the Year."
3. Rich, "Yes, You Are the Person of the Year!"
4. Rich, "Yes, You Are the Person of the Year!"
5. Rich, "Yes, You Are the Person of the Year!"
6. Ephron, "On Being Named Person of the Year."
7. On this poster, see Mitchell, *What Do Pictures Want?*, 36–38.
8. Brusati, "Stilled Lives," 168.
9. Foucault, *Order of Things*, 1–15.
10. Foucault, *Order of Things*, 14–15.
11. Kaganovsky, *How the Soviet Man Was Unmade*, 1.
12. Kaganovsky, *How the Soviet Man Was Unmade*, 2.
13. For a thorough critique of this position, see Roberts, "Positive Women Characters."
14. Huang, "*Azalea Mountain* and Late Mao Culture."
15. Bean, "Technologies of Early Stardom."
16. Van Fleit Hang, "Zhong Xinghuo," 108.
17. Lu, "Zhang Ruifang"; Zhang, "Zhao Dan"; Van Fleit Hang, "Zhong Xinghuo." On Soviet stars, see Taylor, "Red Stars"; and Haynes, "Stalinist Cinema and the Search for Audiences."
18. Van Fleit Hang, "Zhong Xinghuo," 109.
19. Dyer, *Stars*, 34.
20. See chapter 2.
21. Finnane, *Changing Clothes in China*.
22. "Zhao jingzi de 'mimi.'"
23. On the development and significance of the plate-glass mirror in France, see Melchior-Bonnet, *The Mirror*, 7–98. On glass in the Qing, see Curtis, *Glass Exchange between Europe and China*; Liu, "Vitreous Views"; and Yang, "An Account of Qing Dynasty Glassmaking."
24. Cao, "Boli yu Qingmo minchu de richang shenghuo." Also see Bao, *Fiery Cinema*, 197–262.
25. Kleutghen, "Chinese Occidenterie."
26. Liu, "Vitreous Views," 24.
27. For an excellent overview, see Varsano, "Disappearing Objects/Elusive Subjects."
28. See, for example, Dällenbach, *Mirror in the Text*; and Lowrie, *Sightings*.
29. Melchior-Bonnet, *The Mirror*, 133–84.

30. Apter and Saich, *Revolutionary Discourse in Mao's Republic*; Denton, "Rectification"; Gao, *How the Red Sun Rose*.

31. Denton, "Rectification," 59.

32. Li, "The Past Is Not Like Smoke," 83–134. See also Wu, "Self-Examination and Confession."

33. Liu, "Steel Is Made through Persistent Tempering."

34. My thanks to Ying Qian for bringing Bleichmar to my attention. Bleichmar, *Visible Empire*, 9.

35. Yin, "Zhao jingzi yu xilian." My translation.

36. Mao, "On Coalition Government," Marxists.org, accessed June 3, 2020, https://www.marxists.org/reference/archive/mao/selected-works/volume-3/mswv3_25.htm.

37. The same move is taken up in the use of "dirt" (*wugou*) in Yue, "Xilian zhi yu."

38. Douglas, *Purity and Danger*, 44.

39. As translated in Varsano, "Disappearing Objects/Elusive Subjects," 101.

40. Zhang, "'Yi ren wei jing.'" My translation.

41. "Yong weida de Mao Zedong sixiang po si li gong," 4.

42. Zhou, "Geming xue feng."

43. "Lüdashi jiaotongju." My translation.

44. Dobrenko, *Political Economy of Socialist Realism*.

45. Foucault, "Of Other Spaces," 24.

46. Foucault, "Of Other Spaces," 24.

47. See Liu, "Vitreous Views." For related late-imperial experiments with space, perspective, and the painted screen, see Wu, *Double Screen*.

48. Brusati, "Stilled Lives."

49. Mitchell, *Picture Theory*, 16; emphasis in original.

50. Mitchell, *Picture Theory*, 35–82.

51. Elsewhere, Mitchell draws a distinction between images and pictures. He characterizes the former as "any likeness, figure, motif, or form that appears in some medium or other." Pictures, on the other hand, are "understood as complex assemblages of virtual, material, and symbolic elements." Within this formulation, pictures may encompass images, but they also necessarily go beyond them, bringing them into relation with other media as well as discursive and sociocultural practices. Mitchell, *What Do Pictures Want?*, xiii. For simplicity's sake I take *picture* to be basically synonymous with the more restrictive *image*.

52. Dal Lago, "Activating Images."

53. Li, *Utopian Ruins*. For Poole's original formulation, see Poole, *Vision, Race, and Modernity*, 8–13.

Coda

1. Coderre, "The Curator, the Investor, and the Dupe." See also Ho and Li, "From Landlord Manor to Red Memorabilia."

2. On the role of museums in (re)constructing the past in contemporary China, see also Denton, *Exhibiting the Past*.

3. My translation.
4. Ho and Li, "From Landlord Manor to Red Memorabilia," 30.
5. "Chenlie zhanguan."
6. It has since been eclipsed many times over.
7. This claim is articulated, in English, at each entrance.

BIBLIOGRAPHY

Ah Cheng 阿城. "Ting ditai" "听敌台" (Listening to enemy stations). In *Qishi niandai* 七十年代 (The seventies), edited by Bei Dao 北岛 and Li Tuo 李陀, 147–54. Beijing: San lian shudian, 2009.

Akademiya nauk SSSR institut ekonomiki. *Politicheskaya ekonomiya: Uchebnik* (Political economy: A textbook). Moscow: Gosudarstvennoe izdatel'stvo politicheskoy literatury, 1954.

Anagnost, Ann. *National Past-Times: Narrative, Representation, and Power in Modern China*. Durham, NC: Duke University Press, 1997.

Anderson, Benedict. *Imagined Communities: Reflections on the Origin and Spread of Nationalism*. London: Verso, 2006.

Andreas, Joel. *Rise of the Red Engineers: The Cultural Revolution and the Origins of China's New Class*. Stanford, CA: Stanford University Press, 2009.

Apter, David E., and Tony Saich. *Revolutionary Discourse in Mao's Republic*. Cambridge, MA: Harvard University Press, 1994.

Arvatov, Boris. "Everyday Life and the Culture of the Thing (Toward the Formulation of the Question)." *October*, no. 81 (1997): 119–28.

Askew, Kelly Michelle. *Performing the Nation: Swahili Music and Cultural Politics in Tanzania*. Chicago: University of Chicago Press, 2002.

Attali, Jacques. *Noise: The Political Economy of Music*. Minneapolis: University of Minnesota Press, 1985.

Austin, J. L. *How to Do Things with Words*. Oxford: Clarendon, 1975.

Bailes, Kendall E. "Alexei Gastev and the Soviet Controversy over Taylorism, 1918–24." *Soviet Studies* 29, no. 3 (1977): 373–94.

Bao, Weihong. *Fiery Cinema: The Emergence of an Affective Medium in China, 1915–1945*. Minneapolis: University of Minnesota Press, 2015.

Barlow, Tani E. "Buying In: Advertising and the Sexy Modern Girl Icon in Shanghai in the 1920s and 1930s." In *The Modern Girl around the World: Consumption, Modernity, and Globalization*, edited by Modern Girl around the World Research Group, 288–316. Durham, NC: Duke University Press, 2008.

Barlow, Tani E. "Wanting Some: Commodity Desire and the Eugenic Modern Girl." In *Women in China: The Republican Period in Historical Perspective*, edited by Mechthild Leutner and Nicola Spakowski, 312–50. Münster: Lit Verlag, 2005.

Bathrick, David. "Making a National Family with the Radio: The Nazi *Wunschkonzert*." *Modernism/modernity* 4, no. 1 (1997): 115–27.

Bean, Jennifer M. "Technologies of Early Stardom and the Extraordinary Body." *Camera Obscura* 16, no. 3 (2001): 8–57.

Bei Dao 北島. "Changpian" "唱片" (Records). In *Chengmen kai* 城門開 (The city gates open), 41–46. Hong Kong: Oxford University Press, 2010.

Bei Dao 北島. "Out of Context." *Renditions* 1 (2011): 47–71.

Beijing daxue jingjixi pipanzu 北京大学经济系批判组, ed. *Kong Qiu jingji sixiang pipan* 孔丘经济思想批判 (A critique of Confucius's economic thought). Beijing: Zhongguo caizheng jingji chubanshe, 1974.

Benson, Susan Porter. *Counter Cultures: Saleswomen, Managers, and Customers in American Department Stores, 1890–1940*. Urbana: University of Illinois Press, 1986.

Bey, Hakim. *T.A.Z.: The Temporary Autonomous Zone, Ontological Anarchy, Poetic Terrorism*. Brooklyn: Autonomedia, 1991.

Bijsterveld, Karin. *Mechanical Sound: Technology, Culture, and Public Problems of Noise in the Twentieth Century*. Cambridge, MA: MIT Press, 2008.

Birdsall, Carolyn. *Nazi Soundscapes: Sound, Technology and Urban Space in Germany, 1933–1945*. Amsterdam: Amsterdam University Press, 2012.

Bleichmar, Daniela. *Visible Empire: Botanical Expeditions and Visual Culture in the Hispanic Enlightenment*. Chicago: University of Chicago Press, 2012.

Bolter, Jay David, and Richard Grusin. *Remediation: Understanding New Media*. Cambridge, MA: MIT Press, 1999.

Bourdieu, Pierre. *Distinction: A Social Critique of the Judgement of Taste*. Cambridge, MA: Harvard University Press, 1984.

Bowlby, Rachel. *Carried Away: The Invention of Modern Shopping*. New York: Columbia University Press, 2002.

Braester, Yomi. "'A Big Dying Vat': The Vilifying of Shanghai during the Good Eighth Company Campaign." *Modern China* 31, no. 4 (2005): 411–47.

Bren, Paulina, and Mary Neuburger. "Introduction." In *Communism Unwrapped: Consumption in Cold War Eastern Europe*, edited by Paulina Bren and Mary Neuburger, 3–19. Oxford: Oxford University Press, 2012.

Bronfman, Alejandra. *Isles of Noise: Sonic Media in the Caribbean*. Chapel Hill: University of North Carolina Press, 2016.

Brown, Bill. "The Tyranny of Things (Trivia in Karl Marx and Mark Twain)." *Critical Inquiry* 28, no. 2 (2002): 442–69.

Brusati, Celeste. "Stilled Lives: Self-Portraiture and Self-Reflection in Seventeenth-Century Netherlandish Still-Life Painting." *Simiolus: Netherlands Quarterly for the History of Art* 20, nos. 2–3 (1990): 168–82.

Buchli, Victor. *An Archaeology of Socialism*. Oxford: Berg, 1999.

Buck-Morss, Susan. *The Dialectics of Seeing: Walter Benjamin and the Arcades Project*. Cambridge, MA: MIT Press, 1991.

Buck-Morss, Susan. *Dreamworld and Catastrophe: The Passing of Mass Utopia in East and West*. Cambridge, MA: MIT Press, 2000.

Bukharin, Nikolai Ivanovich. *Economics of the Transformation Period*. New York: Bergman, 1971.

Cao Chunsheng 曹春生 and Chen Liping 陈丽萍. *Jingdezhen diaosu ciyi* 景德镇雕塑瓷艺 (Porcelain sculpture art in Jingdezhen). Guangzhou: Huanan ligong daxue chubanshe, 2008.

Cao Nanping 曹南屏. "Boli yu Qingmo minchu de richang shenghuo" "玻璃與清末民初的日常生活" (Glass and everyday life from the end of the Qing to the early republican period). *Jindaishi yanjiusuo jikan* 近代史研究所集刊 (Academia Sinica journal of modern Chinese history) 76 (2012): 81–134.

CCP Central Committee. "The Cultural Revolution—Excerpt from 'Resolution on Certain Questions in the History of Our Party since the Founding of the People's Republic of China.'" In *China's Cultural Revolution, 1966–69: Not a Dinner Party*, edited by Michael Schoenhals, 296–303. Armonk, NY: M. E. Sharpe, 1996.

Chan, Roy Bing. *The Edge of Knowing: Dreams, History, and Realism in Modern Chinese Literature*. Seattle: University of Washington Press, 2016.

Chan, Wellington K. K. "Personal Styles, Cultural Values and Management: The Sincere and Wing On Companies in Shanghai and Hong Kong, 1900–1941." *Business History Review* 70, no. 2 (1996): 141–66.

Chao Feng 巢峰, ed. *"Wenhua da geming" cidian* "文化大革命"詞典 (Dictionary of the Cultural Revolution). Hong Kong: Ganglong chubanshe, 1993.

Chao, Shu-li (Zhao Shuli). *Sanliwan Village*. Translated by Gladys Yang. Peking: Foreign Language Press, 1957.

Ch'en, Jo-hsi (Chen, Ruoxi). "The Big Fish." In *The Execution of Mayor Yin and Other Stories from the Great Proletarian Cultural Revolution*, edited by Howard Goldblatt, 126–38. Bloomington: Indiana University Press, 2004.

Chen Shenqing 陈声庆. "Yanzhe Mao Zhuxi de geming wenyi luxian shengli qianjin—Ji Dengzhan gongshe ge dadui yeyu wenyi xuanchuandui dali puji geming yangbanxi" "沿着毛主席的革命文艺路线胜利前进—记灯盏公社各大队业余文艺宣传队大力普及革命样板戏" (Victoriously advance Chairman Mao's revolutionary line in literature and art—On the energetically popularization of yangbanxi by the Dengshan Commune Brigade amateur propaganda teams). *Sichuan ribao* 四川日报 (Sichuan daily), May 23, 1974.

Chen, Tina Mai. "Dressing for the Party: Clothing, Citizenship, and Gender-Formation in Mao's China." *Fashion Theory: The Journal of Dress, Body and Culture* 5, no. 2 (2001): 143–71.

Chen, Tina Mai. "Propagating the Propaganda Film: The Meaning of Film in Chinese Communist Party Writings, 1949–1965." *Modern Chinese Literature and Culture* 15, no. 2 (2003): 154–93.

Chen, Xiaomei. *Acting the Right Part: Political Theater and Popular Drama in Contemporary China*. Honolulu: University of Hawai'i Press, 2002.

Chen Xin 陈新. "Zenyang chenlie shangpin" "怎样陈列商品" (How to display commodities). *Shangye gongzuo* 商业工作 (Trade work) 7 (1964): 20–23.

Chen, Yinghong. *Creating the "New Man": From Enlightenment Ideals to Socialist Realities*. Honolulu: University of Hawai'i Press, 2009.

"Chenlie zhanguan." *Jianchuan bowuguan juluo*. Accessed December 7, 2018. http://www.jc-museum.cn/display.

Chin, Tamara T. *Savage Exchange: Han Imperialism, Chinese Literary Style, and the Economic Imagination*. Cambridge, MA: Harvard University Asia Center, 2014.

Chinn, Dennis L. "Basic Commodity Distribution in the People's Republic of China." *China Quarterly* 84 (1980): 744–54.

Chou, Yu-Min. "Wholesaling in Communist China." In *Comparative Marketing: Wholesaling in Fifteen Countries*, edited by Robert Bartels, 253–70. Homewood, IL: Richard D. Irwin, 1963.

Chow, Rey. *Writing Diaspora: Tactics of Intervention in Contemporary Cultural Studies*. Indianapolis: Indiana University Press, 1993.

Christensen, Peer Moller. "The Shanghai School and Its Rejection." In *The Chinese Economic Reforms*, edited by Stephen Feuchtwang and Arthur Hussein, 74–90. London: Croom Helm, 1983.

Christensen, Peer Moller, and Jorgen Delman. "A Theory of Transitional Society: Mao Zedong and the Shanghai School." *Bulletin of Concerned Asian Scholars* 13, no. 2 (1981): 2–15.

"Chuangzao guanggao xin fengge, fanying yuejin xin mianmao" "创造广告新风格 反映跃进新面貌" (Create a new style of advertising, reflect the new face of the Great Leap). *Renmin ribao* 人民日报 (*People's Daily*), September 7, 1959.

"Cichang de yi xiang jishu gexin" "瓷厂的一项技术革新" (The technological remaking of a ceramics factory). *Renmin huabao* 人民画报 (*China Pictorial*) 9 (1975): 36–37.

Clark, Paul. *The Chinese Cultural Revolution: A History*. Cambridge: Cambridge University Press, 2008.

Cochran, Sherman, ed. *Inventing Nanjing Road: Commercial Culture in Shanghai, 1900–1945*. Ithaca, NY: Cornell University East Asia Program, 1999.

Coderre, Laurence. "*Counterattack*: (Re)Contextualizing Propaganda." *Journal of Chinese Cinemas* 4, no. 3 (2010): 211–27.

Coderre, Laurence. "The Curator, the Investor, and the Dupe: Consumer Desire and Chinese Cultural Revolution Memorabilia." *Journal of Material Culture* 21, no. 4 (2016): 429–47.

Coderre, Laurence. "A Necessary Evil: Conceptualizing the Socialist Commodity under Mao." *Comparative Studies in Society and History* 61, no. 1 (2019): 23–49.

Connor, Steven. "The Modern Auditory I." In *Rewriting the Self: Histories from the Renaissance to the Present*, edited by Roy Porter, 203–23. London: Routledge, 2002.

Corbin, Alain. *Village Bells: Sound and Meaning in the Nineteenth-Century French Countryside*. Translated by Martin Thom. New York: Columbia University Press, 1998.

Cosentino, Frank J. *The Boehm Journey to Ching-Te-Chen, China, Birthplace of Porcelain*. Trenton, NJ: Edward Marshall Boehm, 1976.

"Cuihui Peng Zhen zai shangye shang de hei judian" "摧毁彭真在商业上的黑据点" (Smash Peng Zhen's black stronghold in commerce). *Hong fan jun* 红反军 (Red rebel army), June 19, 1967.

Currid, Brian. *A National Acoustics: Music and Mass Publicity in Weimar and Nazi Germany*. Minneapolis: University of Minnesota Press, 2006.

Curtis, Emily Byrne. *Glass Exchange between Europe and China, 1550–1800: Diplomatic, Mercantile and Technological Interactions*. Burlington, VT: Ashgate, 2009.

Dai Jiafang 戴嘉枋. *Yangbanxi de fengfengyuyu: Jiang Qing, yangbanxi ji neimu* 样板戏的风风雨雨: 江青、样板戏及内幕 (Storms of the model theater: Jiang Qing, the model theater, and the inside story). Beijing: Zhishi chubanshe, 1995.

Dal Lago, Francesca. "Activating Images: The Ideological Use of Metapictures and Visualized Metatexts in the Iconography of the Cultural Revolution." *Modern Chinese Literature and Culture* 21, no. 2 (2009): 167–97.

Dällenbach, Lucien. *The Mirror in the Text*. Translated by Jeremy Whiteley. Chicago: University of Chicago Press, 1989.

Davis, Deborah, ed. *The Consumer Revolution in Urban China*. Berkeley: University of California Press, 2000.

Deleuze, Gilles, and Félix Guattari. *A Thousand Plateaus: Capitalism and Schizophrenia*. Translated by Brian Massumi. Minneapolis: University of Minnesota Press, 1987.

Deng Kesheng 邓克生. *Shangpin zizhuan* 商品自传 (Autobiography of a commodity). Nanjing: Jiangsu renmin chubanshe, 1960.

Deng Kesheng 邓克生. *Shangpin zizhuan* 商品自传 (Autobiography of a commodity). Nanjing: Jiangsu renmin chubanshe, 1978.

Denton, Kirk A. "Rectification: Party Discipline, Intellectual Remolding, and the Formation of a Political Community." In *Words and Their Stories: Essays on the Language of the Chinese Revolution*, edited by Ban Wang, 52–63. Leiden: Brill, 2011.

Denton, Kirk A. *Exhibiting the Past: Historical Memory and the Politics of Museums in Postsocialist China*. Honolulu: University of Hawai'i Press, 2014.

Dillon, Michael. "Fang Zhimin, Jingdezhen and the Northeast Jiangxi Soviet." *Modern Asian Studies* 26, no. 3 (1992): 569–89.

Dillon, Michael. "A History of the Porcelain Industry in Jingdezhen." PhD diss., University of Leeds, 1976.

Ding Lin 丁林. "Women de gongtong zeren" "我们的共同责任" (Our common responsibility). In *Bi tan Lin hai xue yuan* 笔谈《林海雪原》 (On *Tracks in the Snowy Forest*), 26–29. Beijing: Beijing chubanshe, 1961.

Dobrenko, Evgeny. *Political Economy of Socialist Realism*. Translated by Jesse M Savage. New Haven, CT: Yale University Press, 2007.

Donnithorne, Audrey. *China's Economic System*. New York: Frederick A. Praeger, 1967.

Douglas, Aileen. "Britannia's Rule and the It-Narrator." *Eighteenth-Century Fiction* 6, no. 1 (1993): 65–82.

Douglas, Mary. *Purity and Danger: An Analysis of Concept of Pollution and Taboo*. London: Routledge, 2002.

Douglas, Susan J. *Listening In: Radio and the American Imagination from Amos 'n' Andy and Edward R. Murrow to Wolfman Jack and Howard Stern*. New York: Times Books, 1999.

Du, Daisy Yan. "Socialist Modernity in the Wasteland: Changing Representations of the Female Tractor Driver in China, 1949–1964." *Modern Chinese Literature and Culture* 29, no. 1 (2017): 55–94.

Dutton, Michael. "From Culture Industry to Mao Industry: A Greek Tragedy." *boundary 2* 32, no. 2 (2005): 151–67.

Dyer, Richard. *Stars*. London: BFI, 1998.

Eisenberg, Evan. *The Recording Angel: Explorations in Phonography*. New York: McGraw-Hill, 1987.

Engels, Frederick. *Anti-Dühring: Herr Eugen Dühring's Revolution in Science*. Translated by Emile Burns. London: Lawrence and Wishart, 1936.

Ephron, Nora. "On Being Named Person of the Year." *Huffington Post*, December 17, 2006. https://www.huffingtonpost.com/nora-ephron/on-being-named-person-of-_b_36546.html.

Erickson, Britta. "The *Rent Collection Courtyard*, Past and Present." In *Art in Turmoil: The Chinese Cultural Revolution, 1966–76*, edited by Richard King, 121–35. Vancouver: UBC Press, 2010.

Eyferth, Jan Jacob Karl. *Eating Rice from Bamboo Roots: The Social History of a Community of Handicraft Papermakers in Rural Sichuan, 1920–2000*. Cambridge, MA: Harvard University Asia Center, 2009.

Fang Hai 方海. "Xue yidian zhengzhi jingjixue" "学一点政治经济学" (Study a little bit of political economy). *Hongqi* 红旗 (*Red flag*) 7 (1972): 35–42.

Fang Yun 方耘. *Geming yangbanxi xuexi zhaji* 革命样板戏学习札记 Shanghai: Shanghai renmin chubanshe, 1974.

Fehérváry, Krisztina. "Goods and States: The Political Logic of State-Socialist Material Culture." *Comparative Studies in Society and History* 51, no. 2 (2009): 426–59.

Fehérváry, Krisztina. *Politics in Color and Concrete: Socialist Materialities and the Middle Class in Hungary*. Bloomington: Indiana University Press, 2013.

"Feng shou de yi ke" "丰收的一课" (A fruitful lesson). *Zhuangshi* 装饰 (*Art and Design*) 3 (1961): 50–51.

Festa, Lynn. *Sentimental Figures of Empire in Eighteenth-Century Britain and France*. Baltimore, MA: Johns Hopkins University Press, 2006.

Finnane, Antonia. *Changing Clothes in China: Fashion, History, Nation*. New York: Columbia University Press, 2008.

Fitzpatrick, Sheila. "The Good Old Days." *London Review of Books* 25, no. 19 (2003): 18–20.

Foucault, Michel. "Of Other Spaces." *Diacritics* 16, no. 1 (1986): 22–27.

Foucault, Michel. *The Order of Things: An Archaeology of the Human Sciences*. New York: Vintage, 1994.

Franke, Herbert. "Literary Parody in Traditional Chinese Literature: Descriptive Pseudo-Biographies." *Oriens Extremus* 21, no. 1 (1974): 23–31.

Frazier, Mark W. *The Making of the Chinese Industrial Workplace: State, Revolution, and Labor Management*. New York: Cambridge University Press, 2002.

Freedgood, Elaine. *The Ideas in Things: Fugitive Meaning in the Victorian Novel*. Chicago: University of Chicago Press, 2006.

Friedberg, Anne. *Window Shopping: Cinema and the Postmodern*. Berkeley: University of California Press, 1993.

Friedman, Sara L. "Embodying Civility: Civilizing Processes and Symbolic Citizenship in Southeastern China." *Journal of Asian Studies* 63, no. 3 (2004): 687–718.

Gamble, Jos. "Consumers with Chinese Characteristics? Local Customers in British and Japanese Multinational Stores in Contemporary China." In *The Making of the Consumer: Knowledge, Power and Identity in the Modern World*, edited by Frank Trentmann, 175–98. Oxford: Berg, 2006.

Gao, Hua. *How the Red Sun Rose: The Origin and Development of the Yan'an Rectification Movement, 1930–1945*. Translated by Stacey Mosher and Jian Guo. Hong Kong: Chinese University Press, 2018.

"Geng hao di xuexi Mao Zedong sixiang geng hao di yunyong bianzheng weiwu lun—Shangye zhigong xuexi *Guanyu ruhe da pingpangqiu* de xinde" "更好地学习毛泽东思想 更好地运用辩证唯物论—商业职工学习《关于如何打乒乓球》的心得" (Improved study of Mao Zedong Thought, improved use of dialectical materialism: Trade workers' takeaways from studying *How to play ping pong*). *Shangye gongzuo* 商业工作 (*Trade work*) 7 (1965): 22–25.

Gerth, Karl. "Compromising with Consumerism in Socialist China: Transnational Flows and Internal Tensions in Socialist Advertising." *Past and Present* 218, no. suppl 8 (2013): 203–32.

Gillette, Maris Boyd. *China's Porcelain Capital: The Rise, Fall and Reinvention of Ceramics in Jingdezhen*. New York: Bloomsbury, 2016.

Gladney, Dru C. "Representing Nationality in China: Refiguring Majority/Minority Identities." *Journal of Asian Studies* 53, no. 1 (1994): 92–123.

Goldman, Marshall I. "Retailing in the Soviet Union." *Journal of Marketing* 24, no. 4 (1960): 9–15.

Golomstock, Igor. *Totalitarian Art: In the Soviet Union, the Third Reich, Fascist Italy, and the People's Republic of China*. London: Collins Harvill, 1990.

Goscilo, Helena. "Luxuriating in Lack: Plenitude and Consuming Happiness in Soviet Paintings and Posters, 1930s–1953." In *Petrified Utopia: Happiness Soviet Style*, edited by Marina Balina and Evgeny A. Dobrenko, 53–78. London: Anthem, 2009.

Grossman, Lev. "You—Yes, You—Are Time's Person of the Year." *Time*, December 25, 2006. http://content.time.com/time/magazine/article/0,9171,1570810,00.html.

Gu Dawei 顾大伟. "Shanghai diantai de fangyan (huyu) boyin gongzuo" "上海电台的方言（沪语）播音工作" (Shanghai radio's topolect [Shanghainese] broadcasting). In *Shanghai guangbo dianshi ziliao huibian* 上海广播电视资料汇编 (Collection of Shanghai broadcasting materials), edited by Shanghai shi guangbo dianshi ju "Dangdai" bianji zu 上海市广播电视局《当代》编辑组, 112–16. Shanghai: 1986.

Gu Song 古松. "Wei shangdian pi xin zhuang" "为商店披新装" (Stores get a new look). *Meishu* 美术 (*Art*) 7 (1960): 57.

"Guangfudao shangdian shi Liu Shaoqi zai cai mao zhanxian shang qinzi shu qi de yi mian hei qi" "光复道商店是刘少奇在财贸战线上亲自树起的一面黑旗" (Guangfudao Store is a black flag on the financial and commercial front, planted by Liu Shaoqi himself). *Shi yi ba* 十一八 (October 18), September 22, 1967.

Guo, Hongchi, and Fei Liu. "New China's Flagship Emporium: The Beijing Wangfujing Department Store." In *Asian Department Stores*, edited by Kerrie L. MacPherson, 114–38. Honolulu: University of Hawai'i Press, 1998.

Guo Qihong 郭启宏. "Wo yu *Xiangyang shangdian*" "我与《向阳商店》" (*Xiangyang Store* and me). *Da wutai* 大舞台 (Great stage) 2 (2004): 48–55.

Guo Qihong 郭启宏 and Hu Sha 胡沙. *Xiangyang shangdian* 向阳商店 (*Xiangyang Store*). Beijing: Zhongguo changpian chubanshe, 1974.

Guo Qingsheng 郭庆生. "Jianguo chuqi de Beijing shijian" "建国初期的北京时间" (Beijing time in the early PRC). *Zhongguo keji shiliao* 中国科技史料 (China historical materials of science and technology) 24, no. 1 (2003): 1–5.

Guo Qingsheng 郭庆生. "Zhongguo biaozhun shi zhi kao" "中国标准时制考" (Study of China's standard time). *Zhongguo keji shiliao* 中国科技史料 (China historical materials of science and technology) 22, no. 3 (2001): 269–80.

Hay, Jonathan. *Sensuous Surfaces: The Decorative Object in Early Modern China*. Honolulu: University of Hawai'i Press, 2010.

Haynes, John. "Stalinist Cinema and the Search for Audiences: Liubov' Orlova the Case for Star Studies." In *Cinema, State Socialism and Society in the Soviet Union and Eastern Europe: Re-Visions*, edited by Sanja Bahun and John Haynes, 115–48. Abingdon, UK: Routledge, 2014.

Hessler, Julie. *A Social History of Soviet Trade: Trade Policy, Retail Practices, and Consumption, 1917–1953*. Princeton, NJ: Princeton University Press, 2004.

Hetherington, Philippa. "Dressing the Shop Window of Socialism: Gender and Consumption in the Soviet Union in the Era of 'Cultured Trade,' 1934–53." *Gender and History* 27, no. 2 (2015): 417–45.

Hilton, Marjorie L. "Retailing the Revolution: The State Department Store (GUM) and Soviet Society in the 1920s." *Journal of Social History* 37, no. 4 (2004): 939–64.

Hilton, Marjorie L. *Selling to the Masses: Retailing in Russia, 1880–1930*. Pittsburgh, PA: University of Pittsburgh Press, 2014.

Ho, Denise Y. *Curating Revolution: Politics on Display in Mao's China*. Cambridge: Cambridge University Press, 2018.

Ho, Denise Y., and Jie Li. "From Landlord Manor to Red Memorabilia: Reincarnations of a Chinese Museum Town." *Modern China* 42, no. 1 (2016): 3–37.

Hoffer, Thomas W., and J. D. Rayburn II. "The Broadcast Blitz against Revisionism: Radio and the Chinese Cultural Revolution." *Journalism and Mass Communication Quarterly* 54, no. 4 (1977): 703–12.

Huang, Ellen C. "From the Imperial Court to the International Art Market: Jingdezhen Porcelain Production as Global Visual Culture." *Journal of World History* 23, no. 1 (2012): 115–45.

Huang, Nicole. "*Azalea Mountain* and Late Mao Culture." *Opera Quarterly* 26, nos. 2–3 (2010): 402–25.

Huang, Nicole. "Listening to Films: Politics of the Auditory in 1970s China." *Journal of Chinese Cinemas* 7, no. 3 (2013): 187–206.

Huang, Nicole. "Sun-Facing Courtyards: Urban Communal Culture in Mid-1970s' Shanghai." *East Asian History*, nos. 25–26 (2003): 161–82.

Huang Zili 黄自立. "'Fan Dulin lun' Wu Liangping yiben dui Zhongguo Makesizhuyi zhexue de gongxian" "《反杜林论》吴亮平译本对中国马克思主义哲学的贡献" (The contribution of Wu Liangping's translation of *Anti-Dühring* to Chinese Marxist philosophy). *Makesizhuyi yanjiu* 马克思主义研究 (Studies on Marxism) 3 (2018): 107–15.

Huebner, Jon W. "Architecture and History in Shanghai's Central District." *Journal of Oriental Studies* 26, no. 2 (1988): 209–69.

Inkeles, Alex. *Public Opinion in Soviet Russia: A Study in Mass Persuasion*. Cambridge, MA: Harvard University Press, 1950.

Jiang Qing 江青. "Tan jingju geming—yijiuliusi nian qi yue zai jingju xiandai xi guanmo yanchu renyuan de zuotanhui shang de jianghua" "谈京剧革命—一九六四年七月在京剧现代戏观摩演出人员的座谈会上的讲话" (On the revolution in Beijing opera—Talks at the July 1964 conference on Beijing operas on contemporary themes). *Renmin ribao* 人民日报 (*People's Daily*), May 10, 1967.

Jiangxisheng qinggongye ting taoci yanjiusuo 江西省轻工业厅陶瓷研究所, ed. *Jingdezhen taoci shigao* 景德镇陶瓷史稿 (Draft history of the porcelain industry in Jingdezhen). Beijing: Shenghuo dushu xin zhi san lian shudian, 1959.

"Jianjue huiji wenyijie youqing fan'an feng" "坚决回击文艺界右倾翻案风" (Resolutely counterattack the right-deviationist wind to reverse correct verdicts in the world of literature and art). *Renmin xiju* 人民戏剧 (People's theater) 1 (1976): 10–18.

Jiefangjun Heilongjiang shengchan jianshe budui zhengzhi bu 解放军黑龙江生产建设部队政治部, ed. *Zhishi qingnian zai Beidahuang* 知识青年在北大荒 (Sent-down youth in the northeast). Beijing: Renmin meishu chubanshe, 1973.

Jin Dalu 金大陆. "Guanyu 'piaozheng shidai' de jiti jiyi" "关于'票证时代'的集体记忆" (On "the era of coupons" in collective memory). *Shehui kexue* 社会科学 (Social science) 8 (2009): 127–37.

Jing Chi 景池. *Shangpin zishu* 商品自述 (A commodity's tale). Shanghai: Shanghai renmin chubanshe, 1975.

Jingdezhenshi geming weiyuanhui jihua weiyuanhui 景德镇市革命委员会计划委员会, ed. *Jingdezhenshi guomin jingji tongji ziliao (1974)* 景德镇市国民经济统计资料 *(1974)* (National economic statistical data for Jingdezhen City [1974]), 1975.

Jingdezhenshi geming weiyuanhui jihua weiyuanhui 景德镇市革命委员会计划委员会, ed. *Jingdezhenshi guomin jingji tongji ziliao (1977)* 景德镇市国民经济统计资料 *(1977)* (National economic statistical data for Jingdezhen City [1977]), 1978.

Jingdezhenshi jingji jihua weiyuanhui 景德镇市经济计划委员会, ed. *Jingdezhenshi guomin jingji tongji ziliao (1950–1957)* 景德镇市国民经济统计资料 *(1950–1957)* (National economic statistical data for Jingdezhen City [1950–1957]), 1958.

Jingdezhenshi jingji jihua weiyuanhui 景德镇市经济计划委员会, ed. *Jingdezhenshi guomin jingji tongji ziliao (1958)* 景德镇市国民经济统计资料 *(1958)* (National economic statistical data for Jingdezhen City [1958]), 1959.

Jones, Andrew F. "Quotation Songs: Portable Media and the Maoist Pop Song." In *Mao's Little Red Book: A Global History*, edited by Alexander C. Cook, 43–60. Cambridge: Cambridge University Press, 2014.

Jones, Andrew F. *Yellow Music: Media Culture and Colonial Modernity in the Chinese Jazz Age*. Durham, NC: Duke University Press, 2001.

Jones, Keith. "Music in Factories: A Twentieth-Century Technique for Control of the Productive Self." *Social and Cultural Geography* 6, no. 5 (2010): 723–44.

Judd, Ellen. "China's Amateur Drama: The Movement to Popularize the Revolutionary Model Operas." *Bulletin of Concerned Asian Scholars* 15, no. 1 (1983): 26–35.

Judd, Ellen. "Prescriptive Dramatic Theory of the Cultural Revolution." In *Drama in the People's Republic of China*, edited by Constantine Tung and Colin Mackerras, 94–118. Albany: State University of New York Press, 1987.

Kaganovsky, Lilya. *How the Soviet Man Was Unmade: Cultural Fantasy and Male Subjectivity under Stalin*. Pittsburgh, PA: University of Pittsburgh Press, 2008.

Kaganovsky, Lilya. "Learning to Speak Soviet: Soviet Cinema and the Coming of Sound." In *A Companion to Russian Cinema*, edited by Birgit Beumers, 292–313. Chichester, UK: Wiley Blackwell, 2016.

Kao Ciji 考茨基 (Kautsky, Karl). *Ai'erfute gangling jieshuo* 爱尔福特纲领解说 (Explanation of the Erfurt Program). Translated by Chen Dongye. Beijing: San lian shudian, 1963.

Kautsky, Karl. *The Class Struggle (Erfurt Program)*. Translated by William E. Bohn. Chicago: Charles H. Kerr and Co., 1910.

Ke Zuji 柯祖基 (Kautsky, Karl). *Jieji zhengdou* 阶级争斗 (The class struggle). Translated by Yun Daiying. Shanghai: Xin qingnian she, 1921.

Kelly, Diana. "Perceptions of Taylorism and a Marxist Scientific Manager." *Journal of Management History* 22, no. 3 (2016): 298–319.

Kenney, William Howland. *Recorded Music in American Life: The Phonograph and Popular Memory, 1890–1945*. Oxford: Oxford University Press, 2003.

Kerr, Rose, and Nigel Wood. *Chemistry and Chemical Technology*, part 12: *Ceramic Technology*. Cambridge: Cambridge University Press, 2004.

Kettering, Karen. "'Ever More Cosy and Comfortable': Stalinism and the Soviet Domestic Interior, 1928–1938." *Journal of Design History* 10, no. 2 (1997): 119–35.

Kexuejia tan 21 shiji 科学家谈21世纪 (Scientists discuss the twenty-first century). Shanghai: Shaonian ertong chubanshe, 1959.

Khan, Naveeda. "The Acoustics of Muslim Striving: Loudspeaker Use in Ritual Practice in Pakistan." *Comparative Studies in Society and History* 53, no. 3 (2011): 571–94.

Kiaer, Christina. *Imagine No Possessions: The Socialist Objects of Russian Constructivism*. Cambridge, MA: MIT Press, 2005.

Kleutghen, Kristina. "Chinese Occidenterie: The Diversity of 'Western' Objects in Eighteenth-Century China." *Eighteenth-Century Studies* 47, no. 2 (2014): 117–35.

Kleutghen, Kristina. *Imperial Illusions: Crossing Pictorial Boundaries in the Qing Palaces*. Seattle: University of Washington Press, 2015.

Klochko, Mikhail A. *Soviet Scientist in Red China*. Translated by Andrew MacAndrew. New York: Frederick A. Praeger, 1964.

Kornai, János. *The Socialist System: The Political Economy of Communism*. Oxford: Oxford University Press, 1992.

Lacey, Kate. "Radio's Vernacular Modernism: The Schedule as Modernist Text." *Media History* 24, no. 2 (2018): 166–79.

Lamb, Jonathan. *The Things Things Say*. Princeton, NJ: Princeton University Press, 2011.

Larkin, Brian. "Techniques of Inattention: The Mediality of Loudspeakers in Nigeria." *Anthropological Quarterly* 87, no. 4 (2014): 989–1015.

Latham, Kevin. "Rethinking Chinese Consumption: Social Palliatives and the Rhetorics of Transition in Postsocialist China." In *Postsocialism: Ideals, Ideologies and Practices in Eurasia*, edited by C. M. Hann, 217–37. London: Routledge, 2002.

Latour, Bruno. *We Have Never Been Modern*. Translated by Catherine Porter. Cambridge, MA: Harvard University Press, 1993.

Latour, Bruno. *Reassembling the Social: An Introduction to Actor-Network-Theory*. Oxford: Oxford University Press, 2005.

Leach, William R. *Land of Desire: Merchants, Power and the Rise of a New American Culture*. New York: Pantheon, 1993.

Ledderose, Lothar. *Ten Thousand Things: Module and Mass Production in Chinese Art*. Princeton, NJ: Princeton University Press, 2000.

Lee, Haiyan. "Mao's Two Bodies: On the Curious (Political) Art of Impersonating the Great Helmsman." In *Red Legacies in China: Cultural Afterlives of the Communist Revolution*, edited by Jie Li and Enhua Zhang, 245–70. Cambridge, MA: Harvard University Asia Center, 2016.

Lee, Leo Ou-fan. *Shanghai Modern: The Flowering of a New Urban Culture in China, 1930–1945*. Cambridge, MA: Harvard University Press, 1999.

Lee, Tong Soon. "Technology and the Production of Islamic Space: The Call to Prayer in Singapore." *Ethnomusicology* 43, no. 1 (1999): 86–100.

Li Mowry, Hua-Yuan. *Yang-Pan Hsi—New Theater in China*. Berkeley: Center for Chinese Studies, University of California, 1973.

Li, Jie. *Utopian Ruins: A Memorial Museum of the Mao Era*. Durham, NC: Duke University Press, 2020.

Li, Jie. "The Past Is *Not* Like Smoke: A Memory Museum of the Maoist Era (1949–1976)." PhD diss., Harvard University, 2010.

Li Kuixu 李魁戍. *Zhang Binggui* 张秉贵 (Zhang Binggui). Changchun: Jilin wenshi chubanshe, 2016.

Lieberthal, Kenneth. "Beijing's Consumer Market." *China Business Review* Sept.–Oct. (1981): 36–41.

Liebes, Tamar. "Acoustic Space: The Role of Radio in Israeli Collective History." *Jewish History* 20, no. 1 (2006): 69–90.

Lien, Ling-ling. "From the Retailing Revolution to the Consumer Revolution: Department Stores in Modern Shanghai." *Frontiers of History in China* 4, no. 3 (2009): 358–89.

Lin, Cyril Chihren. "The Reinstatement of Economics in China Today." *China Quarterly* 85 (1981): 1–48.

Litzinger, Ralph A. *Other Chinas: The Yao and the Politics of National Belonging*. Durham, NC: Duke University Press, 2000.

"Liu Deng hei dian—'Hei qi hao'" "刘邓黑点—'黑七号'" (Liu and Deng's racket: Black no. 7). *Jingji pipan* 经济批判 (Economic criticism), April 28, 1967.

Liu, Alan P. L. *Communications and National Integration in Communist China*. Berkeley: University of California Press, 1971.

Liu Guoxiang 刘国祥. *Songhuo lushang (Hunan huaguxi)* 送货路上（湖南花鼓戏）(Delivering goods on the road [a Hunan flower-drum opera]). Beijing: Renmin wenxue chubanshe, 1974.

Liu, Lihong. "Vitreous Views: Materiality and Mediality of Glass in Qing China through a Transcultural Prism." *Getty Research Journal* 8 (2016): 17–38.

Liu, Xinmin. "Steel Is Made through Persistent Tempering." In *Words and Their Stories: Essays on the Language of the Chinese Revolution*, edited by Ban Wang, 85–99. Leiden: Brill, 2011.

Lovell, Stephen. *Russia in the Microphone Age: A History of Soviet Radio, 1919–1970*. Oxford: Oxford University Press, 2015.

Lowrie, Joyce O. *Sightings: Mirrors in Texts—Texts in Mirrors*. Amsterdam: Rodopi, 2008.

Lu, Guang. "Modern Revolutionary Beijing Opera: Context, Contents, and Conflicts." PhD diss., Kent State University, 1997.

Lu Shuyuan 鲁枢元. "Laba yu shijie" "喇叭与世界" (The loudspeaker and the world). *Haiyan* 海燕 (Petrel) 4 (2006): 48–49.

Lu, Xiaoning. "Zhang Ruifang: Modelling the Socialist Red Star." In *Chinese Film Stars*, edited by Mary Farquhar and Yingjin Zhang, 97–107. London: Routledge, 2010.

Lu, Xiaoning. "Villain Stardom in Socialist China: Chen Qiang and the Cultural Politics of Affect." *Journal of Chinese Cinemas* 9, no. 3 (2015): 223–38.

"Lüdashi jiaotongju geji lingdao ganbu jianchi shenru jiceng shenru qunzhong" "旅大市交通局各级领导干部坚持深入基层深入群众" (Leading cadres at every level of the

Lüda transportation bureau resolutely go to the grass roots and the masses). *Renmin ribao* 人民日报 (*People's Daily*), January 17, 1971.

Lupton, Christina. *Knowing Books: The Consciousness of Mediation in Eighteenth-Century Britain*. Philadelphia: University of Pennsylvania Press, 2011.

Lynch, Deidre. *The Economy of Character: Novels, Market Culture, and the Business of Inner Meaning*. Chicago: University of Chicago Press, 1998.

Lyon, Phil, Anne Colquhoun, and Dave Kinney. "UK Food Shopping in the 1950s: The Social Context of Customer Loyalty." *International Journal of Consumer Studies* 28, no. 1 (2004): 28–39.

Mackerras, Colin. *Amateur Theatre in China, 1949–1966*. Canberra: Australia National University Press, 1973.

"Makesi, Engesi, Liening lun wuchanjieji zhuanzheng" "马克思、恩格斯、列宁论无产阶级专政" (Marx, Engels, and Lenin on the dictatorship of the proletariat). *Renmin ribao* 人民日报 (*People's Daily*), February 22, 1975.

Mao Zedong 毛泽东. *A Critique of Soviet Economics*. Translated by Moss Roberts. New York: Monthly Review Press, 1977.

Mao Zedong 毛泽东. "Sulian *Zhengzhi jingjixue* dushu biji" "苏联《政治经济学》读书笔记" (Reading notes on the Soviet Union's *Political economy*). In *Mao Zedong sixiang wansui* 毛泽东思想万岁 (Long live Mao Zedong Thought), 319–99. Beijing: 1969.

Mao Zedong 毛泽东. "Talks at the Yan'an Forum on Literature and Art." In *Modern Chinese Literary Thought: Writings on Literature 1893–1945*, edited by Kirk A. Denton, 458–84. Stanford, CA: Stanford University Press, 1996.

Marx, Karl. "The Fetishism of the Commodity and Its Secret." In *Capital*, 163–77. New York: Vintage, 1990.

McCarthy, Susan. "Ethno-Religious Mobilisation and Citizenship Discourse in the People's Republic of China." *Asian Ethnicity* 1, no. 2 (2000): 107–16.

McGrath, Jason. *Postsocialist Modernity: Chinese Cinema, Literature, and Criticism in the Market Age*. Stanford, CA: Stanford University Press, 2008.

Medley, Margaret. "Ching-Tê Chên and the Problem of the 'Imperial Kilns.'" *Bulletin of the School of Oriental and African Studies* 29, no. 2 (1966): 326–38.

Melchior-Bonnet, Sabine. *The Mirror: A History*. Translated by Katharine J. Jewett. London: Routledge, 2001.

Melvin, Sheila, and Jindong Cai. *Rhapsody in Red: How Classical Music Became Chinese*. New York: Algora, 2004.

Merkel, Ina. "Consumer Culture in the GDR, or How the Struggle for Antimodernity Was Lost on the Battleground of Consumer Culture." In *Getting and Spending: European and American Consumer Societies in the Twentieth Century*, edited by Susan Strasser, Charles McGovern, and Matthias Judt, 281–99. Cambridge: Cambridge University Press, 1998.

Merkel, Ina. "From Stigma to Cult: Changing Meanings in East German Consumer Culture." In *The Making of the Consumer: Knowledge, Power and Identity in the Modern World*, edited by Frank Trentmann, 249–70. Oxford: Berg, 2006.

Michaels, Walter Benn. *The Gold Standard and the Logic of Naturalism: American Literature at the Turn of the Century*. Berkeley: University of California Press, 1987.

Miller, Michael B. *The Bon Marché: Bourgeois Culture and the Department Store, 1869–1920*. Princeton, NJ: Princeton University Press, 1981.

Mitchell, W. J. T. *Picture Theory: Essays on Verbal and Visual Representation.* Chicago: University of Chicago Press, 1994.

Mitchell, W. J. T. *What Do Pictures Want? The Lives and Loves of Images.* Chicago: University of Chicago Press, 2005.

Mittler, Barbara. *A Continuous Revolution: Making Sense of Cultural Revolution Culture.* Cambridge, MA: Harvard University Asia Center, 2013.

Mittler, Barbara. *Dangerous Tunes: The Politics of Chinese Music in Hong Kong, Taiwan, and the People's Republic of China since 1949.* Wiesbaden: Harrassowitz, 1997.

Morgan, Stephen L. "Transfer of Taylorist Ideas to China, 1910–1930s." *Journal of Management History* 12, no. 4 (2006): 408–24.

Murck, Alfreda. "Golden Mangoes: The Life Cycle of a Cultural Revolution Symbol." *Archives of Asian Art* 57 (2007): 1–21.

Murck, Alfreda, ed. *Mao's Golden Mangoes and the Cultural Revolution.* Zürich, CH: Scheidegger and Spiess, 2013.

Nathan, Andrew James. *Chinese Democracy.* Berkeley: University of California Press, 1986.

"New Political Economy Textbook." *Peking Review* 1, no. 35 (1958): 18.

Nienhauser, William H. "An Allegorical Reading of Han Yü's 'Mao-Ying Chuan' (Biography of Fur Point)." *Oriens Extremus* 23, no. 2 (1976): 153–74.

Ollman, Bertell. *Alienation: Marx's Conception of Man in Capitalist Society.* Cambridge: Cambridge University Press, 1976.

Olsen, Bjørnar. *In Defense of Things: Archaeology and the Ontology of Objects.* Lanham, MD: AltaMira, 2010.

Osborne, Peter. *The Politics of Time: Modernity and Avant-Garde.* London: Verso, 1995.

Oushakine, Serguei Alex. "'Against the Cult of Things': On Soviet Productivism, Storage Economy, and Commodities with No Destination." *Russian Review* 73, no. 2 (2014): 198–236.

Pang, Laikwan. *The Art of Cloning: Creative Production during China's Cultural Revolution.* London: Verso, 2017.

Perkins, Dwight H. *Market Control and Planning in Communist China.* Cambridge, MA: Harvard University Press, 1966.

Poole, Deborah. *Vision, Race, and Modernity: A Visual Economy of the Andean Image World.* Princeton, NJ: Princeton University Press, 1997.

Priyadarshini, Meha. *Chinese Porcelain in Colonial Mexico: The Material Worlds of an Early Modern Trade.* Cham, CH: Palgrave Macmillan, 2018.

Prybyla, Jan S. *The Chinese Economy: Problems and Policies.* Columbia: University of South Carolina Press, 1981.

Qiu Ling 邱陵. "Chuchuang de goutu he secai" "橱窗的构图和色彩" (Color and composition in window displays). *Zhuangshi* 装饰 (*Art and Design*) 6 (1959): 48–49.

Randall, Amy E. *The Soviet Dream World of Retail Trade and Consumption in the 1930s.* New York: Palgrave Macmillan, 2008.

Ren Baige 任白戈. "Zuzhi chengshi renmin de jingji shenghuo shi jianshe shehuizhuyi xin chengshi de yi ge zhongyao fangmian" "组织城市人民的经济生活是建设社会主义新城市的一个重要方面" (Organizing the economic life of urban residents is an important aspect of building the new socialist city). *Hongqi* 红旗 (*Red flag*) 5 (1960): 35–43.

Rice, Tom. "Soundselves: An Acoustemology of Sound and Self in the Edinburgh Royal Infirmary." *Anthropology Today* 19, no. 4 (2003): 4–9.

Rich, Frank. "Yes, You Are the Person of the Year!" *New York Times*, December 24, 2006.

Richman, Barry M. *Industrial Society in Communist China: A Firsthand Study of Chinese Economic Development and Management*. New York: Random House, 1969.

Riskin, Carl. "China's Rural Industries: Self-Reliant Systems or Independent Kingdoms?" *China Quarterly* 73 (1978): 77–98.

Riskin, Carl. "Small Industry and the Chinese Model of Development." *China Quarterly* 46 (1971): 245–73.

Roberts, Rosemary. "Positive Women Characters in the Revolutionary Model Works of the Chinese Cultural Revolution: An Argument against the Theory of Erasure of Gender and Sexuality." *Asian Studies Review* 28, no. 4 (2004): 407–22.

Rofel, Lisa. *Other Modernities: Gendered Yearnings in China after Socialism*. Berkeley: University of California Press, 1999.

Rogger, Hans. "Amerikanizm and the Economic Development of Russia." *Comparative Studies in Society and History* 23, no. 3 (1981): 382–420.

Roth-Ey, Kristin. *Moscow Prime Time: How the Soviet Union Built the Media Empire That Lost the Cultural Cold War*. Ithaca, NY: Cornell University Press, 2011.

Russo, Alessandro. "How Did the Cultural Revolution End? The Last Dispute between Mao Zedong and Deng Xiaoping, 1975." *Modern China* 39, no. 3 (2013): 239–79.

Scannell, Paddy. "Public Service Broadcasting and Modern Public Life." *Media, Culture and Society* 11, no. 2 (1989): 135–66.

Scannell, Paddy. *Radio, Television, and Modern Life: A Phenomenological Approach*. Oxford: Blackwell, 1996.

Schran, Peter. "Handicrafts in Communist China." *China Quarterly* 17 (1964): 151–73.

Selden, Mark. "Mao Zedong and the Political Economy of Chinese Development." In *Marxism and the Chinese Experience: Issues in Contemporary Chinese Socialism*, edited by Arif Dirlik and Maurice Meisner, 43–58. Armonk, NY: M. E. Sharpe, 1989.

Shang gang wu chang yi chejian gongren lilunzu 上钢五厂一车间工人理论组, ed. *Lian'ganglu qian de zhengzhi jingjixue* 炼钢炉前的政治经济学 (Political economy in front of the smelting furnace). Shanghai: Shanghai renmin chubanshe, 1976.

Shanghai haiwuju Yangcun pu zhuangxiezhan gongren xiezuozu 上海海务局杨村浦装卸站工人写作组 and Fudan daxue jingjixi gongnongbing xueyuan 复旦大学经济系工农兵学员, eds. *Matou shang de zhengzhi jingjixue* 码头上的政治经济学 (Political economy on the docks). Shanghai: Shanghai renmin chubanshe, 1974.

Shanghai shifan daxue zhengjiao xi 上海师范大学政教系 and Shanghai dengpao chang lilun xiaozu 上海灯泡厂理论小组, eds. *Xuexi shehuizhuyi zhengzhi jingjixue* 学习社会主义政治经济学 (Study of socialist political economy). Shanghai: Shanghai renmin chubanshe, 1976.

Shanghai shifan daxue Zhongwen xi gongnongbing xueyuan diaocha xiaozu 上海师范大学中文系工农兵学员调查小组, ed. *Yizhi changdao gongchanzhuyi: Gongnongbing puji geming yangbanxi diaocha baogao* 一直唱到共产主义: 工农兵普及革命样板戏调查报告 (Singing all the way to communism: Investigative report on the popularization of yangbanxi by workers, peasants, and soldiers). Shanghai: Shanghai renmin chubanshe, 1975.

"Shanghai Tianjin geming xiao jiang he shangye zhigong xiang boxue jieji 'si jiu' fadong zonggong huiqi geming tie saozhou hengsao yiqie jiu xisu" 上海天津革命小将和商业职工向剥削阶级'四旧'发动总攻挥起革命铁扫帚横扫一切旧习俗" (Launching an all-out offensive against the "four olds" of the exploiting classes, revolutionary little generals and commercial workers in Shanghai and Tianjin wield the revolutionary iron broom and wipe away all old customs). *Renmin ribao* 人民日报 (*People's Daily*), August 25, 1966.

Shanghaishi di yi baihuo shangdian chuangzuozu 上海市第一百货商店创作组. "Er shi si xiaoshi" "二十四小时" (Twenty-four hours). In *Guitai fengbo* 柜台风波 (Storm at the counter), 32–46. Shanghai: Shanghai renmin chubanshe, 1974.

Shanghaishi di yi baihuo shangdian chuangzuozu 上海市第一百货商店创作组. "Pei wazi" "配袜子" (Pairing socks). In *Guitai fengbo* 柜台风波 (Storm at the counter), 18–31. Shanghai: Shanghai renmin chubanshe, 1974.

Shanghaishi di yi baihuo shangdian chuangzuozu 上海市第一百货商店创作组. *Guitai fengbo* 柜台风波 (Storm at the counter). Shanghai: Shanghai renmin chubanshe, 1974.

Shanghaishi guanggao gongsi 上海市广告公司, ed. *Zenyang buzhi chuchuang* 怎样布置橱窗 (How to dress display windows). Shanghai: Shanghai renmin meishu chubanshe, 1964.

Shanghaishi Huangpuqu geming weiyuanhui xiezuozu 上海市黄浦区革命委员会写作组. *Shanghai Waitan Nanjing lu shihua* 上海外滩南京路史话 (A history of the Shanghai Bund and Nanjing Road). Shanghai: Shanghai renmin chubanshe, 1976.

Shangye bu baihuoju 商业部百货局, ed. *Zhongguo baihuo shangye* 中国百货商业 (China's department stores). Beijing: Beijing daxue chubanshe, 1989.

Shi Ning 施宁. "Yanchu qianhou" "演出前后" (Before and after the performance). *Jiefang ribao* 解放日报 (*Liberation daily*), April 14, 1974.

Shuo Han 硕翰. "Zhuming tongsu jingji lilunjia Deng Kesheng" "著名通俗经济理论家邓克生" (The celebrated vernacular economic theorist Deng Kesheng). *Xuehai* 学海 (Sea of learning) 1 (1990): 88–91.

Sicular, Terry. "Redefining State, Plan and Market: China's Reforms in Agricultural Commerce." *China Quarterly* 144 (1995): 1020–46.

Silvio, Teri. "Animation: The New Performance?" *Journal of Linguistic Anthropology* 20, no. 2 (2010): 422–38.

Smith, Aminda. "Remoulding Minds in Postsocialist China: Maoist Reeducation and Twenty-First-Century Subjects." *Postcolonial Studies* 15, no. 4 (2012): 453–66.

Smolinski, Leon. "Planning without Theory 1917–1967." *Survey* 64 (1967): 108–28.

Solinger, Dorothy J. *Chinese Business under Socialism: The Politics of Domestic Commerce, 1949–1980*. Berkeley: University of California Press, 1984.

South China Morning Post. "The Famous Mao Slogan That He Never Even Used." February 25, 2009.

Starr, John Bryan. "On Mao's Self-Image as a Marxist Thinker." *Modern China* 3, no. 4 (1977): 435–42.

Steinberg, Marc. *Anime's Media Mix: Franchising Toys and Characters in Japan*. Minneapolis: University of Minnesota Press, 2012.

Stephanson, Anders. *Manifest Destiny: American Expansion and the Empire of Right*. New York: Hill and Wang, 1995.

Sterne, Jonathan. "Sounds Like the Mall of America: Programmed Music and the Architectonics of Commercial Space." *Ethnomusicology* 41, no. 1 (1997): 22–50.

Sulian kexueyuan jingji yanjiusuo 苏联科学院经济研究所, ed. *Zhengzhi jingjixue jiaokeshu* 政治经济学教科书 (Textbook on political economy). Beijing: Renmin chubanshe, 1955.

Sun Dingguo 孙定国. "Xinsheng shiwu shi bu ke zhansheng de" "新生事物是不可战胜的" (Newborn things are invincible). *Guangming ribao* 光明日报 (Guangming daily), September 6, 1959.

Szamuely, Laszló. *First Models of the Socialist Economic Systems: Principles and Theories*. Budapest, HU: Akademiai Kiadó, 1974.

Szendy, Peter. *Sur écoute: Esthétique de l'espionnage*. Paris: Les éditions de minuit, 2013.

Tamen, Miguel. *Friends of Interpretable Objects*. Cambridge, MA: Harvard University Press, 2001.

Tao Youzhi 陶友之. "'Yiyang' yu 'bu yiyang'—tan xianxiang he benzhi" "'一样'与不一样"— 谈现象和本质" ("Alike" and "Unalike"—On appearance and esssence). In *Xue yangbanxi, tan bianzhengfa* 学样板戏, 谈辨证法 (Study the yangbanxi, discuss dialectics), edited by Gong Xuli 巩旭黎, 32–37. Shanghai: Shanghai renmin chubanshe, 1974.

Taussig, Michael. *Mimesis and Alterity: A Particular Study of the Senses*. London: Routledge, 1993.

Taylor, Richard. "Red Stars, Positive Heroes and Personality Cults." In *Stalinism and Soviet Cinema*, edited by Richard Taylor and Derek Spring, 69–89. London: Routledge, 1993.

Teiwes, Frederick C., and Warren Sun. *China's Road to Disaster: Mao, Central Politicians, and Provincial Leaders in the Unfolding of the Great Leap Forward, 1955–1959*. Armonk, NY: M. E. Sharpe, 1999.

Thompson, Emily Ann. *The Soundscape of Modernity: Architectural Acoustics and the Culture of Listening in America, 1900–1933*. Cambridge, MA: MIT Press, 2004.

Tichane, Robert. *Ching-Te-Chen: Views of a Porcelain City*. Painted Post: New York State Institute for Glaze Research, 1983.

Tillman, Margaret Mih. *Raising China's Revolutionaries: Modernizing Childhood for Cosmopolitan Nationalists and Liberated Comrades, 1920s–1950s*. New York: Columbia University Press, 2018.

Tsai, Wen-Hsuan. "Delicacies for a Privileged Class in a Risk Society: The Chinese Communist Party's Special Supplies Food System." *Issues and Studies* 52, no. 2 (2016): 1–29.

Valenstein, Suzanne G. *A Handbook of Chinese Ceramics*. New York: Metropolitan Museum of Art, 1989.

Van Fleit Hang, Krista. "Zhong Xinghuo: Communist Film Worker." In *Chinese Film Stars*, edited by Mary Farquhar and Yingjin Zhang, 108–18. London: Routledge, 2010.

Varsano, Paula. "Disappearing Objects/Elusive Subjects: Writing Mirrors in Early and Medieval China." *Representations* 124, no. 1 (2013): 96–124.

Verdery, Katherine. *What Was Socialism, and What Comes Next?* Princeton, NJ: Princeton University Press, 1996.

von Geldern, James. "Radio Moscow: The Voice from the Center." In *Culture and Entertainment in Wartime Russia*, edited by Richard Stites, 44–61. Bloomington: Indiana University Press, 1995.

Vukovich, Daniel F. *China and Orientalism: Western Knowledge Production and the PRC.* London: Routledge, 2013.

Wang, Ban. *The Sublime Figure of History: Aesthetics and Politics in Twentieth-Century China.* Stanford, CA: Stanford University Press, 1997.

Wang Cuilan 王翠兰. "Hongse guangbozhan" "红色广播站" (Red broadcast station). In *Qing shen ru hai quyi ji* 情深如海 曲艺集 (Feelings deep as the sea: A collection of creative works), edited by Nongcun ban tushu bianxuan xiaozu 农村版图书编选小组, 79–86. Beijing: Nongcun duwu chubanshe, 1974.

Wang Ning 王宁. *Cong kuxingzhe shehui dao xiaofeizhe shehui: Zhongguo chengshi xiaofei zhidu, laodong jili yu zhuti jiegou zhuanxing* 从苦行者社会到消费者社会：中国城市消费制度、劳动激励与主体结构转型 (From the ascetic society to the consumer society: Transformations of the institutions of consumption, the incentives to labor, and the structures of subjectivity in urban China). Beijing: Shehui kexue wenxian chubanshe, 2009.

"Wei gong nong bing fuwu de xin xing shangdian" "为工农兵服务的新型商店" (A new-style store that serves the workers, peasants, and soldiers). *Tongxian gongren* 通县工人 (Tongxian worker), March 14, 1969.

Werner, Jake. "Global Fordism in 1950s Urban China." *Frontiers of History in China* 7, no. 3 (2012): 415–41.

Wilcox, Emily E. "Dancers Doing Fieldwork: Socialist Aesthetics and Bodily Experience in the People's Republic of China." *Journal for the Anthropological Study of Human Movement* 17, no. 2 (2010): 6–16.

Williams, Rosalind H. *Dream Worlds: Mass Consumption in Late Nineteenth-Century France.* Berkeley: University of California Press, 1982.

"Wo guo shehuizhuyi shangye de fangxiang" "我国社会主义商业的方向" (The direction of China's socialist trade). In *Ban hao shehuizhuyi shangye* 办好社会主义商业 (Carry out socialist trade well), edited by Shangye bu xiezuo xiaozu 商业部写作小组, 1–13. Beijing: Renmin chubanshe, 1972.

Woloch, Alex. *The One vs. the Many: Minor Characters and the Space of the Protagonist in the Novel.* Princeton, NJ: Princeton University Press, 2003.

Wu Chang 吴畅. "Xue yidian zhengzhi jingjixue" "学一点政治经济学" (Study a little bit of political economy). *Hongqi* 红旗 (*Red flag*) 8 (1975): 9–11.

Wu, Guo. "Recalling Bitterness: Historiography, Memory, and Myth in Maoist China." *Twentieth-Century China* 39, no. 3 (2014): 245–68.

Wu, Hung. *The Double Screen: Medium and Representation in Chinese Painting.* London: Reaktion, 1996.

Wu, Pei-Yi. "Self-Examination and Confession of Sins in Traditional China." *Harvard Journal of Asiatic Studies* 39, no. 1 (1979): 5–38.

Wu, Yiching. *The Cultural Revolution at the Margins: Chinese Socialism in Crisis.* Cambridge, MA: Harvard University Press, 2014.

"Wuchanjieji wenhua da geming yunyu chu you yi xinsheng shiwu" "无产阶级文化大革命孕育出又一新生事物" (The great proletarian Cultural Revolution spawns another newborn thing). *Hongweibing bao* 红卫兵报 (*Red Guard report*), November 17, 1966.

Xiao Congshu 肖从曙. *Geming xiandai jingju xue chang changshi jieshao* 革命现代京剧学唱常识介绍 (Introduction to the fundamentals of learning how to sing revolutionary modern Beijing opera). Shanghai: Shanghai renmin chubanshe, 1975.

Xie Hechou 谢鹤筹. "Jin yibu jiaqiang minzu maoyi gongzuo" "进一步加强民族贸易工作" (Further strengthen trade work among minority nationalities). *Minzu tuanjie* 民族团结 (Nationality unity) 2–3 (1963): 10–13.

Xu He 徐禾, ed. *Zhengzhi jingjixue mingci jieshi* 政治经济学名词解释 (Explanation of terms in political economy). Beijing: Renmin chubanshe, 1974.

Xu Zhigao 徐志高, ed. *Wenge shigao: Wenge shiliao huibian* 文革史稿：文革史料彙编 (A rough history of the Cultural Revolution: A collection of historical materials). New York: Shijie huayu chubanshe, 2016.

"Xuexi geming yangbanxi de kexi chengguo—ji pingju *Xiangyang shangdian* de xinsheng" "学习革命样板戏的可喜成果— 记评剧《向阳商店》的新生" (The joyous result of studying the yangbanxi: Rebirth of the pingju *Xiangyang Store*). *Renmin ribao* 人民日报 (*People's Daily*), February 5, 1974.

Yan Ru 燕如. "Xinsheng shiwu san ti" "新生事物三题" (Three issues concerning newborn things). *Xueshu yanjiu* 学术研究 (Academic research) 2 (1960): 57–59.

Yang, Boda. "An Account of Qing Dynasty Glassmaking." In *Scientific Research in Early Chinese Glass*, edited by Robert H. Brill and John H. Martin, 131–50. Corning, NY: Corning Museum of Glass, 1991.

Yang Jinyu 杨瑾瑜. "Wei renmin zhan guitai, cong shijian zhong xue benling" "为人民站柜台，从实践中学本领" (Man the counter for the people, learn principle from practice). *Hongqi* 红旗 (*Red flag*) 2 (1966): 36–41.

Yang, Mayfair Mei-hui. *Gifts, Favors, and Banquets: The Art of Social Relationships in China*. Ithaca, NY: Cornell University Press, 1994.

Yang Rong 杨荣. "Zhongguo gongchandang chengli zhi chu Makesizhuyi zhongyiben zhongyao zhuzuo jieshao" "中国共产党成立之初马克思主义中译本重要著作介绍" (Introduction to important Chinese translations of Marxist texts in the early years of the Chinese Communist Party). *Changjiang lun tan* 长江论坛 (Yangtze tribune) 2 (2010): 15–21, 59.

Yao Jin 姚锦, ed. *Yao Yilin bai xi tan* 姚依林百夕谈 (A hundred evening chats with Yao Yilin). Beijing: Zhong gong dang shi chubanshe, 2008.

Yao Nai 姚耐, ed. *Zhengzhi jingjixue jiaocai (shehuizhuyi bufen)* 政治经济学教材 (社会主义部分) (Teaching materials on political economy: Socialism). Shanghai: Shanghai renmin chubanshe, 1961.

Ye Chaohui 叶朝晖. "Ping *Shangpin zishu*" "评《商品自述》" (Criticizing *A commodity's tale*). *Sixiang zhanxian* 思想战线 (Thinking) 5 (1978): 7–11.

Yeh, Catherine. "Guides to a Global Paradise: Shanghai Entertainment Park Newspapers and the Invention of Chinese Urban Leisure." In *Transcultural Turbulences: Towards a Multi-Sited Reading of Image Flows*, edited by Christiane Brosius and Roland Wenzlhuemer, 97–132. Berlin: Springer-Verlag, 2011.

Yin Xingshan 尹兴山. "Zhao jingzi yu xilian" "照镜子与洗脸" (Looking in the mirror and washing one's face). *Renmin ribao* 人民日报 (*People's Daily*), November 5, 1965.

"Yong weida de Mao Zedong sixiang po si li gong—Jiangsusheng Taicangxian Hongjing dadui huoxuehuoyong Mao zhuxi zhuzuo de jingyan" "用伟大的毛泽东思想破私立公—江苏省太仓县洪泾大队活学活用毛主席著作的经验" (Use the great Mao Zedong Thought to destroy the private and establish the public). *Renmin ribao* 人民日报 (*People's Daily*), October 11, 1967.

Yu Jie 喻杰. "Tigao renshi zuo hao minzu maoyi gongzuo" "提高认识做好民族贸易工作" (Raise the efficiency of trade work among minority nationalities). *Minzu tuanjie* 民族团结 (Nationality unity) 2–3 (1963): 8–10.

Yu Zuqiu 余祖球 and Liang Ailian 梁爱莲. *Jingdezhen chuantong taoci diaosu* 景德镇传统陶瓷雕塑 (Traditional ceramic sculpture in Jingdezhen). Nanchang: Jiangxi gaoxiao chubanshe, 2004.

Yuan Shihai 袁世海. "Tantan zhengque di duidai biaoyan fanmian renwu" "谈谈正确地对待表演反面人物" (On the correct approach to the performance of negative characters). *Wenhui bao* 文汇报, October 4, 1965.

Yuan Yunfu 袁运甫. "Chuchuang de gousi" "橱窗的构思" (The composition of window displays). *Zhuangshi* 装饰 (*Art and Design*) 6 (1959): 47.

Yue Yushi 乐于时. "Xilian zhi yu" "洗脸之余" (Beyond washing one's face). *Renmin ribao* 人民日报 (*People's Daily*), July 24, 1963.

Yurchak, Alexei. *Everything Was Forever, Until It Was No More: The Last Soviet Generation*. Princeton, NJ: Princeton University Press, 2006.

Zeng Zhiquan 曾智泉 and Kong Yang 孔洋. "7501 ci—Zhongguo de 'hongse guanyao'" "7501—中国的'红色官窑'" (7501 porcelains: China's "Red imperial kiln"). *Wenwu shijie* 文物世界 (World of antiquity), 6 (2009): 64–67.

Zhang Binggui 张秉贵. "San kan *Xiangyang shangdian*" "三看《向阳商店》" (Three viewings of *Xiangyang Store*). *Guangming ribao* 光明日报 (Guangming daily), February 1, 1974.

Zhang Binggui 张秉贵. "Wei geming zhan guitai" "为革命站柜台" (Man the counter for revolution). *Hongqi* 红旗 (*Red flag*) 5 (1977): 91–94.

Zhang Binggui 张秉贵. *Zhang Binggui guitai fuwu yishu* 张秉贵柜台服务艺术 (Zhang Binggui's art of counter service). Beijing: Beijing ribao chubanshe, 1983.

Zhang Qingying 张清英. "Boxue zhong, quru shen—Huiyi wo zai jiefang qian de shenghuo" "剥削重, 屈辱深—回忆我在解放前的生活" (Grave exploitation, deep humiliation: Remembering my life before liberation). *Shangye gongzuo* 商业工作 (*Trade work*) 13 (1964): 10–11.

Zhang Weici 张蔚辞. "'Yi ren wei jing'" "'以人为镜'" (Taking people as one's mirror). *Renmin ribao* 人民日报 (*People's Daily*), January 18, 1962.

Zhang, Yingjin. "Zhao Dan: Spectrality of Martyrdom and Stardom." In *Chinese Film Stars*, edited by Mary Farquhar and Yingjin Zhang, 86–96. London: Routledge, 2010.

Zhang Zhenguo 张振国. "Zhongguo gudai 'jia zhuan' wenti fazhanshi shulun" "中国古代'假传'文体发展史述论" (A history of the development of the ancient Chinese pseudo-biography genre). *Hua'nan shifan daxue xuebao* 华南师范大学学报 (Journal of South China Normal University) 2 (2012): 109–13.

Zhao Jing 赵靖. "Zhongguo lishi shang de huobi baiwujiao sixiang" "中国历史上的货币拜物教思想" (The historical fetishization of money in Chinese thought). *Jingji yanjiu* 经济研究 (Economic research) 11 (1983): 60–65, 8.

"Zhao jingzi de 'mimi'" "照镜子的'秘密'" *Renmin ribao* 人民日报 (*People's Daily*), May 29, 1973.

"Zhaozhou yiyao shangdian—Qinjian ban shangye de yi mian qizhi" "肇州医药商店—勤俭办商业的一面旗帜" (Zhaozhou pharmacy: A banner for frugal commerce). *Renmin ribao* 人民日报 (*People's Daily*), October 19, 1963.

Zhe Ping 哲平. "Xuexi geming yangbanxi, baowei geming yangbanxi" "学习革命样板戏保卫革命样板戏" (Study the revolutionary model works, protect the revolutionary model works). *Renmin ribao* 人民日报 (*People's Daily*), October 19, 1969.

Zhengque renshi woguo de shangpin zhidu 正确认识我国的商品制度 (Correctly address China's commodity system). Beijing: Zhongguo caizheng jingji chubanshe, 1975.

Zhengzhi jingji xue jichu zhishi bianxiezu《政治经济学基础知识》编写组, ed. *Zhengzhi jingjixue jichu zhishi* 政治经济学基础知识 (Fundamentals of Political Economy). Shanghai: Shanghai renmin chubanshe, 1975.

Zhengzhi jingjixue jianghua (shehuizhuyi bufen) bianxiezu 《政治经济学讲话（社会主义部分）》编写组, ed. *Zhengzhi jingjixue jianghua (shehuizhuyi bufen)* 政治经济学讲话（社会主义部分）. (Talks on political economy [socialist section]). Beijing: Renmin chubanshe, 1976.

"Zhigong yuandi" "职工园地" (The scope of the field). *Shangye gongzuo* 商业工作 (*Trade work*) 10 (1964): 32–33.

Zhong gong Shanghaishi di yi baihuo shangdian weiyuanhui 中共上海市第一百货商店委员会. "Shangpin jingji shi chansheng zibenzhuyi he zichanjieji de turang" "商品经济是产生资本主义和资产阶级的土壤" (The commodity economy is grounds for the production of capitalism and the bourgeoisie). In *Zhengque renshi woguo de shangpin zhidu* 正确认识我国的商品制度 (Correctly address China's commodity system), 18–23. Beijing: Zhongguo caizheng jingji chubanshe, 1975.

Zhong, Xueping, Zheng Wang, and Di Bai, eds. *Some of Us: Chinese Women Growing Up in the Mao Era*. New Brunswick, NJ: Rutgers University Press, 2001.

Zhonggong Jingdezhen shiwei xuanchuanbu 中共景德镇市委宣传部, ed. *Cidu jilang* 瓷都激浪 (Turbulent waves in the porcelain capital). Nanchang: Jiangxi renmin chubanshe, 1962.

"Zhongguo gongchandang zhongyang weiyuanhui guanyu wuchanjieji wenhua da geming de jueding" "中国共产党中央委员会关于无产阶级文化大革命的决定" (The CCP Central Committee's decision concerning the Great Proletarian Cultural Revolution). *Renmin ribao* 人民日报 (*People's Daily*), August 9, 1966.

Zhonghua renmin gong he guo shangye bu shangye zuzhi yu jishu ju 中华人民共和国商业部商业组织与技术局, ed. *Shangdian chuchuang chenlie yu neibu buzhi* 商店橱窗陈列与内部布置 (Store window displays and interior arrangements). Beijing: Caizheng jingji chubanshe, 1955.

Zhou Changzong 周长宗. "Geming xue feng—Ji Zhongguo renmin jiefangjun Changsha zhengzhi xuexiao" "革命学风—记中国人民解放军长沙政治学校" (Wind of revolutionary study: The Changsha PLA political school). *Renmin ribao* 人民日报 (*People's Daily*), March 1, 1965.

Zhou Peifeng 周佩凤. "Zhichi xinsheng shiwu gonggu wuchanjieji zhuanzheng" "支持新生事物 巩固无产阶级专政" (Support newborn things, strengthen the dictatorship of the proletariat). *Renmin ribao* 人民日报 (*People's Daily*), March 12, 1975.

Zi Qun 子群. "Zenyang banhao yangpinshi" "怎样办好样品室" (How to set up a sample room). *Shangye gongzuo* 商业工作 (*Trade work*) 4 (1964): 24.

Zola, Émile. *Au bonheur des dames*. Paris: Presses Pocket, 1990.

Zola, Émile. *The Ladies' Delight*. Translated by Robin Buss. London: Penguin, 2001.

"Zuohao puji geming yangbanxi de gongzuo" "做好普及革命样板戏的工作" (Carry out the work of popularizing the revolutionary yangbanxi). *Renmin ribao* 人民日报 (*People's Daily*), July 15, 1970.

INDEX

abundance, 85, 86, 195; and display, 63, 64
aesthetics, 55, 91, 115, 153, 191; of broadcasting, 35, 39; of display, 90, 108; of language, 126; of Maoism, 127; of mirrors, 180; musical, 31, 32; of porcelain, 97–99, 101, 103; of sculpture, 22; of socialism, 116, 118; of yangbanxi characters, 100, 175
agriculture, 6, 7, 58–60, 65, 67, 82, 91, 116, 122, 129
alienation, 142, 161–63, 166. *See also* Marxism
amateur body, the, 23–24, 30, 141–42, 144–47, 149–51, 153, 158–66, 168–169, 175–76, 178. *See also* performance
animation, 148
artists, 102, 115, 126, 145; and mass production, 97, 98; and mirrors, 172, 174
audio recordings, 28, 30, 31, 42, 45, 150
Austin, J. L., 39
Autobiography of a Commodity (Deng), 132–34, 136, 214

ballet, 15, 30, 102. *See also* dance
Beijing, 7, 44, 48, 70, 71, 73, 74, 76, 82, 83, 99, 105, 119, 155, 156, 168; and broadcasts, 38, 40, 41; Beijing Radio Factory in, 45, 202; *See also* opera; radio; shopping; Wangfujing Department Store
bourgeoisie, 57, 63, 111, 122, 124, 125, 145, 146, 176, 182; effeminization of, 70, 179, 180; materialist associations with, 63, 64, 71, 72, 100, 110; and mirrors, 181; and porcelain, 22, 92, 101; and proletariat dictatorship, 7, 8; and the socialist commodity, 131
branding, 17, 45, 89, 193
bureaucracy, 37, 38, 55, 58, 59, 64
businesses, family-run, 59

Capital (Marx), 8
capitalism, 1, 2, 134, 138, 160, 162–64, 174, 193; and alienation, 142, 162; in China, 24, 25, 51, 68, 71, 106, 115, 116, 131; and commodities, 9, 108, 109, 113, 114, 118, 132, 137, 164; distinctions with socialism, 29, 66, 122, 123, 137; economy of, 17, 117, 119–21, 123, 126; and mediation, 13; and newborn things, 3, 7; and retail, 69, 76; suspicion of, 11; and trade, 56, 57, 62, 78, 80
Central Academy of Craft and Design, 82, 83, 168
Central Radio, 38–40, 42
ceramics, 91, 93, 93–97, 100; history of, 98
China Records, 44–47, 52, 54, 55, 73
Chinese Communist Party (CCP), the, 9, 116, 125, 126; actions and policies of, 20, 21, 33–36, 60, 65, 84, 113, 163, 193; centralization of power under, 40, 47, 51–53, 109; and class struggle, 110; and consumer

Chinese Communist Party (continued)
  desire, 115; history of, 24–26, 54; interpretations of yangbanxi, 15; in Jingdezhen, 91–93, 97; propaganda of, 10, 16; role of the commodity under, 13, 22, 118; and trade, 66, 68
children, 38, 76, 101, 155, 156
"civilizing processes," 51, 52, 56
class, 1, 120; in commercial areas, 22, 69, 72–76, 79, 80, 179; and commodities, 123, 179: consciousness and distinction, 83, 92, 110: differences in, 6, 7, 23, 64, 77, 181; enemies, 41, 55, 78, 157–61; representations in performance, 154–61; in the PRC, 25, 42, 65, 121; representations in porcelain, 102, 103
clay, 23, 92, 94, 102, 103, 149, 153
Cold War, the, 15
collectivization, 6, 7, 42, 62, 116, 118, 121
colonialism, 22, 51–53, 63, 105, 131,
commercial displays, 22, 63, 82, 83, 87, 90, 104, 105, 108, 179; and productivism, 84, 103; and taxonomy, 86, 89
commodities, 8–10, 14, 17, 18, 20–28, 63, 72, 113, 120, 134–38, 164, 166, 193; on display, 106–8, 109–11, 179; and fetishism, 12, 13, 23, 83–90, 108, 110, 114, 123–25, 133, 135, 136–38, 184; Marxian conception of, 12, 18, 62, 113, 114, 132, 193; and mediation, 12–13; production of, 82, 109; sales of, 47, 56, 64, 67, 76, 78; socialist conception of, 9, 11, 62, 87, 109, 113–19, 121–24, 131, 136, 137
Commodity's Tale, A (Jing), 23, 127, 130–37
communes, 6, 42, 59, 61, 68, 118, 122, 123, 144, 145, 151
communication, 32, 41, 165
communism, 8, 115, 122, 175; and commodities, 113, 124; and heterotopias, 184; in the PRC, 25, 131; relationship with socialism, 3, 85, 111, 117, 121; and the yangbanxi hero, 142, 162, 163
consumerism, 37, 134, 193; and the department store, 63; in the Soviet Union, 85
consumer culture, 17, 63, 199. *See also* consumer desire, consumerism
consumer desire, 22, 23, 25, 90, 108, 109, 113, 115. *See also* consumerism, commercial displays

consumption, 11, 26, 80, 115; by the bourgeoisie, 100; and class distinction, 110; of commodities, 17, 22, 24, 67, 77, 78, 84, 108, 112; of media, 22, 32, 39, 42; and mirrors, 180; of porcelain, 23, 96, 97; and productivist display, 90, 106; and production, 109; relationship with socialism, 25, 57, 65, 86, 113, 118, 121; and retail, 66; and the revolutionary hero, 168, 169; in the Soviet Union, 87; and trade, 70
cooperatives, 59, 65, 80, 124
Criticize Lin Biao, Criticize Confucius campaign, 7, 41, 55, 139, 161, 197
cultural production, 10, 11, 15, 31, 32, 38, 55, 65, 127, 145, 161, 163, 177
Cultural Revolution, the, 70–72, 192; class struggle during, 73, 110, 158; and commodities, 13, 14, 26, 56, 114; definition of, 20, 21; and display, 104, 105; ideology of, 10, 11; and Mao, 41, 141; materiality in, 16, 18; and mirrors, 171, 174, 175, 178, 180; newborn things in, 7–9, 111; old things in, 3, 4; political economy during, 118–20, 125, 138; and porcelain, 91, 99–102; rationing during, 61; soundscape of, 31, 32, 35, 37–39, 42, 44, 46, 47, 50, 51, 53; and utopia, 184–188; and yangbanxi, 30, 146–50, 154, 161, 163
cyberspace, 171

dance, 63, 145, 147, 150
Deng Xiaoping, 14, 24, 71, 73, 91, 161
department stores, 1, 3, 58, 60, 63, 67, 70, 71, 105; socialist construction of, 22, 76, 79
discourse: of the commodity, 9, 118; Maoist, 143, 155, 181; of materiality, 4; official, 16, 34, 161, 187; of political economy, 138; of revolution, 41, 66; of socialism, 17, 18; unofficial, 154
dynasties: Ming, 91, 98; Qing, 91, 92; Song, 98; Tang, 91, 98; Yuan, 98

England, 134, 166
education, 53, 181; of the masses, 125, 150, 160
exoticism, 51, 52

factories, 2, 29, 30, 82, 90, 92–98; workers at, 115, 163

fascism, 31, 32
feudalism, 2, 69, 92, 125, 131, 160
film, 12, 14–16, 30, 47, 87, 142, 147, 150, 177
flexi disc, 39, 42, 45, 46
food, 61, 65
Four Olds, 4, 6, 7, 69
France, 63
Fundamentals of Political Economy (Ma), 112–14, 120–24, 130, 131, 135

Gang of Four, the, 7, 13, 20, 73, 119, 120, 130, 153, 161
gender, 175
glaze, 23, 91, 153
Good Eighth Company, the, 63, 64
Great Leap Forward, 6, 7, 15, 29, 68, 73, 82, 96

healthcare, 8, 53
hermeneutics of suspicion, 23, 142, 158, 159, 161
heterotopias, 184–86. *See also* mirrors
historical responsibility, 181, 190, 191, 192
Hong Kong, 48

iconography, 98, 99, 180, 186; Maoist, 13, 14, 96, 103, 106, 188
identity, 12, 142
imperialism, 51
industrialization, 28, 57, 58, 60, 84, 93–97, 116, 121
internet, 174
iPod, 34

Jiang Qing, 7, 15, 119, 153, 155
Jingdezhen, 22, 84, 91–96, 100; *See also* Jingdezhen Jianguo Porcelain Factory; Jingdezhen Porcelain Sculpture Factory
Jingdezhen Jianguo Porcelain Factory, 92, 93
Jingdezhen Porcelain Sculpture Factory, 97, 101–3, 148

kilns, 23, 91, 93, 94, 103, 149, 153

labor, 8, 22, 65; and the body, 153, 162, 164; and commodities, 84, 113, 114, 116, 121–23, 133; and display, 82, 83, 109; exploitation of, 119, 142; freedom to hire, 68; kinds of, 7; practices and structures of, 67, 90, 92–95; salespeople's, 78
language, 11, 18, 19, 117, 125, 126, 131, 137, 138, 152, 156, 179, 184, 188
law of value, 133
Leninism, 3, 24, 117, 166
listening culture, 28, 31–34, 37, 38, 48, 49, 51
literature, 38, 48, 126, 127, 130, 150, 166, 180, 181
Li Tiemei, 139, 141–43, 147, 168
Li Yuhe, 16, 141, 146, 151, 162, 165, 168, 175–77
Liu Shaoqi, 7, 45, 68, 71, 132
loudspeakers, 29, 32, 35, 36, 41–43, 47, 147, 150, 151; and the PRC, 38, 39; and totalitarianism, 33, 34, 48, 50. *See also* sonic saturation
luxury, 32, 46–48, 60, 64, 69, 92, 177. *See also* consumption

M-1022, 54, 55, 75
Maoism, 121, 126, 127, 152, 181, 184, 186, 192; distinctions with Marxism, 163, 208; relationship with contemporary Chinese socialism, 3; and socialism, 25
Mao Zedong, 91, 93, 119; 125; on class enemies, 64; death, 3, 25, 68, 110; directives of, 7, 77, 122; heroic status of, 141, 162; on materiality, 65; newborn things under, 8; on political economy, 117, 118, 121, 123, 126, 143; role in the PRC, 39; on self-criticism, 182, 183; on socialism, 9; teachings, 56, 120, 127. *See also* iconography; Mao industry; Maoism; Mao Zedong Thought; "On the Correct Handling of Contradictions among the People" (Mao)
Mao industry, 13
Mao Zedong Thought, 72, 106, 107, 183
Marxism, 110, 111, 120, 121, 123, 126, 130–32, 142, 162, 163; political economic theory of, 8, 9, 100, 108, 117; theories of the commodity, 12, 18, 62, 113, 114, 116, 118, 124, 136–38, 193
materiality 4, 6, 9, 12, 16–18, 27, 78, 81, 84, 87, 134, 148; and socialist commodities, 136–138

media environment, 4, 14, 20, 91, 141, 171, 178, 186, 188, 189. *See also* Cultural Revolution, the

mediation, 12–14, 16, 17, 19, 26, 148, 192; and the amateur, 161; and mirrors, 189; and sound, 28, 39; and yangbanxi, 147, 153, 164, 166. *See also* remediation

Las Meninas (Velázquez), 172–74

metapictures, 188, 189

microphones, 39, 42

militarism, 38, 45, 47, 60, 101

Ministry of Commerce, 58, 59, 61, 83

mirror gazing, 24, 179, 180, 183–189

mirrors, 14, 24, 147, 172–75, 184–89, 191; and Maoism, 183; and yangbanxi heroes, 178–81

modernity, 28, 50, 63, 67, 78, 113; socialist conception of, 22, 30, 51, 52, 57, 68

modernization, 24, 51, 53, 80, 81, 84, 193; in Jingdezhen, 90–92, 94, 100

museums, 101, 104, 105, 190–92

Nanjing Road, 63, 64, 69, 83, 105

Nazism, 31, 32

Newborn socialist things, 11, 13–16, 28, 30, 53, 81, 142, 147, 192; and capitalism, 3; and commerce, 57, 72, 78, 84; and commodities, 113, 138; definition of, 2; history of, 4–10; and metonymy, 19; and temporality, 111

Ninth Party Congress, 7, 20

October Revolution, 115, 117

"On the Correct Handling of Contradictions among the People" (Mao), 2, 6

opera, 47, 79, 139, 145–47, 151, 152, 154, 155; in Beijing, 15, 30, 112, 151, 152, 155, 156. See also *Xiangyang Store* (Guo)

orchestra, 35

organization: of the CCP, 65, 162; of labor, 22, 93; of state, 37; of the retail sector, 58, 63; of territory, 36

painting, 127–30, 142, 180, 185. See also *Las Meninas* (Velázquez)

Panaudicon, 31, 35

peasants, 7, 8, 41, 46, 64, 121, 163, 179, 182; and consumption, 59, 62, 72, 80; and class solidarity, 65, 67, 125; and amateur performance, 142–45

People's Republic of China (PRC), 24, 38, 50, 51, 55–58, 83, 85, 177, 181; conception of, 39; pursuit of socialism, 3; economy of, 60, 62, 65, 92, 93, 105, 118, 122; relationship with commodities, 8, 9, 67, 69, 115, 124; production in, 44, 46, 96, 119

performance, 10, 41, 143, 154, 167, 181, 186. *See also* amateur body, the; class; yangbangxi

pleasure, 34, 115, 187

political economic structures, 13, 17, 117, 118, 120–24

political texts, discussion of, 35, 114, 123, 125, 130, 138

porcelain, 14, 23, 104, 142, 153, 179; development in the PRC, 100; history of, 91–95, 98, 99; manufacturing, 96, 97, 102–3, 148, 149; political significance of, 100, 101; statuettes, 22, 84, 100, 101, 148, 164; and yangbanxi, 162, 164

post-socialism, 13, 17, 20, 192; definition of, 3

press, 7, 67, 72, 73, 82, 160

prices, 2, 59–61, 64, 65, 71, 85, 89, 108, 116

productivism, 84, 90, 91, 104, 105, 109, 179; definition of, 103

proletariat, 22, 65, 67, 83, 84, 163; and the commodity, 124; dictatorship of, 7, 24, 116, 123, 131; ideology, 69, 74, 176, 179; as models, 149, 160, 167; production of the, 91–97, 100, 103, 122; respect for, 66; responsibilities, 77; and retail, 72

pseudobiography, 135, 136. *See also* literature; *A Commodity's Tale* (Jing)

publicity, 21, 32, 34, 49, 178

radio, 14, 29, 32–34, 37, 44, 48, 51, 73, 135, 147, 150, 151; Beijing Radio Factory in, 45. *See also* Central Radio

radioification, 30

rationing, 59–62

realism, 31, 99–101, 103, 111, 127, 129, 130, 181, 184

record players, 21, 42–49, 52

records, 29, 42, 48–50. *See also* China Records
Red Detachment of Women, The (film), 30, 157, 169, 187
Red Guard, 4, 7, 20, 41, 55, 56, 68–71, 73, 104, 147, 179
remediation; and the amateur body, 142, 146–48, 153, 164, 168, 176–78
retail, 58–60, 73; and display, 89, 90, 105, 106; manifestations of class struggle in, 69, 72–76; and money, 61–63; in the PRC, 65, 70, 71; and socialism, 9, 22, 56, 63, 64, 84; role of workers in, 57, 66, 67, 73, 76–81, 86, 87, 113
rituals, of revolution, 153
rural areas, 68, 91; and loudspeakers, 33, 36, 41, 42

saboteur, 23; and class, 64, 154, 161 *See also* bourgeoisie
salesclerks, 6, 58, 66, 74
salons; of discourse, 48; for hair, 58, 69
sample rooms, 87–90
self-censorship, 181, 184, 188
sex, and commodification, 108
Shanghai, 44, 52, 63, 64, 79, 83, 104–6, 119, 120, 131, 133, 144, 155, 157. *See also* Shanghai Number 1; Shanghai's Number 4 Benefit the People Food Products Factory; Shanghai People's Press; shopping
Shanghai Number 1, 1–3, 77
Shanghai's Number 4 Benefit the People Food Products Factory, 144
Shanghai People's Press, 1, 125, 130
shopping, 22, 56, 60, 63, 88, 193; and women, 70; and class, 76; in Shanghai, 83, 105; and socialism, 109; in Wangfujing district, 82, 105
shortages, 17, 25, 60, 113; socialist associations with, 85, 86,
socialism, 9–11, 24–26, 28, 85, 97–99, 110, 121, 126, 183, 184; in China, 3, 4, 7, 8, 14, 16, 21, 24, 50, 111, 114–19, 121, 126, 192, 193; and commerce, 17, 57, 58, 62, 65, 66, 72, 79, 80, 83, 84; comparisons with capitalism, 29, 108, 113, 122; and modernity, 30, 51, 52, 76; and realism, 127, 130; and trade, 56, 57, 66–68, 78

song, 35, 44, 50, 54–56, 142, 143, 145, 151, 153, 154
sonic imaginary, 30, 36, 39, 47, 53; definition of, 28
sonic saturation, 31, 35–37, 40, 47, 48, 50, 51. *See also* loudspeakers
soundscapes, 28, 31, 32, 34
Soviet Union, the, 17, 24, 91, 99, 114; the bourgeoisie in, 100; consumption in, 87, 89; economy of, 118–21; policies of, 60, 85; socialism in, 116, 117; trade in, 59
space, 182, 185; definition of, 36, 37; kinds of, 30; sonic, 35–37, 42, 46–50; of the stage, 144, 146, 154
spectatorship, 143, 145, 172, 174, 187, 188
Stalinism, 31, 62, 111, 116, 127; political economic approach of, 118–24
store windows, 36; and commodities, 122, 123 193; design of, 96, 97; role of, 103, 104, 119, 120, 127
style, 17, 69, 70, 72, 80, 99, 193
Sun Dingguo, 6
surveillance, 31, 181, 187

technology, 29, 33, 35, 41, 48, 53, 142; of transformation, 153, 159, 160, 162, 164, 175, 176. *See also* mirrors; performance
television, 38, 45, 47, 142, 147, 150
territory, 21, 37, 38; and sound, 36, 42, 46–48, 50, 53
theater, 146, 147, 149, 186
Tiezhu, of "Red broadcast station" (Wang), 41–43
Time magazine, 170–72, 178, 185
tractors, 6, 55, 128; drivers of, 54
trade, 60, 70; associations with capitalism, 57, 62; domestic, 59, 62, 76; and money, 136; socialist theories of, 56, 65, 67, 68, 72, 78; unions, 92. *See also* capitalism; socialism
transistors, 32–34, 45
travel, 49, 78; of broadcasts, 47, 59; of salespeople, 22, 59

United States, 63, 105
urban environments, 37, 42, 48, 59, 61, 106, 108, 109

Walkman, 34
Wangfujing Department Store, 67–69, 71. *See also* Beijing
warehouses, 60, 87, 89
Western thought, 28, 48, 52, 69
wholesalers, 87, 88, 90, 107, 119
women, 55, 69; and shopping, 70; and mirrors, 179, 180

Xiangyang Store (Guo), 22, 73, 74, 75, 77, 80, 112
Xu Yinsheng, 67

yangbanxi, 16; definition of, 15; and revolutionary heroism, 141, 143, 145, 148, 157, 160–67, 175–79; and sculpture, 148, 149; performances of, 30, 73, 146, 147, 150, 151; role of, 139, 144, 146, 154, 155. *See also* aesthetics; Chinese Communist Party (CCP); communism; Cultural Revolution, the; mediation; porcelain
youth, 7, 42, 43, 48, 54

Zhonghua 206, 44